Penguin Books
Living with *Glasnost*

**Andrew Wilson** was from 1986 to 1988 Moscow
correspondent of the *Observer*, of which he is also an Associate
Editor and former Foreign Editor. His books include *War
Gaming* (1969), *The Concorde Fiasco* (1973) and *The Disarmer's
Handbook* (1983), subsequently made Political Book of the Year
in West Germany. In 1986 he was a joint author of *The Worst
Accident in the World*, an immediate account of the Chernobyl
nuclear disaster. He spends much of his time between London,
Moscow and Brussels.

**Nina Bachkatov** is Moscow correspondent of the Belgian
newspaper *Le Soir*. A graduate of the École des Hautes Études
en Sciences Sociales in Paris, and with a joint Russo-Belgian
cultural background, she has spent long periods in the Soviet
Union reporting and researching, and visiting her family. Her
first book, *La Classe ouvrière ne va pas au paradis . . . fiscal*,
appeared in 1978. She also contributes to various publications in
France, Switzerland and Canada.

· Andrew Wilson and Nina Bachkatov ·

# Living with *Glasnost*

### Youth and Society in a Changing Russia

Penguin Books

PĒNGUIN BOOKS

Published by the Penguin Group
27 Wrights Lane, London w8 5tz, England
Viking Penguin Inc., 40 West 23rd Street, New York, New York 10010, USA
Penguin Books Australia Ltd, Ringwood, Victoria, Australia
Penguin Books Canada Ltd, 2801 John Street, Markham, Ontario, Canada l3r 1b4
Penguin Books (NZ) Ltd, 182–190 Wairau Road, Auckland 10, New Zealand

Penguin Books Ltd, Registered Offices: Harmondsworth, Middlesex, England

First published 1988
10 9 8 7 6 5 4 3 2 1

Made and printed in Great Britain by
Richard Clay Ltd, Bungay, Suffolk
Filmset in Lasercomp Bembo

*For those who are trying to change it,*
*truly,*
*there and here.*

# · Contents ·

# · List of Illustrations ·

All illustrations are from the magazine *Krokodil*.

p. 170: 'And where is the sports complex?'
          'In perspective.'
          (no. 19, July 1986)

p. 208: The modern Soviet Laocoön, father and sons caught in the coils of
          consumerism (no. 3, January 1987)

# · Introduction ·

In the second half of the 1980s no Western journalist could have wanted to be anywhere but in the Soviet Union – or so it seemed to those of us who were there. After decades of repression and secrecy, with one false dawn (the short reign of Nikita Khrushchev), the world's first socialist state had come out of its nightmare-ridden sleep and started groping towards the twenty-first century. All over Moscow the telex machines of foreign correspondents were busy reporting the surprising changes that were happening with the advent of Mikhail Gorbachev. In short, not to have been in the Soviet Union in 1985–8 was to have missed one of the great tides of history, though subsequent events were to temper optimism about the speed of the transformation.

It was just before this time – in the interval between the stifling reign of Leonid Brezhnev and the appearance of the new leadership – that one of us (Nina Bachkatov) arrived in Moscow to complete a thesis on the problems of Soviet youth as seen by the Soviet media. But it was not until 1986, when we were both correspondents for our newspapers in Moscow, that the opportunity came to develop this picture of a new generation of Soviet citizens into a book.

It required no great vision to see that Gorbachev's reforms would have an importance far beyond Russia's borders; that by furthering Moscow's interest in stability and collaboration, they could help to transform East–West relations. This is still so. But whether or not they succeed must depend on the generation, still in its teens, that will have to supply the motivation for change. Unless Gorbachev can win its active support, the *perestroika* is doomed. Without it, there can be no committed work-force, no new layer of innovative managers, nobody in whom to rekindle the sense of direction that has been lost for decades.

This new generation has been badly disadvantaged, however: first by the absence of any inspiring example from its parents' generation, corrupted by years of stagnation under Brezhnev, and secondly by being denied experience in responsibility. The latter is in contrast to earlier Soviet history, which in the first years of the Revolution saw every great task devolve upon the shoulders of youth. Even in the

1930s, with their black history of political purges, it was common to find directors of enterprises and leading scientific researchers as young as twenty-five. And still greater responsibility fell on young people in the Second World War, when battle and independent partisan operations put a premium on youthful leadership.

After the war, young leaders were again given a leading role in the work of reconstruction and in the development of Soviet science and technology. But the children of the Brezhnev generation had none of this experience. They were kept in subordinate positions and denied responsibility by the accumulation of age at the top. Where projects absorbed them, like the building of the BAM railway,[g] the purpose was mainly social and political. Their talents were directed towards 'playing the system', avoiding decisions and acquiring whatever they could with no sense of duty towards society.

The question of youth and the *perestroika* thus struck us as one of the most crucial of our time, and not only within Russia itself. But since youth does not exist in a vacuum, it was necessary to take account of other aspects of Soviet life. Our book is therefore not only about youth, but also the problems affecting the whole of Soviet society – and these are huge.

What we have to say about the effect of inertia, the rigidity of the system, the habits of centuries, and the curbing of all kinds of spontaneity and initiative is bound to sadden readers who, like ourselves, look impatiently to Russia's modernization. But although our picture may be far removed from that presented by official propaganda (inevitably, since part of our duty is to expose the system's weaknesses), it is certainly not our aim to portray a future without hope, or to ally ourselves with those who look only for signs that the painfully constructed edifice of socialism is about to collapse.

On the contrary, we hope that objective readers will find the same grounds as ourselves for hoping that the Soviet Union will one day achieve the fairer and more efficient society it proclaims to be its goal. Certainly there are not only negative things to report from Gorbachev's Russia. As we point out in the last chapter, the years since 1985 have seen momentous changes: the easing of censorship, a renaissance in the arts (especially the theatre and the cinema), a transformation of the press, the first experiments in elective democracy. Within the Party, despite the tensions revealed by the dismissal of Boris Yeltsin and the shock of ethnic upheavals in Armenia and

Azerbaijan, there remains a leadership committed to the continuation of reforms.

But no picture of Russia can stop short at politics. Those of us who choose to work in the Soviet Union are often asked, back in London, or Brussels, or wherever is 'home', what it is that repeatedly takes us back there. How is it that, despite the officialdom, the harsh climate, the appalling inconveniences, the many rudenesses, the impoverished diet, the absence of nearly every material comfort that the West takes for granted, one returns again and again, not just voluntarily but with quickened expectation?

The answer is not easy. Partly it is a question of friendships, an empathy with others opposed to the 'system' (in the social, not the political, sense); a sense too of the space that can still be accorded to human relations in the absence of cloying material goods. But an important part is also to do with history.

One cannot walk through Moscow, or Kharkov, or Leningrad, or any other western Soviet city, without remembering that its streets have witnessed some of the most violent events of our century: two wars, two revolutions, two great hungers, uncountable years of political terror. In these cities posterity was saved from Hitler, and we share, however vicariously, in the pride of their people in their unmatched feat of endurance.

In the same spirit, one must set the imperfections of Soviet society against the poverty of what it inherited three-quarters of a century ago.

Of course, the Party claims too much credit for the raising of today's industrial economy from the backwardness and chaos of 1917. (Other societies, more backward then, are today much further advanced, materially and even democratically: witness Japan.) But it requires an act of stupendous ungenerosity to belittle what the country and its people have achieved, at an untold price in sweat and blood.


It has not been our aim to produce yet another Western commentary on what is happening in Russia. We have not applied the facts to any political purpose or attempted to fit them into a neat, theoretical pattern for which there is no basis. Rather we have set out to chart some social cross-currents in the sea of events we as journalists must navigate, with no hope for a long time to come of sighting the distant shore.

In the process of writing we have tried to keep ourselves in the background in order to let Soviet subjects speak for themselves, in private conversation or through the increasingly open columns of the press. But any book, however much it pretends to be without bias, must reflect the authors' views, and readers are entitled to know what they are.

Both of us look hopefully for the ultimate success of Mikhail Gorbachev's 'restructuring'. We believe in its necessity and in its sincerity. But, as we work in Moscow, and travel through the cities and countryside more freely than most of our predecessors were able to do, we can hardly overlook the obstacles in its way.

Yet we are also bound to ask how we would have filled the pages that follow if we had been writing not about Soviet society, but about the West. Certainly, for every word that we devote to the Soviet drugs problem (a matter of grave concern to the authorities), we could have written a thousand on the same problem in the West. And when writing of the December 1986 riots in Alma-Ata, we could hardly fail to reflect on whatever sends Western middle-class youth rampaging through Stockholm, or young British blacks through the burning streets of Toxteth.

In our portrait of the *perestroika* generation we have concentrated on the questions that concern people most directly, what they talk about, and write about to the papers: things like frustration at work, the shortage of flats, the break up of families, the 'rebellion' of youth, the disappearance of 'values' and morality. But we have also accommodated less prominent matters, such as attitudes towards homosexuals and other minorities, which must be included if the *variety* of the arguments raging in the late 1980s is to be shown.

Russian is a beautiful language. One result of this is that Russians seldom talk briefly on any subject. Speakers do not know how to stop, or editors how to cut. We have therefore shortened some direct quotations by speakers and letter-writers. At the same time we have deliberately included some naïve and seemingly simplistic statements where these give an insight into widely held attitudes.

The vast majority of comments in the book are from Soviet citizens, be they officials, friends, 'experts', letter-writers or simply strangers in queues. When they have been made in public, the sources are given at the end of the book. When no source is given, the remarks have come to us privately. Our own comments, where they occur, should be obvious as such.

In addition, in order to explain technical words without forever interrupting the narrative, we have provided a short glossary. Wherever such words first occur, they are marked with a superscript *g*, as are some everyday words whose literal translation from the Russian can be misleading.

Finally we wish to thank all those who have given us help and advice, particularly Zhores Medvedev in London, Gabor Rittersporn in Paris and numerous friends in the Soviet Union who wish, for the moment, to remain anonymous. We also thank *Krokodil* magazine for permission to reproduce sixteen cartoons that, perhaps better than anything else, show the ability of Soviet writers and artists to spot and laugh at the failings of the system in true spirit of *glasnost*.

This, then, is our look at some of the murkier, but also, we hope, brighter, parts of the Soviet scene in the first years of the 'Gorbachev revolution'. In contrast to the improvement in foreign relations, most recently symbolized by the 1988 Moscow 'summit', progress at home is uneven, especially with the economy. But one has only to look at the obstacles – bureaucracy, inertia and past disillusionment – to know that, whatever the final outcome, history must judge the changes begun in the 1980s as one of the bravest undertakings of our time.

*Moscow, July 1988*

# Children of the *Perestroika*

*Birth of* perestroika − *the Twenty-seventh Party Congress* [g] − *the Party in society − urban–rural tensions − generation differences − attitudes of young people − psychological effect of inefficiency − the 'black' economy − beginning of reform −* glasnost *and the arts*

In the great hall in the Kremlin, on 23 February 1986, the 5,000 delegates stood up as one person and, with the precision taught by years of Party discipline, applauded the new General Secretary with prolonged rhythmic hand-claps.

'Comrade delegates, esteemed guests,' began Mikhail Gorbachev, in a speech that was to last four hours,

> the Twenty-seventh Congress of the CPSU [g] has gathered at a crucial turning point in the life of the country . . . We shall not be able to move a single step forward if we do not learn to work in a new way, do not put an end to inertness and conservatism in any of their forms, if we lose the courage to assess the situation realistically and see it as it actually is.

Between the two sentences, joined in one paragraph above, Gorbachev was to give his audience a shattering picture of the failings of Soviet society and to propose drastic steps to remedy them − steps that have become known by two Russian words, *glasnost* (openness) and *perestroika* (restructuring), now as familiar in the West as in the East. Nearly a quarter of those present were women and a third were young people under the age of thirty. Several hundred were servicemen whose green or blue uniforms stood out clearly from the rows of scarlet seats. At important passages the heads of the audience would bend forward and hands reach for pencils with which to note points for emphasis when the hearers reported back to the 19 million members of the Party at large.

The Communist Party of the Soviet Union comprises approximately one-eighth of the adult Soviet population. Among them are the holders of every important position in government, three-quarters of the members of the Supreme Soviet, three-quarters of all deputies in the Soviets (parliaments) of fifteen constituent republics, [g] most regional and local councillors, nearly all factory and farm heads, nearly a third of all citizens with higher education and, of course, key members in every command in the armed forces.

But beyond the Communist Party, Gorbachev was addressing the 280 million members of the Soviet population as a whole. Through radio and television broadcasts, and in identical print to appear the next day in 8,427 newspapers, he was exhorting the country to abandon the cynicism of decades and join the march to the twenty-first century. The participation of the mass of the people was indispensable; for the Soviet Union could not expect to reach the glittering goals set forth in his speech by the efforts of the Party alone.

The variety of Gorbachev's audience would have made nonsense of any attempt to generalize about those who composed it. Apart from cultural and ethnic differences among Russians, Ukrainians, Belorussians, Kazakhs, Tartars, Azeris, Armenians and Georgians – in all, 160 nationalities speaking 131 languages\* – it was divided across the whole country by education, age, environment, privilege and differences in material welfare. To draw any useful conclusions as to the impact of his appeal, it would have been necessary to make at least three distinctions.

The first basic line that divides Soviet society (about which we shall say more later) is between Party members and the rest. Not all Party members have a deep political dedication, and many join out of sheer material self-interest: for status, advancement or simply 'perks'. But all must follow events with scrupulous attention if they are not to be caught out by unexpected policy changes, and this in itself marks them off from most people outside the Party.

Among the more highly educated, the decision not to join the Party requires a deliberate resolution. Those who remain outside include private social democrats and religious believers as well as some Marxists who reject the bureaucracy of the Party. In 1988 nearly all 'non-Party' intellectuals remained deeply sceptical of the Party's ability to change this, and of the country's ability to attain its economic goals, at least within the proclaimed time.

The same scepticism is shared by most workers, who recall the Party's failure to make good its promises in a whole succession of Five-year Plans from Khrushchev's time onwards. This scepticism is

---

\*Including such ethnic groups as Yukaghirs and Tofars, numbering less than 1,000 each. The largest groups are Russians (140 million), Uzbeks (13 million) and Belorussians (10 million).

compounded with natural inertia in a system where jobs, however ill-performed, have traditionally been guaranteed for life (though in 1988 there were signs that this might not be so for ever).

The second division is between established urban communities and the grossly underprivileged countryside. But lest this be mis-understood, it is necessary to say more about the actual condition of the cities.

A visitor landing at Moscow's Sheremetyevo airport may catch a distant glimpse of high-rise buildings. Presently, as he drives past them, he may imagine that he is entering the equivalent of a modern Western capital. It is only later, if he looks more closely at the exterior or, more revealingly, the interior of one of these blocks, with its flaking paint and rusty cladding, dirty windows and grimy stairs, that he will see the reality of which Soviet citizens complain.

Street life is similarly deceptive. The signs on the shops may proudly say 'Gastronom' or 'Vegetable Bazaar', but, except for a few show-places, the shelves contain the same tins of 'fish products', bruised tomatoes and mouldy potatoes that are to be found in the small neighbourhood stores. The only difference is that the latter are even more frequently closed – for sanitary days,[g] 'stock-taking', a *remont*[g] or some other, generally unexplained reason.

With luck, the same goods may be sold from one of the numerous wooden pavement kiosks that have appeared since 1986, or passed out, against rouble notes, from a hole in the wall. Or, if it is summer, a lorry may deposit a crate in the street, and people will stop whatever they are doing and converge on the vendors like a swarm of ants. Better-off shoppers usually go to the local 'peasant' market, where produce abounds in season, but prices, being uncontrolled, are very much higher than in the unappealing State shops. (For example, it is not unusual to pay fifteen roubles* for a kilo of tomatoes in winter.)

At night, above the boulevards, neon signs glow with the names of State enterprises, and illuminated slogans extol democracy and progress. But the sidewalks below are dark and dead. Restaurants,

---

*In 1988 the official rate of exchange was approximately one rouble to the pound, or sixty-five kopecks to the US dollar. But, as we explain elsewhere, such rates can be misleading. The average Soviet salary is less than 200 roubles a month. This means more than it seems, because of very low housing and service charges. Nevertheless, to shop in the market almost certainly requires an income from unofficial sources. Party functionaries, government officials, army officers and other privileged groups have the use of special shops selling better quality goods at fixed prices.

guarded by imperious doormen, are effectively closed to most ordinary citizens, and the so-called cafés, selling little except fruit juice,
bear almost no resemblance to anything by that name in the West.
As for the great cultural spectacles, such as the ballet and opera, all
but a fraction of the seats are sold to visitors, mainly hard-currency
holders, at five times the 'Soviet' price, and the average Muscovite
has a chance of a ticket to the Bolshoi once in thirty years.[1]

Nevertheless, to the inhabitants of the surrounding countryside
the Soviet capital is a magnet – a cornucopia for a whole range of
goods that the countryside never sees, including, amazingly, meat.
Every day trains from the country disgorge tens of thousands at the
mainline railway terminals. Half carry bags of vegetables or fruit to
sell on the street or in the markets. The rest fan out with empty
suitcases and rucksacks, crowding with office-workers into the
Metro, and making for the GUM and other department stores. In
the evening one sees them going back, laden with packages of smoked
sausage or fresh beef, wallpaper, children's dresses, bags of nails,
bicycles, saucepans, electrical goods and furniture.*

The differences between town and country cause friction and
mistrust, evidenced wherever the two meet, as in the markets. The
urban housewife ostentatiously examines every apple and potato,
convinced that she is being swindled by the crafty peasant, whom the
country goes to huge lengths to support. 'All *I*'ve got is my pension,'
grumbles a typical city pensioner.

But the peasant can be just as bitter. 'It's us that rears the cows, and
Moscow that eats the butter,' goes a typical grouse. Or 'There go our
cattle. Now we'll have to manage on eggs, because the city softies
need our meat.'

It's an old story. The peasant is forever being forced to do without
in order, as he sees it, to feed the townsman who won't soil his hands;
while the townsman sees the peasant getting fat at the workers'
expense and cheating the poor, whom he regards as useless mouths.

In fact, the Russian village is a strange mixture of affluence and
poverty. Rural wages approach the national average. The small, de-
tached village houses may lack many facilities, but they are distinctly
more spacious than city flats. A private plot and a little scrounging
can provide the peasant with economies the town never knows.

Yet despite a huge effort to make village life more acceptable to

*Out-of-town visitors may buy only individual pieces of furniture, such as tables
and chairs. Larger items, such as suites, require proof of at least four years' residence in
the city.

young people, it is still necessary to be born in the country in order to be able and willing to live there. Distances are enormous. Roads are often mere dirt-tracks where cars dare not venture once it rains. Broken-winded trains, and scarcely better buses, run to timetables that frequently depend on the whim of the driver. To finish any journey, one must finally rely on an armada of trucks and farm-machines, or one's feet.

The men, with nothing better to do after work, console themselves with a bottle of *samogon*.[8] For women it is the opposite. After their jobs (generally on the collective farm), looking after the family plot and doing the housework (including going to the public pump for water), they have no free time to fill. Young people are left without anything at all, especially in so-called 'villages without perspective', which, being denied any improvement, are falling entirely into the hands of the old, before being abandoned completely.

The third way of dividing Soviet society (and the one with which this book is particularly concerned) is by age. Of the 200 million or so Soviet viewers who might have been expected to hear and see Gorbachev's Party Congress performance on television, about a sixth would have been old enough to remember the sufferings of the Great Patriotic War and the Stalinist terror. A very much larger group, well over half, would have come to maturity during the stagnant years under Leonid Brezhnev. About a quarter were still under thirty and thus, perhaps, capable of rescue from the collective demoralization.

This last was the key-group whose allegiance Gorbachev had to win if he was to get anywhere near the bold economic targets set for the year 2000: a doubling of productive capacity, a 130–50 per cent increase in labour productivity and a 60–80 per cent increase in per capita real incomes. For this he would have to find a new generation of administrators, managers and brigade-leaders,[8] as well as simple workers, who, according to the new economic thinking, would need to be moved by material incentives to raise quality and output rather than by time-worn appeals to ideology and patriotism.

Soviet sociologists avoid dividing society into precise age groups. In particular they refuse to consider youth a class in itself, developing separately from the whole. Youth, they argue, is no more homogeneous than other social groups. In sociological jargon it is an 'inter-class' group,[2] meaning a layer of society with particular characteristics. As a leading authority put it, 'We use the words "social group" to denote elements in the social structure from different classes (working class, peasantry or intelligentsia). It would not be correct to designate young people, women or pensioners, as social classes.'[3] This outlook explains a whole series of attitudes that come up for attention in the chapters that follow.

All the same, certain ages can be taken as markers in the young Russian's progress from infancy to adulthood. Thus:

— *At fourteen:* A young person can be proposed for membership of the Komsomol youth organization.[g] Having completed the basic education course, he or she must choose between taking two more years of secondary education or going to a vocational–technical school (PTU).[g]

— *At sixteen:* Receives a passport, and can choose which nationality[g] to adopt if the parents are from different nationalities.

— *At seventeen:* Finishes with compulsory schooling.

— *At eighteen:* Ceases to be a minor, can vote, marry, become a probationary Party member, be elected to any office except membership of the Supreme Soviet and generally, if a boy, becomes liable for military conscription.

— *At nineteen:* Can become a full Party member (in which case Komsomol membership is given up).

— *At twenty-one:* Can be elected a deputy of the Supreme Soviet.

— *At twenty-eight:* Reaches the Komsomol age limit and must choose whether or not to enter the Party.

Given the peculiarities of Soviet society, the years fourteen to twenty-four could be taken as 'youth'. Fourteen is the age of one's first important choice (what kind of further schooling to follow), while joining the Komsomol from the Pioneers[g] marks the end of childhood. Twenty-four is when young people reach what the social scientists regard as a mark of maturity, their 'insertion into the world of work'. By this time students in higher education have done their military service, and those who have gone directly into employment have had time to climb the first steps of the qualification ladder. Most young people will also have married and many will have had their first child.

In 1988 young people aged fourteen to twenty-four, i.e., those born in 1963–73, formed a sixth of the population. But whereas 1960 had seen a record number of births (5.3 million), 1970 saw a record low (4.2 million). Subsequently the rate stabilized, but at a relatively low level (in 1980, 4.8 million). The decline was caused partly by the

arrival at child-bearing age of the reduced number of children conceived during the war years, but also by a steady diminution of the
size of families in the European part of the country. So people of this
age group came from smaller families, were often only children, and
were the first generation of this kind.

In the same period Soviet society underwent rapid urbanization.
In 1958 less than half lived in cities and 52 per cent in the country. By
1970 the ratio had changed to 56:44, and by 1986 to 66:34, at which
level it showed signs of stabilizing. This means that many of today's
young people are first-generation city-dwellers, born of parents who,
by quitting the countryside, have forsaken the traditional large family
group, and with it the support the family used to provide for the
upbringing of young children. All that these uprooted parents have
been able to pass on to their children is the dreams of urban newcomers. Their links with the past have been totally destroyed.

The division between rural and urban society is vastly more significant than the differences, also often considerable, between the conditions of youth among various Soviet nationalities. 'For example,'
says one of the country's best-known sociologists, Igor Bestushev-
Lada, 'I find it more difficult to have contact with country people in
my native Russia than I do with my Armenian and Uzbek colleagues.'

The break with family tradition resulting from the exodus from the
countryside is regarded by many as one of the main reasons for the 'lost'
condition of Soviet youth. This is a matter of passionate debate in the
Soviet media. Witness the diatribe of a fifty-year-old writer against his
generation's *bête noire*, 'metallist' hard-rock groups: 'They hate and
despise our whole system, all our values. That's why they're dangerous,
and why I'm pessimistic about the future.' Or another intellectual: 'The
young pick up all that's most artificial, most empty, in the West . . . It's
particularly serious in the case of young Russians. Up to now other
nationalities have been better at preserving their traditions. We Russians
used to be a cultured, hospitable people, but we've lost all that. We've
even forgotten how to cook.' Even young Lena, only twenty-two,
talking about the new generation of fifteen- to twenty-year-olds, has a
word on the subject: 'They reject everything and propose nothing. For
them it's enough to say "No" and drown in material acquisitions, rock
or pop, aping the West.' But then she has an afterthought: 'All the same,
they do have the courage to say "No", whereas we, at the same age,
chose to hide our feelings for the sake of peace. In a way they're sincere,
whereas we were hyprocrites. If they're given the chance, they'll do
better than us, with more generosity and conviction.'

The weightier voice of the celebrated poet Andrei Voznessensky was to speak on behalf of the new generation in a row at the 1987 plenum of the Union of Writers, after some delegates had fulminated against the rock 'cult'.

> And now, let's talk about youth. A poet was grieving because, in BAM work camps, young people dance to rock and roll in the evenings. But why shouldn't these youngsters dance after a hard day's work? After all, what is rock and roll? Chiefly it's rhythm. Why accuse rock of every sin? It's like decrying iambics. You can write marvellous verses in iambics or you can write trash. It's the same with rock . . . Young people want a new culture. We have heard the young writer Yuri Sergeev attacking the new generation, blaming rock for all that's wrong . . . But who faced the fire at Chernobyl, when we didn't give them the proper protective equipment? Those young firemen died to save us – and you too. So, let their generation dance to whatever music it chooses! [4]

To grow up at all in the Soviet Union of the 1980s is indeed hard. (The problem was treated with rare sensitivity and insight in a documentary film *Is It Easy to be Young?*, released in Moscow at the onset of the *glasnost* campaign in 1987.) But to grow up in the exemplary image demanded by Gorbachev's reform programme will be even harder.

There are at least six areas in which emotional turmoil, heavy-handed bureaucracy or simply the want of any means of self-realization are enough to destroy whatever potential may exist for the making of tomorrow's citizens:

– the parental family, whose over-extended support deprives millions of young Russians of the need to develop the sense of responsibility that is a *sine qua non* of social and economic progress;

– a general education system that, despite so-called reforms, continues to squander time on old ideological fads (such as 'manual work-experience') at the expense of real learning;

– military service, which, though it may help foster a spirit of 'internationalism',[g] is for most young men a soul-destroying waste, delaying for two years the commencement of a productive job;

– work, where disillusionment with reality, after all the propaganda of political education, breeds an ineradicable suspicion of all that the system promises;

– leisure, where the Party's heavy hand on every form of activity drives adolescents into 'negative' alternatives;

– marriage, where prospects of happiness are threatened from the start by sexual ignorance and the resort to abortion because of the lack of contraceptives.

These social disaster areas are the subject of the chapters that follow. But there is one further aspect of Soviet life that is so widespread and harmful to loyalty and responsibility that it requires special mention. This is the pretence that, for all its faults, the official economy works, that there is a tolerable relationship between wages and prices, and that there is no justification for resorting to the black market.

Occasionally the newly liberated press prints reports of economic and industrial inefficiency so breath-taking that if published in any Western newspaper, they would strain credibility. An extreme, but by no means isolated, case was that of Evgeny Osipov's car, published in June 1987 by the sober-minded *Izvestia*. It is worth a short digression.

According to *Izvestia*, Osipov took delivery of a new Volga, but he was unable to drive it away because the ignition failed. After four months of telephone calls, the Ministry for the Automobile Industry authorized the Moscow garage to make free repairs. It then found that the car had twenty-six other defects. These took three months to rectify. The rear axle was changed four times, as each replacement was found to be worse than the first. The ignition was changed three times, and the carburettor twice. Similar changes were also made to other parts of the engine and suspension. 'Drive it while the wheels still turn,' advised a mechanic cheerfully when Osipov finally returned to collect the car.

Only then, however, did he see the reason for the delay. On the clock were 3,500 kilometres, and, although the car had originally been white, a wing and a door were now grey. It was explained that one of the mechanics had had 'a small accident'; the grey was a mistake, and the garage agreed to 'rub it off' by running the car through a car-wash for half a day. Unfortunately, due to a defect, the upper brush of the car-wash worked the roof so hard that, according to *Izvestia*, 'it came out looking like a sheet of corrugated iron'. This time the Automobile Ministry was obliged to admit negligence and ordered a complete body replacement, with the result that, after nearly a year, almost nothing was left of the original car but the wheels.

For the last time Osipov came to collect it. But just as he got behind the wheel, a mechanic staggered up drunk and demanded a lift. When the station manager told him to clear off, the man gave

Osipov a parting gift: 'four hefty thumps on the roof, leaving four deep dents'.[5]

*Izvestia*'s story says plenty about standards of quality control, the workings of bureaucracy, customer relations, and so on. But one of the more interesting details might pass a foreigner by. This was what Osipov paid for the car: the official price of 17,000 roubles. The average monthly wage at that time was 180 roubles, with only a minority of workers and officials earning double that sum. So any law-abiding ordinary citizen who bought a Volga at the official price (black-market prices are much higher) would have needed to save nearly eight years' pay. Quite a number of private citizens own Volgas, and a vastly greater number Zhigulis (Ladas), costing nearly 8,000 roubles. Possession of a Volga, a Zhiguli or even a primitive Zaporezh therefore means that the seemingly law-abiding owners (or their indulgent parents) are liable to be deriving a substantial income from the illegal parallel economy.

Although new legislation permits limited forms of 'individual enterprise', and some co-operative ventures in services and agriculture, the gap between legal incomes and the price of almost any form of 'luxury' consumer goods – cars, motorcycles, refrigerators, washing-machines or colour television sets (800 roubles or more) – strains all belief in the rule of the official economy.

So long as the system of self-deception continues, there can be no honest planning, and no realistic incentives to lay before young people (or anyone else) in order to win their co-operation in reconstruction.

Were this all to Soviet life, the existence of anyone not operating in a big way outside the law would be almost unbearable. Gorbachev's task would be hopeless, and Western propagandists justified in the belief that if all frontier barriers were lifted tomorrow, 280 million Soviet citizens would vote for free enterprise with their feet. But it is not quite the whole picture.

In fact, it is doubtful whether more than a fraction have any real wish to exchange the shabby security of their country for the uncertainties of life in the West. (Most of those who do so have religious reasons.) And if they were given the freedom of movement enjoyed by the citizens of most other countries, the number would be reduced even further.

The reasons are prosaic, and hardly flattering to the Leninist ego. Most Russians now know, from Western broadcasts or from those who travel and have contact with foreigners, that Western unemployment is not just a fiction of their own propaganda machine. They know about the homeless adrift on the streets of American cities, the workless youth of Western Europe, and the hungry millions of capitalist Latin America. They know that even in times of prosperity, there is something the West calls a 'rat race' for promotion and pay.

The Soviet citizen, by contrast, is assured of a job of some kind, regardless of performance, as long as he is of working age; and, however enervating this security may be for the economy, it does permit the majority of Russians an agreeably relaxed attitude, a freedom from what they are taught to regard as socially destructive tensions in the world outside. 'Here we have money, and nothing in the shops; there you have fine shops; but if you're unemployed, how can you enjoy them?' is a common observation. Pressed to say which is worse, the vast majority will say it is better to be sure of a job and put up with shortages – because possibly, just possibly, the dream will come true, and one day the shops will fill up with Western-style luxuries.

But there are other factors to enliven this negative picture and make life more than just tolerable, particularly for the privileged urban intelligentsia. Among these are developments of recent origin, like the easing of censorship and a revival of the arts. The year 1985 saw the start of a series of plays like Mikhail Shatrov's *The Dictatorship of Conscience*, which explores previously forbidden subjects like the citizen's right of access to history.

The changes in the cinema had the widest impact, because of the size of the audiences. In 1986 the Film-makers' Union threw out the bureaucrats who had stifled their industry for decades. It was too late to bring back the dying Andrei Tarkovsky, but there were long queues for Chengiz Abuladze's *Repentance* and the documentary *Is It Easy to be Young?* (we say more about this in chapter 4). The easing of book censorship in 1986 was slower to be felt, because of the time taken to get new books printed, or serialized in magazines like *Novy̆ Mir*. But 1987 saw the appearance of Anatoly Rybakov's great anti-Stalinist novel, *The Children of the Arbat*, and 1988 the first Soviet edition of Boris Pasternak's *Doctor Zhivago* (see chapter 13).

Even on television, the slowest to reform of the media, there are now live arts and discussion programmes that compare favourably with the diet of violence and banality transmitted in many countries of the West. All this finds an audience in youth, and particularly urban youth, with access to cinemas and clubs.

But many of the conditions that ease and brighten what would otherwise be a grey existence have nothing to do with recent change. For the town-dweller there are virtually free transport services to take him to Palaces and Parks of Culture,[g] where occasionally, just occasionally, one can see the socialist dream working, as in Gorky Park on a warm summer evening, when laughing couples sail up in the Big Wheel, and teenagers crowd the concerts and poetry recitals.

For the less privileged countryman there are huge preserves of nature: the Caucasus, the Urals, the Siberian tundra, the endless miles of western Russia where, thanks to a shortage of chemical herbicides, meadows and corn fields still glitter with wild flowers, and ducks still run free as they do in the story-books. Here is the Russia where, despite all shortages and frustrations, people can still find joy in living: fall in love, marry, bear children, even, in some cases, find fulfilment in their work – a Russia full of complexes and imperfections, yet far from the unrelievedly grim picture drawn by years of hostile propaganda.

Central to it all is the role of the family, to which Gorbachev, amid a mountain of economic and managerial problems, found time to devote a substantial passage in his Congress speech. The problems of the family comprise more than half the problems of Soviet life; and it is with these that any look at tomorrow's Soviet society must begin.

# The Cradle of Society

*The concept of the family — income and budgeting — diminished birthrates — problems of size — inequality of fathers — one-parent families — basis of matriarchy — conflicts with children — frequency of divorce — abandoned children — 'problem' children — scandal of children's homes*

The family has always played a central role in Russian society. It is also central to the Soviet social concept, which sees it as the child's, and citizen's, first collective.[g]

The constitution devotes Articles 35 and 53 to it. In addition a 'family code' governs marriage and divorce, the rights and duties of parents and children, rules for adoption, and so on. But since this is the Soviet Union, the role of the family cannot be reduced to a strictly family dimension. This is where the child learns to live in society,[1] and its unique task is to demonstrate those moral and social principles that cannot be imparted by theory alone.[2]

At the back of every Russian mind is the notion of the traditional, extended family, which still exists in rural European Russia — a mutually supportive complex of individual households, which may also include members who have moved to towns but not yet cut their roots. In the harshness of rural conditions, such a family provides the conditions for a tolerable life. Parents and grandparents, cousins and in-laws, can be called on in matters of everyday need and for moral and practical support in emergencies. Thus a car, however old or new, becomes the means of transport for the whole family; and when a house has to be built, or furniture moved, or grass cut for winter cattle-feeding, there is an unquestioning supply of voluntary labour.

In many ways the extended family predates the notion of the Soviet collective — the social model in which the citizen will always have a place, and which becomes both a protective cocoon and a suffocating controller. But in recent years, with urbanization, the family has become limited to the small circle of parents and children, enjoying better material conditions but losing out socially and emotionally.

It is almost perverse to speak of a 'typical' family in a country so divided by cultural differences. But for a norm on which to focus, one could legitimately start with the 'ordinary household' portrayed in Soviet text-books for students of Russian. This consists of a husband and wife, evidently in their late twenties, and their two children, living in (to judge from the pictures) Moscow or Leningrad. In the widely used *Russian for Everybody* course, the parents are called Ivan Ivanovich and Anna Petrovna, and the children Nina and Maxim. They also have a dog.

Ivan is a bus-driver and Anna a teacher. This should bring them a joint income of 350–450 roubles a month – more than a couple of doctors or engineers of the same age could hope to earn, and enough to put them in the category of tax-payers. In all, some 15 per cent of their wages will go in income tax and dues, such as trade union subscriptions. From the balance, they will have to pay thirteen roubles for a flat of two rooms (plus kitchen, bathroom and toilet) and about four roubles for gas, electricity and telephone. These very low charges, like those for urban public transport (five kopecks per journey), make any comparison with a Western family budget very difficult.

Other items are very much more expensive than in the West, even at the official exchange rate (see page 18) and hugely expensive when measured against income – especially clothing. A pair of men's shoes costs a tenth of their monthly income, and a medium-quality overcoat about half. Nevertheless, Anna Petrovna will contrive to dress neatly in something like the Western fashion of a few years earlier, and scour the shops to provide the children with warm winter coats and the small extras that will not disgrace them at school. (Only the school uniform is cheap, and not very good.)

With only two children, the couple receive no family allowance, and, because of their relatively high income, they will have to contribute to the cost of Maxim's crèche (ten roubles per month) or kindergarten (thirteen roubles). If Anna allows another pregnancy to develop – which is most unlikely – she will receive the usual one-off maternity grant of a hundred roubles (fifty for a first child), two months' paid leave from her employer and a grant of thirty-five roubles a month as a mother at home for twelve months. After that she can take up to twelve months' unpaid leave. On her return to work, her employer will be obliged to give her back her old job, upgraded for seniority.

Anna and Ivan have nothing to pay for their children's schooling (after kindergarten), or for social insurance, or for medical treatment. But the last is free in principle only. As we relate elsewhere, it is necessary to bribe hospital staff, including surgeons, for all kinds of attention. Things were so bad that in October 1987 the authorities allowed Moscow's first paying hospital.

To help her through a long day – job from nine to six, mother from six to nine, wife from nine to ten – Anna will have some, but not all, of the household appliances taken for granted in the West: refrigerator, vacuum-cleaner, electric iron, washing-machine (though in the case of the last many women still prefer the apartment block laundry, charging a few kopecks a kilo). All these items will be of basic design and liable to need frequent repair. For a freezer she will be able to use the balcony or window-sill during a northern winter that lasts from November to March, with temperatures reaching anything down to $-25°C$. Winter is when the flat seems most cramped, when the children have nowhere to play out of doors, and the suburban park is no longer a substitute for a garden.

For shops Anna and Ivan will need to walk only a block or two. There may even be a shop as part of their block; but Anna will try to buy as much as she can near her school, or take part in a lunch-hour shopping pool with colleagues. Nevertheless she will not be able to avoid altogether the long queues that Russians have grown to accept as a normal part of life.* For recreation there will be the local House of Culture,[g] a public library and, in cities like Moscow, a fair choice of cinemas. But, as we explain below, husband and wife are likely to have separate friendships and interests.

Couples like Ivan Ivanovich and Anna Petrovna actually exist, though they are likely to have less living space and fewer Western-style luxuries than the text-book suggests. Their welfare is a result of the consumer boom of the eighteen-year Brezhnev period, when living standards rose by one third.† They do sit down regularly to well-laid dinner tables, husbands do play chess with neighbours in the

*A housewife can spend up to two hours a day shopping. This is partly because of shortages, partly because of a lack of sales staff, but also because of the rarity of self-service arrangements. In most shops it is necessary to queue three times: to inspect the goods, to buy a ticket for them, then to receive them at the counter. More time can be taken as the customer heading the queue examines every item for soundness. Since housewives seldom carry a list or stock up, shopping becomes an almost daily chore.

†In the mid-1980s 95 per cent of households had a television set (a third of them colour), 95 per cent a radio, 90 per cent a refrigerator (101 in towns, 76 per cent in the country), 68 per cent a washing-machine (78 in towns, 58 in the country), 35 per cent a tape-recorder (43 per cent in towns, 24 in the country), 30 per cent a camera (41 in towns, 18 in the country), 34 per cent a vacuum-cleaner (48 in towns, 20 in the country), 15 per cent a car (14 in towns, 15 in the country), 16 per cent a motorbike (8 in towns, 15 in the country), 62 per cent a bicycle or moped (44 in towns, 79 in the country), 66 per cent a sewing-machine (63 in towns, 70 in the country).[3]

evening, and wives relax elegantly at the recreation centre. There may even be families where, as in *Russian for Everybody*, a younger sister, a crane-driver in Vladivostok, comes up twice a year to Moscow for meetings of the Supreme Soviet, of which she is a deputy.

But the picture presented by *Russian for Everybody* says nothing of the warmth, disorder, impulsiveness, humour and vitality of Russian family life when it works, or the squalor, intolerance and misery when it does not. Nor, being a Russian picture, does it carry any hint of the wide cultural differences among the many Soviet nationalities.

One of the reasons for Gorbachev's concern for family welfare was the increasingly serious imbalance between the birth rates of European Russia and Central Asia. If current trends continue, some time in the next century the European part of the Soviet population will be outnumbered by the Central Asian part, with serious implications for Russian culture and the dominant position of Russians in the Soviet Communist Party and State. It will then be necessary to give a place in the country's power structure to a new, non-European elite – the first in Soviet history – particularly when Asian rural regions catch up in the development of education. Both to check this imbalance and to sustain the labour-force needed for economic development, it has long been official policy to encourage Russian parents to raise larger families.

But in a country where the wife is expected to provide half the family income, this can be hard to follow. Child allowances have scarcely changed since 1947. A mother receives only four roubles a month on the birth of a third child, and six on that of a fifth. The allowance increases gradually thereafter. Additional help takes the form of vouchers for the purchase of clothing and other items for young children in local shops, at reduced prices and with priority.

A mother of thirty-five explains: 'Everywhere you hear about help for large families. I used to believe it. But after my third or fourth, I lost my illusions. You sit at home and all you get is fifty roubles a month for six months, and for a further twelve if the only income is your husband's pay.' A mother of five, Tatyana Kiseleva, desperately needing to get back to work and recover an income, tried to get her infant son into nursery school, but there were no places. 'Managing on less than the national poverty level is harder than you'd think,' she concluded, especially with the cost of clothes for growing children. 'Buying them in the Novosibirsk [Siberian] climate is like throwing a wardrobe on the fire.' Each winter her elder daughter wears out a pair of boots that cost two weeks' salary. 'And where can I find tights which will last even a month, when

— Милая, не верьте разговорам, что любовь зла!

Рисунок А. СЕМЕНОВА.

'Don't believe what they say about love being bad for you, dear.'

nylon ones last only a week?' So Kiseleva sits at home knitting garments to sell at a market.

Until regulations were eased in 1987, this 'private enterprise' was illegal. Once she was detained by the militia[g] and fined twenty-five roubles. 'They sent a report to my work-place, saying I'd been detained. The management immediately concluded that I was a black-marketeer. I was so ashamed that I handed in my notice.'[4]

Not surprisingly there are scarcely any Russian or Baltic names in the monthly list of women honoured with a medal on the birth of their seventh child or the title 'heroine mother' on that of their tenth. In fact, in European Russia the norm is rapidly tending towards the one-child family – and, because of the high divorce rate, the one-parent family also, a phenomenon still almost unknown in Central Asia. In 1986 the psychologist V.V. Stolin estimated that in the USSR there were 8 million one-parent families in a population of 280 million.*

For an increasing number of Soviet citizens, the chief concern is not to enlarge their families, but to hold together what they have.

*According to *Sotsialistitcheskaya Industria*,[5] there are 70 million families in the Soviet Union, and 700,000 children under eighteen are left in single-parent families every year due to divorce alone.

The Russian couple differs from the Western in almost every respect. First, it is not a social unity. In many ways the partners retain great autonomy. It is quite normal to take separate holidays, have different friends, go out separately, have independent leisure activities. Their separate circles, like their work- or study-groups (and, in the case of boys, the army), remain important emotional poles, as do the families of their parents. This concept of family relationships can be one of the stumbling-blocks in relations between Soviet and non-Soviet partners in mixed marriages.

There is also an in-built inequality of roles. Compared with the wife and mother, whose role is clear, the husband finds it hard to set himself up as a man and father. The mother is everywhere, and her relationship with the child emotionally strong. But the father is not supposed to intervene in the child's life until later, and then in a cerebral way, with a more critical kind of love. Young boys quickly fall in with this picture of the father as the one who imparts a philosophy of life and the mother as the giver of affection – something that appears regularly in the essays turned in by young pupils on the set theme 'When I Become a Father'.[6]

In other cases, particularly in European Russia, there may simply be no man. Not only is the male image missing in so many divorce-struck homes, but a whole generation of future grandfathers was devoured by the war. Again and again, in post-war films and literature, the father is the missing figure: gone off to the front, fallen in combat, vanished to found another family. 'Couldn't a writer depicting our own generation of fathers paint the same kind of picture?' asks a writer in *Komsomolskaya Pravda*.[7]

This has a further repercussion. For decades history ensured that more men were killed than women. So there remains at the back of a woman's mind a fear of not finding a man to take her, and in a man's the reassuring thought that, whereas he can always turn down a prospective partner, she cannot afford to do the same. So he need make less effort, on the old principle that scarce goods will always find a buyer. Mothers used to tell their daughters that 'there won't be enough men to go round', so they had to seize a man whenever the chance came. This hunt for husbands was vividly portrayed in a film about the 1950s, *Moscow Doesn't Believe in Tears*. The subconscious memory of it has survived with today's young girls, who, while paradoxically quite ready to live alone after a divorce, are afraid of remaining teenage spinsters.

Boys can also be victims of the unmanned society. In an excessively feminine environment, they have every bump in the path smoothed out for them, with the assurance that, no matter what, there will always be a woman – mother, grandmother, sister, aunt, neighbour or eventually (it is well understood) wife – prepared to forgive their faults.

It is perhaps not surprising that, racked by all these contradictions, Soviet society in the European half of the country should have developed into a *de facto* matriarchy existing on a foundation of machismo.* An ironical, but apt, example is the attitude of many Soviet women towards alcoholism. Those who are its first victims are also very often the first to lay in a bottle for their man, so that 'he'll be happy when he comes home', and who, since the restrictions on vodka sales, have turned to making *samogon*, 'so that he won't poison himself with goodness knows what stuff he gets outside'. There is more than just humour in the story of the elderly aunt who asked her young niece, 'Your husband, does he drink?' and, on hearing that he didn't, cried 'Thank God' – only to exclaim, when the young man refused vodka at breakfast next morning, 'But what kind of a man are you!'

Another expression of the man's inferior status is his exclusion from everything to do with childbirth and baby-care. The father is even barred from visiting the maternity ward on the pretext of sparing the mother 'psychological shock' or 'exposure to infection' (a touch of black humour to anyone knowing the prevailing state of Soviet hospital hygiene). He may leave a message or a gift at the hospital reception desk, but not see his wife and child till they come out. In desperation young fathers have been known to climb trees so that their wives can show them their newly born babies from second-floor windows.

For the woman, the absence of any kind of sex education (see chapter 11) is matched by the lack of any preparation for the delivery. In the country that was one of the pioneers of painless birth methods, tradition has been turned on its head, leaving mothers with grim memories of confinement in ancient and decrepit hospitals, without drugs, in a deplorable psychological environment.

Future parents receive no preparation for their baby's upbringing. A host of traditions, often verging on superstition, continues to

---

*But in rural Asia and the Caucasus the pattern remains strictly patriarchal. A Soviet friend of one of the authors recalls visiting a colleague in a provincial town in Uzbekistan. The man's wife was the equivalent of a Ph.D. But after serving the meal, she retired to the kitchen. When the friend inquired if she would not be joining them, his host replied, with some embarrassment, that it was 'not the custom'.

weigh women down, like the obligation to give up to six months' breast-feeding. True, there is a shortage of powdered milk, and supplies are uncertain. But why the superstitions? Lydia is sure that her four-year-old son's allergy was caused by her having been unable to feed him for more than three weeks. Natalie, whose parents are both doctors, went on feeding her baby for months, despite being seriously ill with a lung infection.

Svetlana's husband was never told about post-natal depression, because 'babies are a woman's business'. So he was chagrined when, showing friends her little daughter, she would say: 'When I learned it was a girl, I wept to think, yet another unhappy creature for the future.' As frequently happens, Svetlana was looked after by her mother, who came and stayed for weeks. During this time the two women kept guard lest the poor father should have anything to do with his offspring, and even – a subtle precaution against a premature new conception – occupied the marital bed, so that he was obliged to sleep beneath a blanket in the kitchen.

Another inferiority of men is simply cultural. Because more boys than girls enter PTUs after the eighth grade (fifteen to sixteen), the last two years in urban schools are dominated by the female element. The disproportion is continued in higher education, which more girls enter than boys. As a result, women occupy six out of every ten places in 'intellectual' employment; go more often than men to exhibitions and concerts and, according to the magazine *Smena*, consider their male partners grey and not very interesting personalities. The situation is sufficiently serious for some sociologists to have called for the raising of men's cultural levels as a means of combating divorce.[8]

'Mama, what has come over you?' exclaims the young bride, seeing tears in her mother's eyes. 'Sergei and I love each other. Why must mothers cry at their children's weddings? You should be happy.' Wiping away her tears, Nadezhda Vassilievna remembers saying the same to her own mother on her wedding day. Yes, why *does* a mother cry on that day of all days, asks *Pravda* rhetorically? 'Because only then does she remember all those important things she never told her daughter – how a woman's happiness consists of patience, kindness and caring; and how keeping and not losing that happiness on life's road full of ambushes is not easy.'[9] This picture of the sweet and patient wife, and the strong and virile husband, is at variance with reality. The comedy of Soviet manners continually shows the opposite: the aggressive wife frustrated at having to shoulder all the family cares; the husband forever expecting her to be the sweet mother, while he shuns any kind of decision, is more involved with his mates than with his wife, and is incapable of taking his place in the home, as a husband or even as a man.

Even the young are not free of ambiguity on the subject. During a discussion with a group aged seventeen to twenty-two in Leningrad, the girls, rather than the boys, insisted on the harmful effects of too much moral licence. For them, more than boys, it was a serious lapse to drink, use drugs or sleep around – things that 'leave more of a mark on a girl'. Girls were 'future mothers', and those who misbehaved 'degrade all of us'. But one girl was moved to say she hoped that in the next generation her own daughter would be 'liberated from all those Turgenev heroines who still weigh on us. I enjoy Turgenev; but that nineteenth-century literature is a thing of the past.'

The gap between reality and these clichés about men and women undoubtedly contributes to many of the divorces attributed to 'lack of preparation for life together', as does the myth of the mother, solid as a rock yet possessed of boundless compassion, which weighs on Soviet women and traps their men in a kind of emotional infantilism.

The role of the woman in the Soviet family is, in fact, very complex and beset with contradictions. At the 1987 Congress of Soviet Trade Unions, Mikhail Gorbachev returned in detail to something he had said about women and work at the previous year's Party Congress. Unless something was done to improve their lot, with its 'double day' of work in the factory and in the home, there could be no revival of the economy or improvement in social conditions. And despite what has been said about matriarchy, this is surely true.

Women often complain of having to shoulder all the burdens. Their menfolk, meanwhile, give the impression of helping by taking the children for a Saturday walk, so that women can get on with the housework 'in peace'. Bestushev-Lada calculates that the wives work an average of eleven hours a day and husbands only eight to nine hours.

Male and female roles are also very stereotyped, as these typical divisions of household tasks show.

– In the Kuzmitchev family, the husband, an army engineer, and his wife, a vocational schoolteacher, share tasks 'according to inclination'.

– Kolya Juravliev, a *kolkhoz*[g] driver, 'does all the man's work' about the house.

– Sasha Glouchenko, a skilled craftsman, says: 'There's always something to do in the flat. Things happen of their own accord.'[10]

At least these examples exhibit a new trend – that of the 'helping husband' – to be found in some urban households. But the opposite is still the rule.

– Olga Kolesnitchenko complains that her husband thinks housework is only for women and that anyway they 'do it better'. 'And strangely, many women agree with him.'

– Galina X, typical of so many Soviet women, creates obligations and then complains. Told by her son that 'nothing comes up to your cooking, Mum,' she comes home after long hours of work (and an hour in the Metro) to cook for him, though there is a perfectly good canteen where he could eat at his institute.[g][11]

Walking round any Moscow suburb towards midnight, one can see lights in innumerable kitchen windows, and the moving silhouettes of Galinas as they prepare tomorrow's meals. In other parts of the country the stereotype of the female in the household is even more rigid. Indeed, some everyday tasks are regarded as so 'unmanly' in Central Asia and the Caucasus that army conscripts arriving from those regions are given a lecture (where possible by a veteran of their own kind) and told that military life is exceptional, and that no stigma is attached to such duties as making one's bed.

Many of the problems of women in the home are to do with the family's need of a second pay packet. Half the workers in industry and nearly half of those in agriculture are women. Thus, in addition to fulfilling family duties, women perform more than their fair share of work in the least well-paid occupations. Nor is there any justification for the long-standing boast that three-quarters of Soviet doctors, and nearly all teachers, are women. These too happen to be among the poorest-paid professions.

Many women work from choice: out of genuine interest in the job or because their whole education has conditioned them to the idea of the 'working woman'. But surveys show that 20–30 per cent, particularly young mothers, work only because they need the money and that they have no wish to devote themselves to a career.[12] After their legal maternity leave they would prefer to go back to work part-time until the child reaches the age of ten. This supposes a change in labour legislation, which is also desired by some employers, especially in business and the service industries, who would like to have part-time staff for work during peak hours. It also calls for the organization, in apartment blocks for example, of activities to provide a social life for women who stay at home looking after children, particularly mothers of large families whose pregnancies mean long stretches out of work. But so far all the authorities have done is to increase family allowances and extend maternity leave.

In 1986 a round-table conference discussed the case of mothers who sacrifice their children's welfare to getting on in their professions. 'For years we were obliged to direct women's thoughts towards their jobs, and motherhood was given second place,' a psychologist, Dr Yuri Orlov, told the participants.

> We developed a network of nurseries and kindergartens in which we have since brought up several generations – and not badly. What is bad is that the mother now thinks that the nursery and kindergarten can take her place. Society should be alarmed by this debasement of motherhood. Concern for careers and dissertations has pushed children into the background. More and more women are refusing to have a second one.

Another speaker, a writer, observed drily: 'We must be one of the first generations in history to have to teach parents how to love their children.'[13] The round table also received the information that there are now some 8 million single-parent families in the Soviet Union.

But often the troubles of Soviet families, particularly 'model' ones, involve a quite different area: the failure of parents to treat their children as responsible beings. With married children there are rows about parents' interference (see chapter 11); with growing ones it is a question of authority[14] and the absence of dialogue.[15] Children complain that they cannot talk to their parents about intimate matters,[16] 'all the things you share with your friends'. Parents complain that their children are 'strangers'. To which the newspaper *Komsomolskaya Pravda* replies: 'Whether we like it or not, it is time for a new approach to the generation problem.'[17]

Asked why children seek advice from outsiders, a Moscow University sociologist, Adolf Khadrach, explained: 'All parents want their children's good. We want our children to be happier than ourselves. But when children and parents have different notions of happiness, conflict arises, and there's often a need for somebody who can look at the situation from the outside.' But does this lessen the need for the parents' example? Of course not. 'Where do happy families mostly come from? From happy families.' Khadrach also warned parents against acting dictatorially. 'You can't pass on life experience by commanding "Do this" or "Don't do that". What's needed is not judgement but understanding.'[18]

'The thing is to find a mutual understanding,' says the director Rolan Bykov, maker of many films among young non-conformists, including a classic called *Scarecrow* (see page 47). 'Confidence generates responsibility. We grown-ups say that this or that is good or bad. Wouldn't it be better if young people said it themselves? Why should they always be supposed to look among *us* for models?'* Bykov also has another fresh thought: parents should keep some private life of their own.[19]

It is a well-recognized fact among Soviet sociologists that young people are slow to learn how to bring up a family due to coddling by their own parents and society generally. Parents who have known a hard life, particularly mothers, want their children to have the best possible future. Grandparents, who remember what it was like in the war, can be even worse. Soviet teachers have to tell parents to make an early start by giving children small household tasks, and later letting them earn pocket-money – things that the West takes for granted (see chapter 4).

'Parents are there to help.' In 1987 *Pravda* seized on these commonplace words as the source of endless trouble. 'For many young people they promise a life free from all difficulty,' it declared – and, hoping to bring parents to their senses, offered some salutary information. Moscow University had just worked out that bringing up a child to the age of eighteen now cost parents and the State 17,000– 25,000 roubles, a sum that would have been unthinkable in the early 1970s. What was more, young people thought all this was only their due. When, as part of a demographic survey, a group of teenagers had been asked by their parents to list all the things they needed to buy urgently, they had ended up with an average bill of 700 roubles, nearly four times the average monthly salary.[21]

When a marriage can go no further, Soviet law makes separation easy. If both sides agree and there are no children, the formalities can

---

* *The novel idea that confidence leads to responsibility, and that excessive regimentation leads to a failure to grow up, also appears in a mid-1980s symposium.*[20]

be completed at the registry office. Otherwise divorce requires court approval. There are a few restrictions. A husband may not proceed against the wishes of his wife if she is pregnant or has a child of less than one year. And to limit impulsive divorces, there is a three-month delay between the written application and the act of separation (as much as six months if the court sees a chance of reconciliation). But divorces are never finally refused. They also cost very little: a hundred roubles, shared between the parties in cases of mutual consent, paid by the 'guilty' in others.

The number has now stabilized at about a million annually, after reaching a peak at the end of the 1970s, when there were two divorces for every five marriages. Previous annual levels were 300,000 in the late 1950s, 600,000 in 1966 and 700,000 in 1974. According to the latest census (1979) one woman in six aged thirty to sixty is divorced. But distribution is irregular. 'Catholic' Lithuania has one of the highest rates and 'Moslem' Uzbekistan one of the lowest.

There is no shortage of explanations for the large number of broken marriages. In 1984 a writer in *Nedelia* attributed it to 'improved living conditions and the more demanding standards of partners'.[22] But in 1985 specialists working in Brest produced more illuminating findings.[23] In 1983 there were 777 divorces in the city, compared with 1,974 marriages, a slight drop from the previous year. The majority of couples had been together three to five years, and had not more than one child. The commonest reason for breaking up was 'Lack of preparation for married life', given by 60 per cent of women'; the second alcoholism, given by 31 per cent of women and 23 per cent of men; and the third infidelity. Three-quarters of the divorces had been on the wife's initiative. Sixty-eight per cent of the men, but only 28 per cent of women, had subsequently remarried.[24]

But although divorce may be easy for the parents, it is often very hard on Soviet children. These are generally placed in the care of the mother, that is to say, in a home without the permanent presence of a man. Half of all couples lose contact after the divorce, which makes visiting rights uncertain. And many children of divorced couples are repeatedly dragged hither and thither, obliged to change home, school and friends. Some simply become unwanted, particularly when their mother remarries.[25] If lucky, they may be taken to live with their grandparents; if not, they can become the object of painful wrangles: 'cases' to be decided by 'minors' commissions'.[g]

A typical case was that of Lena, born as the result of an overexuberant evening when her nineteen-year-old mother was celebrating her admission to drama school. Her mother had dreamed of becoming an actress; but then came this unwanted child. Soon after birth, Lena was taken to live with her grandparents. Later, her mother married; Lena was brought back, and a second daughter was born. But the marriage broke up. 'Her mother never wanted her,' wrote a *Moskovski Komsomolyets* reporter. 'Her childhood ended at six, that terrible day when she left her grandmother to come to Moscow. But who asks the opinion of a six-year-old child? Her subsequent life was a story of absconding, petty-theft and alcoholism.' She finally got out of it, but 'this kind of itinerary is nothing unusual'.

Then there was Ekaterina, who told *Sobesednik* magazine: 'A year after I was born my mother sent her son from an earlier marriage back to his father. Then her marriage with my father broke up. I thought she was going to marry for a third time and send me to my father too. But unfortunately she didn't.' The wretchedness of her childhood so traumatized Ekaterina, now a grown woman and a doctor, that she was afraid to have a child of her own. She blamed the almost automatic award of custody to the mother: 'How can one be so sure that the mother is the right person?'[26]

The question of custody provoked a long debate in *Literaturnaya Gazeta*,[27] which decided, with a hint of male partisanship, that it was wrong for the father to have to pay maintenance but have no say in the child's upbringing. 'Even if the mother is guilty of negligence, so long as she is not a chronic alcoholic, the father has no chance of obtaining charge.'

More opinions on the subject of love and marriage:

– From *Komsomolskaya Pravda*: 'You need only see a film to know what happens when "love" intervenes. You see a wife at home with three children, squeezed between the housework, her job and bringing up the family. Then along comes a pretty girl, and the hero, the man, finds an escape with her – from his work, his wife and the children. How often do you hear on television: "I can tell just by reading a letter if it's from the wife or the lover." Does that mean that you can't be both at the same time?'[28]

– From Ludmila of Leningrad, talking about married friends at her institute: 'Nearly everyone agrees that everything in the household falls on the wife; husbands soon forget to show affection and can't even buy a loaf by themselves.'

– From *Pravda*: 'And then they complain that their wives can't make borsht "like mother does".'[29]

For years the vast number of children left abandoned in the Soviet Union could be explained by the vicissitudes of war and famine. But this is no longer possible. These children left voluntarily by their parents are one of the worst scandals of Soviet society. The scandal is all the greater in that this is a society in which all traditions are for once united, from one end of the country to the other, in making the child a cradled, cherished, pampered being. 'Children are our wealth' is not just another political slogan but a cry that echoes a deep popular sentiment. In hotels or in the street, the presence of a child ensures the parents endless pieces of advice but also opens studiously locked doors.

At the time of the Chernobyl disaster, newspapers were deluged with letters offering temporary shelter or holidays in the country: 'Here they'll find open air, good food, a grandfather ready to teach them how to fish' or 'Our flat isn't large, but our children of eight and thirteen have decided to give up their room to children of the same age evacuated from Pripyat.' Most writers asked for their names and full addresses to be printed so that parents could get in touch directly.[30]

But abandonment is not always by choice, and some mothers resign themselves to it with death in their hearts – like A.X. from near Moscow.

> My mother was dead, my father was an alcoholic, and my husband left me before the baby was born.* The factory where I worked had three shifts, and I couldn't change this. The only help I got from my collective was to put my son in a home. But I always went to visit him, and when I finally found a different job, and a room, I took him back. My pay was sixty-five roubles. I didn't draw any allowance because I didn't want to register as a single mother. That lasted for years. Aloysha went to school and I went to the university, still working on night-shift in order to keep us both. I'm not complaining. But I can't forget the day I had to put my boy in a home.[31]

It is in a children's home that children without parents usually end up. This may be as a result of abandonment or the consequence of a court decision in cases of ill treatment or moral danger, generally alcoholism.† Older children are put into a State boarding school (*internat*[g]). In principle their parents share the cost of their keep. But

---

*Nearly 10 per cent of births in the Soviet Union are to single women, but the law makes no distinction between legitimate and illegitimate.

†In 1987 there were 422 'infants homes' (*dom rebionka*) for children under three, 745 'children's homes' (*dom detska*) for children above this age and 237 *internats*.[32]

only in principle. Newspapers are constantly getting angry letters about single mothers who abandon their children and continue to draw allowances, or parents who spend all their pay on drink while the State keeps their children for free. Only 10 per cent of the children in these schools and homes are orphans. The rest have living parents, and some are put there as late as twelve or thirteen.

The institutions themselves face enormous problems, none of them new: emotional deprivation among their charges, teaching problems, a shortage of qualified staff. The work is hard and discouraging. In 1985 the warden of a children's home in Varaklian, Lithuania, accepted thirty applications from students graduating from teachers' institutes – applications full of enthusiasm after the appearance of an article in *Komsomolskaya Pravda*. In January 1987 only twelve were still at work. 'Let's not mince words, the work here is tough', the head confided. 'There's no apprenticeship to freedom, because everything's regulated, from getting up to going to bed. Even the bright ones find it difficult to learn anything.'[33] There are also serious problems of overcrowding and lack of equipment; in 1987 *Komsomolskaya Pravda* reported that eight children were crowded into bedrooms meant for four, and that the lavatories were 'as bad as those in railway stations'.[34] Student-teachers coming for the first time were said to be so overcome by the conditions that they volunteered to do spare-time jobs in order to buy the children some toys.[35]

Despite such prompt and valuable help, the Soviet press has made the condition of children's homes one of its favourite targets. In August 1986 the newspaper *Moskovski Komsomolyets* published a devastating account of conditions in the Dedenevski home near Moscow. The roof was collapsing, there was damp in the walls, and the cellar where the children's showers were located was knee-deep in water. After an earlier scandal the children had been promised fresh fruit. But in the intervening two months they had received none at all, apart from some apples given by local villagers. Their only meat had been stewed beef from tins.

But the worst scandal concerned so-called discipline. The head teacher, a woman called Faiha Mirgovan, had punished children caught smoking by mixing tobacco in their food. 'Some could not face this; others were so hungry that they swallowed it all down.' When Mirgovan found one child smoking in a lavatory, she had taken the burning cigarette and tried to force it down his throat. When he turned his head, she had dropped it down his collar. The children told the newspaper that if they committed a more serious offence, they were taken to a 'punishment cell' and beaten with a rubber hose. Girls who had tried to run away had their heads shaved.[36]

Because of the shortage of places in homes, many 'orphans' are put into children's hospitals. In 1986 a scandalized mother wrote to the magazine *Smena* after visiting her sick child in hospital in Yaroslavl: 'Every day I saw the sad faces of children who were not ill at all.' Following up her letter, the magazine went round various hospitals in the town and found numerous cases of perfectly healthy children who had been deserted by their parents or put there because their parents were alcoholic. 'Deserted and rejected, they lie there on their beds. The orderlies try to put them away from infection, but it doesn't always work. So they catch every conceivable kind of illness.'[37]

But above all it is the emotional desert of these children, their feeling of rejection, that preoccupies the country. Referring to a moving book, *Children's Home* by Larissa Mironova, *Literaturnaya Gazeta* observed:

> It is not a question of money. The government spends plenty on the young. It is an emotional problem. Only a minority are orphans, the others are abandoned children from broken homes or have criminal parents. They develop a feeling of dependence ('I'm in an orphanage, so everything is my due') and have no apprenticeship in freedom and responsibility. Hence their difficulties in becoming part of society.[38]

'How many unhappy children have I not seen in *internats*; we've got to face the problem of birth control,' wrote an educationalist, I. Kortcheva,[39] shortly after four nurses at Nijni Tagil in the Urals revealed that twenty-four babies had been abandoned at birth in their hospital in a single month.[40] But while there is endless talk about 'lack of moral education' and similar clichés, the real, social causes – lack of contraception, alcoholism (particularly of mothers, whose condition determines custody) and now the problem of young mothers on drugs – remain to be tackled at the root.*

---

*Noting the rising number of babies born with neurological malformations, an official of the Russian Federation's Health Ministry, Antonia Gratcheva, proposed a law requiring pre-marital medical checks and 'obligatory contraception' for young women alcoholics and drug addicts. She also called for changes in the law to cover situations in which alcoholics' children are informally adopted by kind-hearted neighbours, and later their parents come back and claim them.[41]

# · 3 ·

# A 'Communist Education'

*The Soviet education system – reforms of 1984 and 1987 – vocational training – universities and institutes – prestige institutions – abuse of 'collective' concept – lack of careers guidance – mystique of manual training – campaign against 'special schools' – unequal opportunities – 'cramming' – crisis in P T Us – decline of night schools – handicapped and 'problem' children – further reform*

Few things will more directly affect the character of tomorrow's Soviet citizens than the Soviet education system, which sharply distinguishes the Soviet concept of society from that of the West.

The main difference is the completeness of the Soviet system. Though public education in the West may devote some effort to producing decent citizens, even be touched with a little patriotism (as in the United States), it is primarily a system for implanting knowledge. Soviet education, on the other hand, is concerned with the production of citizens. It aims to be a 'total education', to produce 'good citizens of our country' with an adequate 'philosophy of life' [1] (see chapter 10) who know that 'there is no "I" without "we"'.[2] Youth is the future, as the Party is fond of saying. Hence the interminable arguments about education, and particularly the two reforms, in 1984 in secondary education and in 1987 in higher, of which more is said below.

Compulsory schooling now begins at six and lasts for eleven years. The first eight are spent in a general educational school. Then, at fifteen, pupils have three choices:

– They can remain with the general education course for ninth and tenth grades, finishing with a 'certificate of maturity', which is part of the requirement for entering higher education.

– They can leave the general stream for a 'secondary specialized school' (*tekhnikum* [g]) that combines general education with professional training in anything from electronics to nursing, office work to the arts. (Courses at secondary specialized schools are normally for four years; but pupils can also enter after finishing the whole general cycle, in which case, since they require only professional training, they attend for only two.)

– Or they can go to a vocational–technical school (PTU) for training as skilled craftsmen. PTUs also give some general education, but the standard is low. As explained later, they have also tended to become a dumping ground for 'difficult' and less talented children.

The Soviet constitution requires instruction to be available in one's mother tongue. But since curricula are uniform throughout the country, what happens in practice is that most pupils start by being taught in their own language, and Russian is introduced later.

The system of higher education distinguishes between universities, institutes, *tekhnikums* and pedagogical institutes, collectively known by the acronym *vuzy*,[g] whose Russian initials stand for 'higher educational establishments'. Universities, in addition to their research function, have numerous specialized faculties for training teachers in higher education. Institutes train higher specialist[g] or technical staff and are often helped financially by the Ministry they serve (thus the Ministry of Energy assists the Institute of Energy). The *tekhnikums* train middle-level technical staff. The pedagogical institutes, for example language institutes, train secondary-level teachers.

Access to *vuzy* is subject to a highly competitive examination. First-degree courses are for four or five years and lead to the award of a diploma. The more brilliant students may then go on to write a thesis and became a Candidate of Science (roughly corresponding to the Western Ph.D.) or, beyond that, a Doctor of Science.

The real distinction is not between universities and institutes (which until 1988 came under separate ministries) but between 'prestige' *vuzy* and others. One must undergo a merciless selection process to enter a *vuz* like MGIMO (the Institute of Foreign Affairs), MIFI (the Moscow Higher Physical Institute), the Kiev University foreign languages faculty or the Kalinin Polytechnic Institute in Leningrad. In addition, as we explain later, it is useful to have good family or Party connections, to be an active Komsomol member, and to be able to call on other non–academic references.

For those who have had to interrupt their studies or who want to change direction or jobs, there is a parallel system of night schools, which begins at ninth-grade secondary level, and, starting at higher level, correspondence courses.

At first sight the system works, particularly in the scientific and linguistic fields, with which Westerners have the most contact. They are invariably impressed by the fluency of Soviet participants in international seminars and conferences, while in the higher branches of science and mathematics the standing of Soviet scholars is unquestioned. But these are the country's foremost representatives, survivors of a system in which millions must waste time in symbolic ideological pursuits or have their talents misdirected to inappropriate jobs.

The trouble with the system is its over-generosity. A lifetime or more after the October Revolution, Soviet education still carries the emotional baggage of the early drive for knowledge, when the 'battle to liquidate illiteracy' became a kind of a crusade. Progress with a capital $P$ came to be measured by the extension of the period of universal education, while the university or institute beckoning at the end became a symbol of the conquest of knowledge by the people. This has resulted in a decline in the standing of manual skills, an inflation of diplomas and degrees, the growth of an army of underemployed and disenchanted youth, and the flooding of factories with secondary school-leavers who have to be trained from scratch.

As the second collective after the family, school is supposed to teach collectivism in practice, with all it entails in both security and constraint. To this have been added elevated notions of 'moral', 'atheistic', 'internationalist', 'patriotic' and 'work' education (see below), all judged indispensable for 'learning collectivism and humanism'.[3] In this way the young Soviet citizen is supposed to be immersed in a global educational environment in which school, family and youth movements all participate.

Of course, the authorities know well enough that the ideal of the collective, in which the stronger and cleverer pupils are supposed to take care of the weaker, can be subverted. There can be rejection and cruelty; this has been vividly depicted in Rolan Bykov's film *Scarecrow*, in which fellow-pupils persecute a young girl. And everyone knows about anti-social 'superniks' who must always be top – like Evgeny, who, on the eve of a vital physics paper for entrance to Moscow's Bauman Institute, stole the alarm clock of his competitors.[4] Yet the ideal of the collective persists.

One of the less agreeable consequences of the collective idea is the liability of children to be subjected to humiliating interference in their private affairs. Slava Gromadski, in School Number 10 in Belgorod, was humiliated by his teacher in front of the whole school Komsomol for having a 'modern' hair-cut. At another school, a pregnant girl, Olia, wanted to continue her studies at night school. She concealed her pregnancy and asked for her school documents 'because she was going to live with an aunt in Siberia'. When the falsehood was discovered, the head sent her before the local Party Committee, to whom she had to reveal her condition. She was then sent, like a delinquent or drug-taker, before the minors' commission to be reprimanded for 'loose behaviour'.[5]

In order to preserve the collective's good name, schools frequently hush up scandals. Thus when Sasha Traskin, a pupil in a school near Pskov, was so badly beaten up by bullies that he had to be hospitalized for psychiatric treatment, the whole school closed ranks to smother the affair, which only became known through the disclosures of the victim.[6]

'Delighted to see you,' beamed the Head of Simferopol PTU Number 26 – before he learned that the *Komsomolskaya Pravda* reporter had come about a vicious attack by a group of his teenage pupils on a party of young campers. The Head then pretended it was a matter of no consequence. The newspaper subsequently published the story under the sarcastic headline 'Nothing Happened'.[7] In the same 'good cause' of protecting the collective, schools have been known to provide pupils with false alibis when brought up before minors' commissions for misbehaviour and law-breaking.

A scarcely less subtle form of deception is practised by teachers in order to 'fulfill the plan' in terms of scholastic achievements. Since the failure of one pupil becomes a failure of the whole collective, the teacher feels responsible for having prepared his charge badly. The feeling of guilt can have disastrous consequences. So as not to fall short in the eyes of the school management or parents, the teacher over-marks exam papers, knowing very well that the poor performer should really be given an honest mark as an alarm signal.[8]

All this results in big arguments about the respective roles of parents and the school. Sociologists say parents today are encouraged to surrender their responsibilities.[9] Teachers accuse parents of not having enough interest in their children's performance.[10,11] And parents accuse parent–teacher meetings of too often being like public executions of those unlucky enough to have a lazy or undisciplined child.

The 1984 reform lowered the starting age of school from seven to six. It also introduced a number of other changes, including a new marking system, a better balance between scholastic and other activities (at least in theory), a better ratio of teachers to pupils, and less

Child in tears: 'I'm lost – up to now I was driven to school in my father's official car.'

pontificating and learning by rote. Teachers were instructed to encourage discussion in class,[12] and to develop a new relationship with their pupils, based on friendship and mutual respect. They were also promised better training and awarded more pay: a 30 per cent increase in 1985 and another in 1987.

All this was intended to make teaching more attractive, and especially to bring more men into a profession that, because of poor pay and lack of prestige, has become almost wholly feminized. (In the Russian Federation in 1986, nine-tenths of secondary schoolteachers were women.) Feminization adds greatly to the problems of upbringing caused by the absence of fathers. How extensive this is was disclosed in an inquiry by the review *Smena*,[13] which found that a quarter of all seventeen-year-olds and more than half the children in PTUs were from single-parent families.

In September 1986, the new Moscow Party boss, Boris Yeltsin, delivered a devastating attack on the condition of schools in the city. It was a fighting speech of the kind that was to be his undoing, and could well have applied to schools throughout the country. 'Why does everything revolve around the question of preparing pupils for *higher* education?' he demanded. 'How shall we fill out the ranks of the working class in the capital? How can we reconcile the demand for special schools [*spets-schkoly*]⁸ with the demand for social justice? How long will some children come to school in their parents' official cars [*sluzhebni*]?' (see page 59). He attacked the practice of over-crowding for the sake of good statistics. 'Instead of one room for teaching, and others for sleeping and recreation, the smaller children are given only one room. Forty per cent of our schools are like this. Provision of proper food and health care has been sacrificed to figures and percentages.' He then turned to the question of juvenile crime and drug addiction. 'Drugs have become a serious problem. For a long time we closed our eyes to it. This ostrich-like policy has led to our having 3,700 registered addicts in Moscow. One hundred and sixty-four have been found in schools and PTUs this year alone, and crimes by teenagers are steadily increasing.' Yeltsin also referred to corruption among teachers. In one case, he said, a head had been given a five-year sentence for systematically extorting bribes from staff members guilty of absenteeism, and 330 other Moscow teachers had been sacked for drunkenness and breaches of discipline.¹⁴

As well as attempting improved teaching methods, the 1984 reform also introduced a number of new subjects – not all with conspicuous success, as in the case of 'Ethics and Psychology of Family Life', an emasculated attempt to introduce sex education (see chapter 11), and 'Elementary Informatics and Computer Technology'. Another in-novation was a course on citizenship and the law.★

'Ethics and the Psychology of Family Life' has caused considerable bewilderment, not least among teachers. 'Here I am, a chemistry teacher, supposed to be talking about "mutual respect" and similar notions,' said one schoolteacher (a woman). 'Half the class have already had sexual experience. The other half simply want to know

★In August 1986 the television programme *Youth and the World*, using live street interviews, asked passers-by if they knew their rights as citizens. All replied 'No'. Commenting on the results, a lawyer deplored the small number of copies of the Soviet criminal code on sale and called for the rapid distribution of millions of copies in the form of pocket books.

how to have it without ending up in a catastrophe at the registry office. They'd be astonished if I were to tell them how I avoid pregnancies myself.'

The computer course was quickly given high-flown descriptions, such as 'a challenge without historical precedent'[15] and 'how to meet the new expectations of Soviet society in the new technological age'.[16] But those who knew the facts were less sanguine, especially as the Soviet Union produces very few personal computers, lacks technicians to repair them, and has very few teachers trained to give computer lessons to young children. 'More and more one hears that the study of informatics is just hours thrown to the wind,' wrote a *Sobesednik* contributor.

> Imagine someone being taught to ride a bicycle. He diligently learns that this bicycle consists of a frame, two wheels, handlebars, pedals and other bits and pieces, and that it serves as a vehicle for travelling short distances. But he can only straddle a chair and pedal his legs in the air. Absurd, you say! And quite rightly so. But this is more or less how informatics is taught in school, and nobody finds it ridiculous.
>
> I have seen a teacher, blushing and looking in confusion at her text book, tell sixth-graders about word-processors and discs with hundreds of kilobytes of memory. And the star pupils were sitting in the front rows, racking their brains in a vain attempt to imagine what this mysterious word-processor looks like – never having seen a computer, let alone discs, and wondering whether hundreds of kilobytes means a lot or a little.[17]

In Armenia, where no prospect exists of obtaining 1,500 computers for 30,000 schools, the authorities are experimenting with classrooms in buses,[18] a solution that has also been adopted in some other republics, including Belorussia. Another obstacle to implementing the reform has been the absence of new text-books. These will not be ready before 1992. 'So the transition will have to be made with the old ones,' says L. Chakhmaev, head of the State Pedagogical Laboratory, 'and their poor content is no secret.'


The reform of higher and middle education was the logical complement of the changes in secondary schools, for which the universities supply teachers. But, like the further reforms introduced in 1988, it also had an economic purpose: to step up the training of engineers and high-technology specialists. (The minister appointed to oversee the whole process is a trained engineer and former rector of Moscow's Mendeliev Institute, which has caused some misgivings in other departments, afraid of losing attention.) The reform imposes stiffer conditions on students, and gives greater autonomy to teaching bodies. On the whole it promises to be more successful.

University entrance has ceased to be an almost automatic ticket to eventual graduation, and matriculation now involves a quota of compulsory papers designed to 'reduce the element of chance' [19] and cut out the time-honoured system of favour-swapping (*blat*[g]). Nor is it possible any longer to carry over exams from one term to the next. Those who have not taken and passed their annual test by September are sent down, a measure that was expected to cut the student population by a third.

There are still lively arguments between those who want admission to depend less on examination marks and more on personality, and those who think there is already too much emphasis on non-academic factors. But at least the reformers are agreed on the need to eliminate one other method of qualification – that by corruption.

A spate of dismissals, begun under the short-lived leadership of Yuri Andropov and renewed under Gorbachev, put an end to the breath-taking sums obtained from the sale of diplomas in some Caucasian and Asian republics. (At the Odessa Medical Institute it formerly cost 700 roubles to pass without even attending the course.)

But in April 1986 a Leningrad court sentenced a Professor Kurbatov to twelve years with confiscation of property for taking bribes totalling 13,550 roubles. And eighteen months later *Moskovski Komsomolyets* described a system of illegal entry into higher education institutes in Moscow. Under this system, substitutes, known as 'stuntmen', take and pass entrance exams on behalf of unqualified 'clients'. In March 1987 a pair of smart-alecks called Braga and Omarovich were sentenced to prison for running a 'firm' for the purpose. The business began in 1980 when they met with a citizen called Timur, who was willing to pay 6,000 roubles to be enrolled at the Moscow Polygraphic Institute. Braga and Omarovich hired a 'stuntman' to take the enrolment exam for 500 roubles, and pocketed the difference. 'Not bad for two hours' work,' observed *Moskovski Komsomolyets*, adding that news of the facility 'spread like an avalanche'. The newspaper blamed the poor system of control and the negligence of institute staff: 'How else could one not notice that there were students who passed the enrolment exams . . . but who during examination sessions could not properly put together two Russian words?' Without stricter control and stricter punishment, the system of 'stuntmen' and 'clients' would continue.[20]

The 1987 educational reform also contained an industrial require-ment. Enterprises had to reimburse the State for training the young specialists they engaged. This was to discourage managements taking on many more than they needed as an insurance against a shortage. The practice was the cause of great bitterness in the past. A year later it had not been entirely eliminated. It was also responsible for a shortage of specialists in other enterprises.

The difficulty of placing the right person with the right qualifica-tions in the right job is a part of nearly every Soviet educational and industrial problem.

At the beginning of each academic year newspapers print pages of notices from universities and institutes, giving conditions of entry, subjects, dates of registration, details of entrance exams, and so on. This is the student's only practical guide in choosing which direction to follow, apart, that is, from the 'manual work' courses at school. These are supposed to keep him in touch with employers, but in practice they are seldom taken seriously, because parents would be shocked at the idea of their offspring choosing a blue-collar job.

In some sectors economic development is totally paralysed for want of skilled personnel, while others have a surplus. In 1987 *Pravda* reported that because of bad planning, Georgia had produced 55,000 surplus specialists, who were having 'one long holiday'. Party investigators found that institutes in the Black Sea 'sunbelt' were turning out historians, architects, psychologists and mathematicians without any reference to the number of positions available, at a time when there was a desperate shortage of skilled technicians in energy, mechanical engineering, electronics, automation and other vital fields.[21]

A 1986 all-Union conference on 'careers guidance' found that most students chose their profession for the wrong reasons. They were gravely disappointed when they took up their jobs, either be-cause these were not what they had expected, or because there were no skilled vacancies when they arrived. As a result the economy was wasting precious human resources.

Any attempt at better orientation is frustrated by the tendency of young people to prolong their studies to the maximum and by the romantic appeal of 'prestige' jobs. But there is also a woeful absence of any organized system for testing students' aptitudes. The Soviet authorities for years opposed the general use of psychological tests, which, they said, measured knowledge rather than personality and reflected the subject's current environment rather than his or her future potential. Today they are more open-minded. But tests must be used 'liberally' and not for any quick placing of subjects in rigid categories of 'talented' or 'limited'. The young person must be given time to develop, to discover his own inclinations,[22] and it must all be done within an interdisciplinary approach, because final judgement cannot be left simply in the hands of the psychologist.[23,24]

Subject to these 'safeguards', the Psychological Institute of the Soviet Academy of Sciences has begun to investigate 'the psychological aptitude of students for professions', and Moscow University Psychology Department has started a research and consultation centre, using a list of 600 trades and professions being taught in the city and *oblast*.[g][25]

But when it comes to the point, and a fifteen-year-old has to choose which job-oriented stream to follow, any advice the psychologists (or anyone else) may give must contend with the influence of parents, whose obsession with diplomas and 'prestige' is the despair of economic planners.


It should not be supposed that Soviet young people enjoy equal opportunities when choosing their futures. Not many academicians' sons are to be found in P T Us, and only a minute fraction of special-school pupils (see below) come from working-class families. We speak about string-pulling elsewhere. But Gennadi Yagodin, the Minister supervising education reform, thinks accusations of 'patronage' are exaggerated. Of course, he says, institute and faculty heads sometimes receive telephone calls 'recommending' this or that pupil, and they do not always resist – a situation that they are the first to deplore, but which they say is beyond them. However, a son joining his father's faculty does not automatically benefit from the connection. 'There are dynasties of workers, officers, actors . . . So why speak of favouritism when a son quite logically follows in his father's academic footsteps?'[26]

In August 1986 *Smena* published the results of a poll among 4,000 young people about their futures. Not surprisingly, most wanted higher education and an interesting job, and to become members of the intelligentsia. But their specific choices were interesting. Asked to evaluate different professions on a scale of 1 to 10, they gave 'actor' and 'journalist' first place with 8. 'Sailor' and 'pilot' came next with 7. Former 'prestige' professions came lower on the list: 'doctor' with 5.7 and engineer with 4.6. 'Secondary schoolteacher' received only

4.5 and physicist 4.8. In both 1963 and 1973, young people taking part in a similar poll in Novosibirsk gave 'engineer' 10. Ten years later they gave the same profession only 5.[27]

The 'hierarchy of jobs' reflected by such surveys was studied in greater depth by a group of Leningrad psychologists who asked a cross-section of young people why they wanted to become motor mechanics, salesmen, sailors, doctors, etc. The result was a cold douche for anyone believing in high motivation. From the replies it appeared that the future mechanics were mainly interested in jobs 'on the side'; the future salesmen in access to 'deficit' goods; the sailors in bringing back sellable purchases from abroad; and the future doctors in 'presents' from patients. In another inquiry applicants for places in the Plekhanov Economics Institute were found to be thinking not of the 'honour' of the economic professions but of finding a job where, in the homely Russian phrase, 'one is never without butter on one's bread'.

Letters to newspapers show that no one has any illusions about the cost to society of young people's eagerness to make a quick kopeck. 'Who has the smartest apartments, the best books?' asks a typical reader. 'Everyone knows that it's the easy money that attracts young people to work in restaurants and the like. What's so disgraceful is that many of them have engineering diplomas in their pockets.'[28]

The authorities do what they can to counter it. But, trying to boost unpopular jobs, like those in agriculture, they can overreach themselves. In the early 1980s the papers blossomed with pictures of coquettish girl farm-hands. A favourite film hero was the clean-limbed young countryman who, on completing his studies (brilliantly, of course), renounced the bright lights of the city to return to his native *kolkhoz* as an agronomist or vet. Papa was proud, and mama shed a tear. But very soon, the audience could be sure, the handsome vet would meet a pretty young dairy-maid and the couple would live happily ever after.

Sometimes local authorities act on their own initiative in seeking to attract young people back to the land. In the Kuban they appeal to local patriotism and open up institutes that teach new agricultural specializations.[29] Others think hopefully that with so many diploma-holders, the attraction of 'respectable' jobs will eventually give way to a thirst for real knowledge unconnected with one's work, and that blue-collar jobs will come back into favour.[30] But of this, so far, there is signally little evidence.

A serious crisis is meanwhile brewing in the PTUs. Intended to provide a skilled labour reserve, these are no longer fulfilling their role. Instead they are becoming a scrap-heap for unpromising pupils who arrive through rejection rather than by choice – a situation making for long-term social tensions. 'The low standing of working-class trades is the calamity of our economy,' says the economist Viktor Perevedentsev. 'Not only are they undermanned, but those who work in them are often people who could find nothing better.'[31]

But much of the talk about restoring the respectability of blue-collar work is ambiguous. One of the main aims of the reform of secondary education is to furnish the economy with badly needed specialists. Whole factories are paralysed by the shortage of skilled staff, while doctors of science have to wash test tubes for want of laboratory assistants. But no one dares to come out with the obvious solution. This would be for millions of young people to leave general education at fifteen and go into vocational and technical training of their own volition. For this to happen, the switch to the P T U would have to be 'positive' and not, as at present, carry a stigma of rejection or even of punishment.[32]

Heads of P T Us deplore the schools' practice of sending them all their 'bad elements': pupils accused of laziness, indiscipline, vandalism, alcoholism and other forms of misbehaviour. So does the National Institute for the Prevention of Delinquency, whose Director told *Ogonek*: 'You get the horrible paradox that schools use the P T Us to unload their worst pupils, just when society is making huge efforts to improve industrial discipline – yet the P T U is where workers are trained.'[33]

The result is a fear of two separate layers of society developing: the bright and the lucky, who take the royal road through the complete cycle of secondary education to university or institute, and the un-lucky and less talented who are forced back on second-class establishments. 'When will we stop centring everything on superqualification and the big *vuzy*?' asked V. E. Chukchunov, Rector of Novocherkask Polytechnic – a sentiment widely echoed by other educationalists.[34] But the P T Us at the bottom of the scale and special schools at the top are far from being the only instances of inequality in the system.

Pupils nearing completion of the full secondary school course are today made increasingly aware of what Russians call 'the scissors': the gap, as described by diverging lines on an imaginary graph, between what they know and what they are required to know in order to pass university and institute entrance exams. In recent years this has assumed alarming proportions, at least for those without strings to pull. 'Cramming' has become indispensable, even for those attending the best schools. Group tuition costs five roubles an hour, and individual teaching ten. To make things easier, many university faculties now offer tuition by their own staff, at only twenty roubles for a complete course. But this is beyond the reach of students in places far away.

Country schools are seriously short of teachers in essential exam subjects such as languages, science and maths. The rural exodus has reduced the number of pupils, and *kolkhozes* jib at finding the money for teachers of small classes. In the Baltic republics the problem has been solved by standing it on its head – first reopening schools and thus attracting back parents. In Estonia, Latvia and Lithuania there are now prosperous *kolkhozes* with young populations. But *kolkhoz* heads elsewhere react less imaginatively.

Night schools, begun before secondary education became compulsory and once highly successful, are now facing a crisis. Apart from young women obliged to leave general school for family reasons, most of the students now taking these 'second chance' courses do so from the wearisome need to obtain a certificate for their jobs. The lack of enthusiasm by the students is equalled by that of the teachers. There are few applicants for teaching positions and those recruited are often of indifferent quality.

Girls soon discover that, for all the talk about equality, by no means are all careers open to both sexes. Two bastions fell in the mid-1980s: the Police School and the Institute of Marine Engineering at Murmansk. But there are still pitifully few women in industrial management positions and senior administrative posts.

Married students with children (whose numbers doubled in the early 1980s) have formidable problems of accommodation and child-care. Often young wives have to abandon their studies or put up with going to night school. One of the few institutes to take note of the situation is Moscow's Gubkin Institute, which is building a 350-family hostel to be ready by 1990. But this is a 'prestige' institute supported by the Gas and Petroleum Ministry.

Spared most of the problems that beset other parts of the education system are the special schools so fiercely attacked by Yeltsin in his Moscow speech. Their existence and privileges have caused argu-

Son of string-pulling official: 'And did you get the permission of the head to give me only two out of five?'

ments out of all proportion to their numbers. Not to be confused with another kind of specialized school for blue-collar trades, the special schools were created in one of those bursts of enthusiasm for 'intellectual excellence' that have punctuated Soviet history as frequently, and as erratically, as drives to open the universities to workers and peasants. Special schools were opened (and, despite increasing criticism, continue to exist) for promising linguists, scientific and mathematical prodigies, budding artists. Entry is intended to be competitive but is often clearly helped by parents' connections and social background. There are some ninety in Moscow, and they are distributed very unevenly: most are located in white-collar districts, while some blue-collar districts often have none at all. In 1987 *Moskovskaya Pravda* reported a survey in which pupils at Moscow's Special School Number 10 were asked where their fathers worked. Typical answers were: 'in the Council of Ministers'; 'in an institute'; 'in a ministry'; 'his job is secret'. Not one child came from a blue-collar family, and all were proud of their parents' prestigious positions. Probing further, the newspaper found that in all Moscow's special schools, only six in one hundred first-year pupils had worker parents – a proportion that shrank as one went up the age scale and on graduation often dropped to zero.[35]

Challenged to defend the system, the head of Moscow's Special

School Number 1 agreed that special schools were 'strongholds of social injustice' that embraced two kinds of 'illegally enrolled' pupils. 'But what can one do?' he asked. One category consisted of the children of former pupils: 'Condemn us if you like, but teachers have a right to be proud if parents send their children to their old school.' The second category – the 'phone callers' (dosvonochniki) – had to be taken in because of a word in the right ear. No school wanted them; their standard of intelligence was 'often far from high'. And it was they who caused the most trouble, 'never letting anybody forget who their daddies and mummies are. But can you blame the school? We can't refuse local bosses.' Such are the pupils who, until Yeltsin's speech put a stopper on it, were collected from school in their fathers' official cars, and met by 'mothers or grandmothers in Canadian sheepskin coats'.[36]

When the special-school students finally graduate, their parents can nearly always be relied on to get them into 'prestige' institutes, like the Institute of International Relations, where a knowledge of languages is a huge advantage in entrance examinations. But none need feel guilty. 'I went to one of the best special schools in Moscow,' says a former pupil, now a faculty dean. 'Later I entered an excellent institute. All my friends did similarly. The circle of people I belong to today are not rogues, but friends who enjoy giving public service. Since we all have positions that allow us to do that, we have a good life.'

Meanwhile, general school pupils are, in some cases, reduced to only one foreign-language lesson per week, compared with eight in the 1950s and 1960s.[37] In 1986 this caused Moscow University Party chiefs to note that 'the standard of language-teaching in general schools is not answering modern needs, whereas in the vast majority of special language schools it is so extensive that other subjects suffer'. The Party therefore proposed that the system be changed.*[38]

A marked feature of the general run of schools is excessive regimentation. In 1986 an Ogonek reporter, examining a list of 'Rules of Behaviour' set out by the Moscow Education Directorate, was astounded to find that minors were 'forbidden to ice-skate along railway

---

*Other Party members observed that special schools were centres of free-spending and snobbery, where the ultimate goal was to have nothing Soviet. In the lavatories of Special School Number 9 they sold 'everything from chewing-gum to badges featuring Fascist rock groups. They also steal one another's foreign-made clothes' – practices conducive to 'drink, drugs, sexual dissipation and foreign currency speculation'.[39]

tracks . . . to hawk flowers and plants (but not, apparently, cassettes and cassette-recorders, which the militia say they do all the time), not to climb on roofs not designated for games ("Are there such roofs?" asked the reporter), and not to play games with knives and firearms [*sic*].' The same rules included the notorious regulation forbidding children under eighteen to be on the streets after nine in the evening.

It was recommended that the reporter visit School Number 734, considered to be 'exemplary' for its standards of discipline. At the door she found thirty more Rules of Behaviour, consisting almost entirely of pettifogging prohibitions. For example: 'during breaks, it is forbidden to walk down the corridors more than two abreast'; 'it is forbidden to loiter on the stairs'; 'on receiving their [outdoor] coats, pupils will leave the premises without dawdling'. While reading the list, the journalist was startled by the stentorian voice of a woman with a red arm-band telling her to go 'buzz off'. As she did so, she met a parent who had been summoned for an interview. Her son had committed a serious act of hooliganism: racing down the school corridors, and not having the right kind of indoor shoes.[40]

What 'hooliganism' means in popular terminology can be learned from scandalized letters to the press about how children throw balls of paper out of school windows, smoke in the street and hold satchel-throwing contests – trifles that would hardly cause a sigh among Western teachers. There is, however, a serious problem of delinquency – and 'delinquent', 'deprived' and physically or mentally abnormal children present the system with special problems.

The first two categories are sent to *internats*. In these, about 80 per cent are the children of alcoholics. Delinquents convicted of more serious offences are sent to corrective 'colonies', where they receive a scanty training for a manual trade and, as in adult camps, frequently learn to become real delinquents. Their emotional plight was sympathetically explored in yet another of the films inspired by *glasnost* for the benefit of domestic audiences, *Children of School Age*.

The lot of abnormal children varies more widely. Some are sent to special schools, often of high quality, for the physically handicapped, while others go to schools treating severe mental problems. The less obviously handicapped come off worse, usually finding themselves at the bottom of a normal class before being sent to a vocational school.

In 1986 the educational newspaper *Uchitelskaya Gazeta* published a much discussed article by two experimental teachers, the Tikhonovs, who have been dealing with retarded children for many years. They wrote:

> Every teacher knows that 20–25 per cent of pupils are in some degree mentally backward because of parents' alcoholism, a birth trauma or hereditary illness.* The [official] principle that all children have the same potential, and that consequently bad results are the fault of the teacher, is against the facts. The child who because of illness cannot meet the school's 'common requirements' is constantly condemned to low marks, morally humiliated in class and pounced on by the staff.

The Tikhonovs proposed a new kind of school where retarded children would receive special teaching and medical assistance. 'At present only the most handicapped are sent to such schools, whose very name – "special schools for the retarded" – is humiliating. Everybody knows that it is precisely this kind of humiliation that drives children into the street, where they can prove themselves by bullying more gifted classmates.'[41]

In 1988 Soviet education was recognized to be in such a state of crisis that it was made the subject of a plenary meeting[g] of the Central Committee. The previous so-called reform of general education had meanwhile not ceased to be attacked for being timid and piecemeal by both teachers and the press. There was, however, one area of hope that has since received official recognition. This is a method of teaching based on a series of new principles: creativity, more time for the teaching of the specific rather than the general, the abolition of rigid programmes, individuality of approach and work rhythm, spontaneity, limited discipline and no punishments during the first four years. The pioneer of this new method is the Georgian Slava Amonachvili, who freely acknowledges the earlier work of the pedagogue Zankov and the psychologist Davidov. The system is now applied in primary schools in Georgia and on a limited scale in other regions.[42]

But any reform is doomed to failure if left to the Ministry of Education alone. A whole series of solutions to the problem of schools is dependent on action by other authorities in quite different sectors of government. New and renovated buildings are needed, new

---

*Experts have pointed out that alcoholic parents in their twenties (the commonest procreation age) are not yet so damaged as to be able to transmit physical defects to their children. The effect of alcoholism on the children is more likely to be emotional and psychological.

equipment, up-to-date text-books and teaching materials. Above all, it is necessary to provide accommodation for teachers – and not just accommodation but, in many regions, a tolerable cultural and social life. For it can no longer be assumed that simply raising pay will attract better people to a whole backward area of the system.

Moreover, the reformers have yet to curtail the oversolicitude resulting from their belief in children's basic goodness, derived from the beliefs of Rousseau; that, surrounded by constant care and attention, children will always find useful work to perform for the society that taught them; that imperfections are perfectable; and that strays are never so lost as to be beyond hope of reunion with the flock. At present this dangerously unqualified optimism remains unchecked, despite the fact that putting so much weight on the effect of education directly contradicts the Party's declared intention of combating 'infantilism' among the young, who are thus deprived of all responsibility for their successes and failures.

# 4

# Defenders of the Faith

*The Soviet army — daily life — system of call-up and deferment — selection of officers — role in political and 'patriotic' education — reduced popularity of army careers — operational efficiency — prohibition of alcohol — service in Afghanistan — problems of return to civilian life — veteran vigilante groups — the army and sport*

The typical day of a Soviet conscript soldier begins with a bugle call at 6 am in some dusty garrison near the borders of China or Mongolia, or, if he is luckier, in some former *Wehrmacht* barracks in the German Democratic Republic. (For a small, but important, fraction of 100,000 or so it began for most of the 1980s on the parched plateau near Kabul or Kandahar – but that is another story.)

Reveille is followed by physical training, room-cleaning and ablutions. After breakfast there is a regimental parade, after which companies disperse to undertake the morning's tasks: drill, weapon-training, vehicle-maintenance, political education or possibly fatigues, including, in remoter places, looking after the regimental livestock. Afternoons are similarly spent, perhaps with a break for sport. After six, and again after supper, the soldier is 'free'.

There is a good camp library, an up-to-date film show once a week, a football pitch and gymnasium for the athletic. But not much else. The canteen, called 'soldiers' tea-room', sells only what it says, plus cheese or sausage sandwiches to supplement the cookhouse meals, whose quality depends on the honesty of the cooks. Visits to the nearby town, if there is one, require a sparingly granted pass. Outside, the soldier must always wear parade uniform, never smoke while walking, and be ready to be checked by military police wherever he goes. In fact, nearly all 'free time' is spent in camp following one of the pursuits mentioned or lying in one's bed in the barrack room.

'Sleep is the nearest thing to home,' runs an old Red Army saying.* And home is much dreamed of. Unless he has an urgent compassionate reason, such as the death of a near relative, or is specially rewarded with a ten-day leave as an exemplary soldier, the conscript will not

*Since the Second World War the official title of the army has been the Soviet Army.

see home for the whole two years of his service. The only link with parents, wife or girlfriend will be a fast and efficient postal service – though, if they can afford the fare, the relatives may visit the camp for one of its rare 'family days', for example when conscripts take the military oath.

This is the sombre view, typically from the standpoint of a town-bred European. But there is also another. After the hyper-protection of parents and school, the army is generally the conscript's first break with his background – the first and sometimes the last. For some, it offers a welcome change, a breath of fresh air, a touch of the exotic. When collective farm-hands were still denied passports, quite a few took advantage of their army service not to go back to their villages when released. For young Europeans, military service is often the only chance to see Asia and the Caucasus. And you need only observe young Asiatic soldiers sight-seeing in Red Square or the museums of Leningrad to understand that they too are discovering another world.

It is also a break for the millions of young men who will afterwards start work and get married; a watershed between carefree youth and the responsibilities of adulthood. Hence so many pictures in uniform in the Soviet citizen's photograph album: snaps on excursions with room-mates, in the company of smiling girls, on manoeuvres, on the firing ranges, and so on. They bring back a feeling of comradeship that, even for those who detested their service, remains the most positive aspect of their time.

Many keep in touch with their comrades all their lives. 'Those were the ones I shared nearly everything with,' recalls a young university teacher. 'We lived together, depended on one another, went through the same experiences. We ate rough, slept rough, gave each other moral support. This one showed me how to do electrical repairs. That one, an Uzbek, I gave Russian lessons to. Another taught me Caucasian cooking.' In all other respects the speaker hated it.

There are two annual call-ups, April to June and October to December, when railway stations bristle with the close-cropped heads of young men on their way to their units. Earlier they will have appeared before their local military service board and been passed fit; they will then have waited for a letter telling them where and when to report, but not saying the arm in which they will serve. In more colourful days friends would sometimes escort them to the barracks, with force, vodka, songs and guitars.

Call-up is at eighteen, except for some students, who may obtain a deferment by doing military training at their universities or institutes: 150 to 360 hours, according to the length of their study courses. They then serve for a short period as officers. But since the early 1980s, because the army is short of ordinary soldiers, the number of 'military chairs' overseeing this pre-service training has been steadily reduced. Most students are now called up as soon as they have completed their first university year, and serve like everybody else.

Well before call-up, boys between fifteen and seventeen receive instruction in drill and weapon-handling at school, and girls are taught first-aid. At seventeen, young people may join the Armed Services' Auxiliary Association (DOSAAF$^g$), where they can learn to ride motorbikes or become radio hams. Every year 500,000 receive training at DOSAAF centres. Or they may join the Preparation for Work and Defence Programme (GTO$^g$), which puts emphasis on sport. But since the 1950s both programmes have lost much of their military meaning, and Russians find it difficult to understand why the West still represents them as an element in the 'militarization of Soviet society'.

Nevertheless, young people who do this premilitary training can be promoted directly to soldier first class or corporal. If they re-engage at the end of their service, they are made sergeants, while university graduates are made lieutenants. To make good the shortage of qualified technicians, there is an intermediate rank between non-commissioned officers and regular officers – that of *praporchiki*.

Under the *praporchik* system, a young man after completing his conscription service may take a three to six months' course; if he passes, he is offered a five-year contract renewable every two years. The *praporchik* is responsible for technical tasks indispensable to a modern army but that need a continuity of service impossible with conscripts. The high pay and the flexibility of the formula, which does not tie a man to the army for life, attract many young people and the system is said to have given the army a noticeably higher technical level.

Those bent on a lifetime's career in the service follow a different pattern. Regular officers come up through military schools and academies, of which there are about 150 spread across the country, giving courses of two to six years. A select number, about one in twenty, mostly the sons of officers, pass through elite Suvorov academies, where entry begins at the age of ten.

It is Suvorov cadets who, with set features and impeccable precision, traditionally head the October Revolution parades in Red Square. Other cadets are reputed to be marginally less traditional, and some (see chapter 8) have even been accused of reading West German rock magazines.

About a quarter of the army's regular cadre consists of non-commissioned officers and soldiers who opt for a service career while conscripts. Their contact with recruits can be rough, and in 1987 the Soviet press reported cases of bullying. In one instance (reported directly to the authors) a young soldier was so badly beaten up that he had to be discharged on medical grounds. His molester was charged and sent to prison. More came to light when in November the same year the review *Yanost* serialized the novel about army life *100 Days do Demobilization* by Yuri Poliakov. In it the author describes relations between conscripts and non-commissioned officers, the humiliations heaped by 'second-year soldiers' on new recruits, and the liberties taken with regulations. Its appearance after a wait of nearly ten years was hailed by some delegates at the Twentieth Komsomol Congress (see chapter 7).

It is also common, as in many other armies, for working-class non-commissioned officers to pick on conscripts from the intelligentsia. So disturbing were the facts when fully revealed by 1988 that Dr Andrei Sakharov made a point of them during a 'post-summit' Moscow press conference.

While newspaper articles and television programmes (like the Sunday morning army programme *I Serve the Soviet Union*) deal with military day-to-day life and occasionally show, with considerable honesty, the gap between rhetoric and reality, official literature leaves no doubt that 'the breast of the soldier is the defence of the motherland', and that in the army the recruit will discover the 'brotherhood of arms'. 'The highest ambition a man can have is to serve his country,' declared the head of the Moscow military commission,[g] Major-General Nikolaevich Illarionov, in the magazine *Nedelia*.[1] But he had to admit that some conscripts regarded their military service as 'lost years – lost as regards their studies and education'.

An indication that the army is not always so popular is a decree, dating from the mid-1980s, fixing penalties for helping young men to evade service. Those guilty often include housing officials who, for a service or consideration, 'forget' to notify the military commission when a boy reaches age.[2] One of the explanations offered for this lack of military enthusiasm is the higher educational level of today's recruits. Before the war, boys who had completed primary education were immediately made sergeants. After the war, seven years of education was sufficient. Now all recruits must have at least ten years behind them. They are also less prepared to be ordered about – which may explain why in 1987 General Alexei Lizitchev, head of the army's political department, called for better communication between ranks and the dropping by officers of 'an imperious tone of command'.[3]

Today's changed attitudes are also reflected in a decline in the prestige of the regular military career. Though uniforms still have glamour, at least for the wearers, the attraction of an officer's career is not what it was. Amazingly, in so militarized a country, there is no published study of the social status of military life. It is therefore necessary to resort to expedients. A study in the 1970s showed that even then, when up to 33.9 per cent of workers had set out wanting a white-collar profession, only 2.1 per cent had contemplated a military career. Even agriculture and the despised 'service' occupations rated higher.[4] The same coolness towards the army has been found among students in upper secondary grades. For them the only white-collar professions less esteemed than the military are reportedly those of light-industrial engineer, agronomist and schoolteacher.[5] Taken with similar studies in some sixty countries, this makes the army less prestigious in the Soviet Union than in most others.[6] The military career has also received low marks in surveys dealing with prospects of promotion and 'creativity'.[7]

Whenever research discovers a military career attracting young people, it nearly always turns out to be that of aircraft pilot – pilots being on a par with artists and well above generals. So, when the Soviet Defence Ministry says there are three times as many applicants to military academies as there are places for them, it is glossing over the difference between army academies and those of the much more popular air force. Moreover, according to the Ministry's Director of Staff Administration, the majority of cadets are workers', farmers' and officers' sons – that is to say, from social groups of low or medium standing, with limited chances of ascending the hierarchy. Further evidence of difficulty in filling the ranks of the officer corps is the fact that since the mid-1980s boys have been allowed to enter cadet schools below the age of seventeen.[8]

Account must also be taken of the constant moves army service imposes, often from one end of the country to the other, something that particularly upsets rural families. And, a sign of the times, young officers taking up their first postings now have at their disposal an official manual dealing with problems of 'adaptation'.

The image of the armed forces presented by their own propaganda – parades, films, speeches, demonstrations – is one of great efficiency. The ceremonies in particular can be very impressive. In Red Square during the 7 November parade, when the guns behind the Kremlin crash out salvo after salvo in salute, and the massed bands strike up the national anthem, one senses to the full the mystique of a great, highly disciplined fighting force.

But the workaday reality is inevitably less perfect. Units on field exercises have the same quota of collisions, misunderstandings and general confusion as in Western armies – a situation, however, with which the Soviet soldier is comfortably at home, since it replicates the common state of Soviet industry.

In 1974 a defecting Soviet officer described the confusion resulting from an exercise in which members of the Politburo[g] were to be shown a mass crossing of the river Dneiper. The tanks were fitted with breathing apparatus and, to help them steer underwater, strips of steel matting were laid on the river-bed. As a further precaution, the vehicles were crewed by officers wearing overalls without rank badges.

All went well until the infantry began following in amphibious carriers. When they were half-way across, the artillery should have lifted its covering fire and moved to targets in depth. But it did not, either because the artillery observers had missed the right moment, or because the battalion had started crossing too early. 'In any case, it was impossible for the armoured carriers to continue, and they started to circle in the water, crashing into one another in the current.' Eventually the Defence Minister shouted into a microphone and the guns stopped. But the armoured carriers continued pirouetting in the water, since the battalion commander dared not give the order to advance. 'When finally . . . the battalion moved towards the bank, not one carrier managed to get out, because the guns had cut the opposite bank to pieces. Eventually the battalion commander did the only thing he could: he ordered the crews to get out and wade or swim ashore.'[9]

Sometimes operational mistakes are too big to hush up: like the 1985 shooting down of the KAL airliner and the 1987 failure to prevent the young German, Mathias Rust, invading Soviet air space and landing his light plane in Red Square. Such disasters are most likely to be the result of a whole series of disciplinary failures that in different circumstances would normally be concealed. The same tendency to hush things up noted earlier in the case of schools is found in companies and battalions, where even in the case of quite serious offences, every effort is made to keep punishments within the unit itself, rather than send offenders to a civil prison or to one of the more dreaded penal battalions.

Life in one of the latter was described in December 1987 in *Sovietski Voin* (the bi-monthly journal of the main political administration of the Soviet army and navy). 'The convicted men march measuredly in columns to and from supper . . . They wear no decorations or medals. They are guarded by men with automatic rifles who escort them to work, stand over them at work and escort them back from work.' Rather surprisingly, the article revealed that nearly all the military prisoners were Komsomol members, the commonest recorded charges being assault and battery, insults and mockery. The magazine gave the case of a sergeant reduced to the ranks for striking a subordinate. In most cases social immaturity was associated with a well-to-do family background, it added.

It might well be asked what a new generation of more serious-minded young Russians thinks of the army professionally. In the higher echelons, a group of officers, described as 'Young Turks', is said to be pressing for the military *perestroika* that has yet to take place. In this they may have been helped by a series of promotions following the 1987 replacement of the ageing chief of the defence forces, Marshal Sokolov, over the Rust affair. But the military bureaucracy remained opposed to any cut in the call-up.

At the same time the day is long past when Western observers could characterize the 5 million members of the armed forces as an army of vodka-swillers, and a former battalion commander could unblinkingly tell us that his unit, stationed in the Far East, was 'drunk from morning to night'. The picture brought back by today's conscripts is totally different.

Not only do barracks canteens serve only tea, but even the sale of loose tea is frequently stopped, because in concentrated form it can be used as a narcotic – the famous *chiffir* of crime stories and tales of the 'camps'. Recruits from drug-using areas like Central Asia are regularly searched for 'grass' or, more often, the narcotic paste called *dour*, after the Russian word for 'crazy' (*dourak*).[10] Alcohol can sometimes be smuggled into camp, but penalties are heavy. Doubly strict controls were imposed in Afghanistan, where from the mid-1980s onwards the Soviet colony was supposed to be totally 'dry'. In 1987 alcohol was withdrawn from sale in every district, causing black-market vodka to fetch contraband prices. Deprived of all stimulants in more conventional forms, conscripts have had to fall back on old army recipes for extracting alcohol from toothpaste and boot polish.* The substitute *par excellence*, eau-de-Cologne, is, of course, banned from sale.

In addition to defence in the accepted sense the army serves a variety of non-military functions. It must:

– be ready at all times to defend the 'revolutionary conquests of the Soviet people';
– help to extend the 'overall process of communist education, the production of a harmoniously developed citizen and internationalist patriot, and the active building of communism and its sure defence';[11]
– promote ethnic integration by bringing together the Union's many nationalities, and by deepening familiarity with the Russian language;[12]
– perform a political function through its political instructors, who continue the political training given in school;
– fulfil a social role by performing public services – hence the common sight of young soldiers on building sites, at work on the roads and railways, and in the fields to help with the harvest;[13]
– serve a cultural purpose through its garrison cultural centres, museums and theatres, its publishing house and *Red Star* newspaper – and institutions like the famous Red Army Choir and CSKA sports club.

The army's work in patriotic education begins through DOSAAF, mentioned earlier, and the voluntary activity of ex-soldiers. DOSAAF introduces young people to war veterans and arranges visits to places connected with the early revolutionaries. It also helped to originate two military sports games called 'Lightning' (*Zarnitsa*) and 'Eaglet' (*Orlonoiok*), which are played at military sports camps. These are now coming back into popularity and are used by the militia in their battle with delinquency.[14] But DOSAAF's con-

*The polish is spread on a piece of bread. This is then placed on a stove or heating radiator. When the bread has absorbed the alcohol, the polish is scraped off, and the bread eaten. Toothpaste is dissolved in a glass of water.

nection with military life can be thin. Practical activities range from dirt-track racing, which enables a boy to get a motorcycle licence, to aeroplane modelling.[15] War veterans are enlisted to address young people in schools and 'Houses of Youth', and take them on tours of barracks and ships.[16] But there is far from unanimous enthusiasm about this.[17]

The Second World War remains an inexhaustible source of patriotic material, but the constant harping on it in films and books bores today's young people. 'There's no need to repeat the same thing all the time,' says a young student in a Moscow cinema queue. 'We know how our grandparents suffered. My mother never knew her father, and nobody has to tell me why. My friends know all about the war too.' Besides, today there are other young men who have fought in another war – in Afghanistan. And they have something to say as well . . .


Afghanistan has been like an infection, providing Soviet society with a variety of problems for which it lacks any previous experience. By 1988 more than a million young men and their families had been directly touched by it. Yet one could still pass weeks, or even months, in the Soviet Union without meeting any public sign of the personal anguish that was evident in the United States during the war in Vietnam.

The Afghanistan veteran remains a hero *par excellence* and his image has little in common with Western versions. From the first, the official vocabulary made sure of this; it was never a question of war but of 'events around Afghanistan'. The Soviet forces were 'performing their internationalist duty in a friendly country', prey to attacks by 'armed bands from abroad'. The latter consisted of 'bandits' and '*dushmans*',[g] out to destroy a progressive regime. The soldiers were saving human lives and helping the Afghans to build a juster society. There were no deserters, no drug problems, no frictions between Afghan and Soviet soldiers. The so-called *mujahideen* were real criminals, with cruel medieval customs, who did not spare women and children and who destroyed villages, schools, hospitals and mosques.

But in a system where words are of great importance, it was not only a question of terminology. Everything had to be done to prevent young soldiers from finding themselves in a moral dilemma that could destroy the values that had been instilled in them from childhood.

This was important for parents also. The burden of the fighting in Afghanistan fell on conscripts serving under the direction of specialized troops. Every family with a boy of eighteen knew that he could quickly find himself in Afghanistan and die there. Alternative, longer service in the navy, which had once been considered a catastrophe, became welcomed by parents with the classic phrase 'Better endure three years of waiting and see him come back in one piece.' It was therefore necessary to convince parents that their sons are performing a great task in this 'friendly country', and that those who died there did not die in vain. But many refused to see why such a cruel war should be waged with young conscript soldiers barely out of basic training. 'It's a disgrace; they should send special forces to do those dangerous patrols. It's like sending baby chicks into the forest,' grieved a Soviet mother who, as the saying goes, was obliged to 'live from one letter to the next'.

Everything was done (and still is) by way of patriotic education to make Afghanistan part of an historic continuity. Sometimes the attempt succeeded, as in a letter to *Komsomolskaya Pravda* from a young woman in Kuibishev at the height of the fighting:

> War didn't spare my family. Both my grandfathers died at the front. My parents grew up in occupied territory and suffered all the things I've seen in the film *Go and See*. So then we had forty years of peace. Now people can go to bed and dream of the future, of evenings at the disco or the club. How much strength of character it takes to go and risk one's life. I read articles and stories about Afghanistan, and listen to poems and songs about the young men serving there. Those mountains and valleys are like a magnet to me.[18]

The Soviet press took nearly two years to get round to mentioning the war. Then, in the course of time, it became almost daily material. The image of the soldier was surrounded with an atmosphere like that in films about the Great Patriotic War[g] and the civil war: a mixture of soldierly virtues, awareness of comradeship, splendid feats of arms, tours by artists, visits by propagandists, the hero's letters home, memoirs by his old schoolfriends. And, of course, Nostalgia, with a capital *N*: for the woman in his life (mother, wife, fiancée, sister); for his old home; for the world of nature around him; and for the Motherland − 'nostalgia that could never be stronger than the soldier's'.[19] And finally, less exciting matters: like the difficult readjustment awaiting returning veterans, the problems of the disabled, the lot of bereaved families.

★

Not all returns were the same, as any glance through contemporary newspapers shows.

There is the Happy Return.

> Alexandra Tchmourova had just come back from night shift, when her son Igor telephoned. 'I'm in Moscow.' She woke the family, sighed at not having bought bread the day before, and set to work making his favourite dish. He had lost weight, been given a medal. Now he was on his way home. News travels fast. Friends came, neighbours came; a classmate also back from Afghanistan, a former teacher, a veteran of 1945. Then Igor went to knock on the door of his girlfriend Sveta . . .[20]

The mother features in nearly every story. At Tashkent airport she is being embraced by her son Yakub – the classic picture of the soldier's return.[21]

There is the Historic Return, as when, under the gaze of the Soviet and foreign press, the first contingents left Afghanistan in October 1986, with fanfares, flags flying, flowers in the muzzles of their Kalashnikovs, and ringing goodbyes from their 'Afghan brothers'.[22]

There is the Sad Return – of the wounded or disabled. Igor was picked up for dead by his comrades in the field. 'Their Son Returns a Hero,' said the *Pravda* headline. He had volunteered to serve in Afghanistan but, once there, wrote seldom to his parents: only twenty letters in two years, each one shorter than the last. He always reassured his parents that 'everything was fine', even after he received his terrible wound.[23]

And then there are those who don't come back at all. Right to the end, the start of the Soviet withdrawal on 15 May 1988, the authorities refused to give the figure, on the pretext of military secrecy.★ But newspapers abounded with heroic stories of young soldiers and officers,[24] even political instructors,[25] fallen in combat. And with each came the leitmotiv, 'War is the most terrible thing on earth.'[26]

Ironically, the first intimation of official recognition of the mounting number of deaths in Afghanistan was the devious wording of a government announcement about improving the condition of veterans. It was issued on the fortieth anniversary of the end of the Second World War. The list of those who would benefit included 'families of soldiers fallen in combat while doing their military service'. The only place where, in 1985, a Soviet conscript could have been killed in combat was Afghanistan.

★The total, as of 15 May, was finally given as 13,310 killed, 35,478 wounded and 311 missing in action.

But even in the best conditions, coming home from Afghanistan could be difficult. 'You can't go back to the factory or the university as if you were returning from a long holiday,' observed one veteran.[27] Many homecomings have been followed by a change of plans for study or work. Finding a job you could live with was likely to involve trial and error, as the young man in the film *Is It Easy to be Young?* discovered. In the end, after some weeks of hitting the bottle, he decided to become a fireman, because 'It's a bit like "down there" – saving lives, facing risks, answering emergencies.' Some have chosen to stay on in the army and make it a career. Others have joined the Party. 'They've accepted me . . . It's a communist who's coming home,' wrote one conscript excitedly to his parents.[28] Others have formed veterans' construction brigades, proud that their 'norms' are high above the national average. But others continue to suffer from the 'Afghanistan syndrome', which got its name long before the veterans' shock on home-coming was officially recognized.

In Afghanistan Soviet soldiers saw both poverty and violence. Soviet society may not be affluent, but it does not know utter deprivation. And, although much of a young man's education is to do with weapons and the history of war, violence, even in films and books, is reduced almost to abstraction. The conjunction of all these particulars helps to explain the shock experienced by these very young men, and their often expressed sentiment: 'that people could shoot to kill, not like it happens on exercises – how can you forget it?'

'You can easily recognize the ones who've come back,' says a young veteran, writing about his contemporaries in *Sobesednik*. 'When they look at you, they seem to be seeing something else. They're seeing blown-up trucks, famished children, the snarl on the face of a *dushman*, the mangled body of a friend.'[29] But perhaps too they're seeing their own country with different eyes: they were in the middle of a war, and now they are suddenly back in a country of 'normality' and peace. 'It wasn't like that in 1945,' wrote another young veteran (in 1987).

> Then men came back to a country where everyone had been through the war and occupation. Everyone spoke the same language. People could talk about it. Today you come home and see people living as if the war wasn't happening and you ask yourself why your friends died. They ask you to talk about it. But you can't. There's no communication. You want to forget it all and start living again, but in the end you find yourself back with your mates. Because it's only among ourselves that we can talk about it.

Young returned veterans have become very sensitive about respect for 'revolutionary standards' and deeply resent the liberties being taken with the socialist principles they went to defend. They become uncompromising 'maximalists', to use the fashionable phrase, prepared to carry the fight for these principles to the heart of society.

This phenomenon was first recognized when, in January 1986, after four months' hesitation, *Komsomolskaya Pravda* published a letter about a young veteran called Anatoli. Shocked to find that all that his former classmates were thinking about was how to get a 'cushy' job, Anatoli began, as in Afghanistan, to divide people into 'us' and 'them': comrades and 'contras'. Other veterans started to do the same. Together, they began to hunt out black-marketeers. Then one day they learned that, despite ample proof of guilt, a big speculator had been freed by the local court.

At this point Anatoli sought out the prosecutor in charge of the case (it was the prosecutor himself who later wrote the letter, published under the heading 'An Encounter that Changed My Life') to say that there were too many 'contras' at large and that the State should authorize their liquidation. The copious mail following the letter's publication showed that the case was far from isolated, and that many other young men were wondering how to put their Afghanistan experience to better use.[30]

The debate raged for months. Most of the published contributors agreed that no group of citizens, however well-meaning, could be allowed to put themselves above the law, but that these young men were confronting society with questions that could not be put off with facile references to psychological traumatism. In time, a number of hardened and 'puritan' veterans formed regular vigilante groups with the self-appointed task of purging Soviet towns and cities of 'non-socialist' elements, among them punks and prostitutes. So far did things go that in August 1987 a decorated Afghanistan hero, who had since become a student of forestry, was sentenced to eight years for murder. With two companions, the veteran had attacked a group of young people who, according to his evidence, 'were leading a Western-style life and had no place in our society', killing one and gravely wounding another.[31] Other veterans, disquietingly for the authorities, took to organizing what looked like paramilitary camps.*

*In 1986–7 Afghanistan vigilante groups were imitated by neighbourhood teenagers interested in martial arts (whose unofficial practice is illegal). A group in Dnepropetrovsk learned judo and karate from books in order, they claimed, to see off a gang offering drugs to young children.[32] In another case, a Muscovite identified as 'V. Kh.' joined a group called 'Law and Order'. His first task, allegedly, was to help the

There is virtually no discussion about psychological help for the returnees, perhaps because the authorities feel that the collective society makes therapy unnecessary. The tendency has been to treat them like any other veterans, respected and integrated in the national memory. This, moreover, is what most want themselves – or so it appeared at the 1987 Komsomol Congress.

Already in 1987 some institutes started to put up informal memorials, using pictures of students who had not returned. In the cemetery at the 'artists'' village of Peredelkino, just outside Moscow, a temporary plinth was erected by unknown hands and dedicated simply to 'the fallen in Afghanistan'.

But the young want much more. 'We can't allow our heroes to become "unknown soldiers",' a delegate from Donetz told the Komsomol Congress. 'We must give their names to roads and public places. Books must be published and films made about this war.' (Afterwards the director Elim Klimov said scenarios were under study, but in 1988 there was still no film, and it was not until June that veterans laid the foundation stone for Moscow's first memorial.)

It was partly to meet the demand for recognition that in 1987 the authorities organized a national rally of 'Young Reservists' near Askhabad in Turkmenistan. Delegates came mostly from so-called 'Internationalist Clubs', which sprang up in 1986 to help victims' families and 'actively participate in the patriotic education of youth'. But Askhabad showed that the young Internationalists had no wish to fall into the trap of 'formalism'. According to *Pravda*, the rally was stormy; delegates declared that there was no question of copying the established Veterans' Association; what was wanted was 'not to tell war yarns, but to find a way back'. They wanted equally to 'find their place in the *perestroika*'.[35]

On the material plane, there were angry demands for the bureaucracy to pay prompter attention to the needs of victims. A former parachutist, Yuri Zubin, was profoundly shocked when one of his friends who had lost both legs in Afghanistan had been unable to get a ground-floor flat.[36] In Tadjikstan, the Central Committee itself accused bureaucrats of lacking sympathy; in 1987, 374 veterans and their families were still awaiting rehousing, including fifty

families of dead soldiers. He then received orders to spy on gamblers at a Moscow race-course.[33] A Novosibirsk group claimed to have taken action against fifty-three 'corrupt' citizens and to have destroyed the property of a 'citizen N.'.[34] The militia, probably correctly, dismissed most of the claims as romantic nonsense.

invalids and thirty-three families of soldiers who had been killed.[37]

Since it is only through military service that most Soviet citizens now take direct part in sport, the army is an appropriate context for a postscript on the subject.

In the task of creating 'patriots sound in mind and body', sport naturally has a place. But unfortunately all theories come up against an obstacle. Young people are becoming less and less interested in sport, as is shown by the inquiries of journalists and researchers among university students.[38] Criticism is aimed at the lack of sports facilities, though these are often more luxurious, for those entitled to use them, than in some Western countries. Whether or not this is a reason, the fact is that Soviet adults are becoming more and more sedentary and unfit, and the young finding other ways to spend their free time. There has also been an emphasis on competitive professional sport, which has absorbed resources and enthusiasm to the detriment of sport among the masses.

The revival of the army-organized GTO programme, mentioned earlier, is intended to rectify this. Created in 1917 to democratize sport and prepare young people to work and defend the gains of the Revolution, it was based on a network of clubs holding competitions among themselves. Members could spend all the free time they wanted using the club. But then, after the war, the GTO started to build huge facilities; these became the preserve of local champions and the mass of young people were forgotten. There were empty stadiums, and young people turned to less 'socially useful' forms of leisure.

At the beginning of 1987, therefore, it was decided to have another look at the GTO with a view to restoring it to its original purposes. Ministries were called on to help, and plans made to link sports activities to work-collectives and factories. This led to arguments about participatory and championship sport. 'Popular sport is not at odds with sport with a capital S,' declared *Pravda*, evidently under some pressure. 'On the contrary, it provides an inexhaustible reserve for our national competition teams.'[39]

Sport is always portrayed as a component of cultural progress. A contrast is drawn between 'capitalist' sport, which is a sop to workers suffering under enforced industrialization, and 'socialist' sport, which promotes 'creativity' and 'vitality'. Sports champions quickly become the idols of the young, taking the floor at Komsomol Congresses and 'peace rallies', and receiving important material advantages.[40]

Contests that 'demonstrate the moral, as much as the physical, qualities of our sportsmen' are hailed as helping to teach a 'creative attitude'.[41] However, to judge from the number of police uniforms at big football and ice-hockey matches, and the prohibition on carrying any potential weapon, including little flags, into the spectators' stands, sport in the Soviet Union, no less than in the decadent West, involves more than just teaching a correct attitude.

Such is the fear of spontaneity that when the football-fan movement reached Russia at the end of the 1970s, the Moscow city authorities issued a special decree forbidding fans to shout in the stadiums or to gather in the streets outside. The words of the decree were recorded on tape and played over loudspeakers before every match.

One fan told the sports writer Yuri Shchekochikhin: 'No one wants a fight – not us or the militia. But it's forbidden to support your own team. They take away your hat and confiscate your scarf. That's how fights start.' Fifteen-year-old Igor, another T C S K A fan, agreed: 'Fights flare up because we're forbidden to cheer our teams. But it's not only a question of being allowed to shout "Spartak are champs!" We just want to be together.'[42] Sportsmen started writing to the newspapers, saying there was no harm in letting fans show their enthusiasm, 'so long as it was kept within bounds', and pleading for the formation of supporters' clubs 'to canalize passions and enliven matches without the risk of incidents'.[43]

In 1987 the authorities relented, with the result that one can now see T-shirts with the legend 'I'm Crazy for Dynamo' (or 'Spartak', or 'Torpedo') – or read about 'football hooliganism, as when Kiev Dynamo fans hurled bottles and stones at a train waiting to take home supporters of Moscow Spartak'.[44]

# 5

# The Worker-bees

*Right and obligation to work – the Soviet 'working class' – work as social therapy – disillusionment of young with reality – migration as a form of protest – balance of work and leisure – graduates in manual employment – problems of work in development zones – protests at 'voluntary' work – 'subbotniks'*

Article 40 of the Soviet constitution guarantees the right to work, the quality of the job offered and a minimum wage. It also guarantees the right to choose one's kind of employment, subject to capacity, education and training. There is also a 'right to rest', contained in Article 41, which governs hours of work. But rights never come without duties, for, as Article 60 lays down, 'It is the duty of, and a matter of honour for, every able-bodied citizen of the USSR to work conscientiously in his chosen, socially useful occupation, and strictly to observe labour discipline. Evasion of socially useful work is incompatible with the principles of socialist society.'

Work starts immediately on leaving school. Article 81 of labour regulations stipulates that pupils from trade schools must be engaged within one week and assigned within the five days following. It also says that young technicians cannot be assigned to administrative work and must be helped to acquire practical experience and proficiency.

In institutes and universities newly graduated students wait anxiously for the results of 'allocation' meetings that decide where they will be posted for up to the next three years in return for receiving their higher education. This will be where the economy most needs them: often in places where few would risk going of their own accord, in case they are barred from returning to live in a major town or city, and have to spend the rest of their lives in some God-forsaken hole without prospects.

One of the simplest ways to avoid this kind of exile, unless you already have helpful connections, is to come out near the top of the class, which gives you priority of choice. Another is to have a family obligation. Thus many women students contrive to become pregnant just as they are about to be sent to the far end of Turkmenistan; they then use their maximum entitlement to maternity leave to occupy three fateful years.

The legal minimum age for starting work, sixteen, is now purely formal. Girls generally start at eighteen to nineteen, and boys two years later, after doing military service. But there is also a system of apprenticeship, combining study and paid work, that permits young people to leave school earlier without losing their chances of getting a certificate, and another kind of dispensation that allows some young people in rural areas to start part-time work on farms from the age of fourteen.

It is reckoned that the young worker needs two or three years to settle into his trade and work-collective.[1] Though most manage to do this by twenty-four, there are always some who even then have not yet achieved the 'insertion into society' by means of work that is the ultimate purpose of Soviet education.

Retirement is at sixty for men and fifty-five for women, with entitlement to earlier retirement in some heavy occupations. But pensioners are encouraged to continue working, at least part-time, to help meet the labour shortage. In 1987 nearly a fifth of the country's 58 million pensioners were doing so, including 600,000 out of 2 million in Moscow.[2]

Soviet literature makes a sharp distinction between the working class in the socialist and capitalist systems. 'Strong in revolutionary tradition [the working class in socialist societies] is distinguished by its collective awareness and ideology, which makes it, of its nature, a new class.'[3] And just as there are no classes, since there is no exploitation, so there are no special-interest groups, but a homogeneous working class.[4]

This constant harping on 'the worker' is astonishing in so far as the development of the Soviet employment structure has led to a contraction of what could strictly be called the working class. Yet 'education for work' continues to receive an important place in general education and is subtly given from kindergarten onwards. At the same time, the later age at which young people now start jobs because they stay longer at school causes innumerable arguments between two schools of thought: those who put the stress on study, so as to provide the economy with more competent specialists, and those who believe in 'roughening one's hands', i.e., bringing students early into contact with the 'real' world of work.[5]

The argument is an important one since two key ideas – that the young person becomes aware of his social role through work,[6] and that work determines a person's place in society[7] – lead to a very Soviet way of assessing jobs. The young Russian gives priority of importance to the content of his work. 'Interesting' work is what allows the fullest use of his abilities.[8] Among his criteria are the quality of the work-collective (45 per cent), the opportunity to learn (36 per cent), the importance of the job for the overall production (27 per cent) and satisfactory pay (22 per cent).

So it is not surprising to find Soviet theorists conceiving work as a form of social therapy. They see it as indispensable to the formation of character, and its neglect as risking the development among the young of negative attitudes, like predilection for a petit-bourgeois consumerist life-style.[9] This concept of work extends to the treatment of delinquency and criminality. Hence labour camps are a means both of repaying one's debt to society and of re-education. There are inevitable idylls about the young worker who 'shoulders his responsibilities' (a key-phrase), takes it on himself to change a production process,[10] is promoted to a higher position, and sets a moral as well as a professional example.[11,12]

'Shouldering responsibility' proves one's fitness to enter the world of adults. There are also countless improving tales of the old foreman who courageously volunteers to take on a difficult adolescent and teach him his trade but also, more importantly, raise his moral capacity. Where all others have failed, the old man succeeds. In the best cases the former potential delinquent becomes a Komsomol or Party member, and goes on to help others who have taken the wrong road.

The all-important process of integrating the individual with the 'world of work' is helped by the creation within the enterprise, and particularly the brigade,[g] of a socio-industrial micro-climate. This enables young people to enter into full membership of the collective,[13] where they are supposed to learn to function socially, taking part in all that goes on.*[14] More than their elders, the young are liable to develop a feeling of dependence on their enterprise. It

---

*Nevertheless, participation in the life of the enterprise varies greatly with qualifications and age. The period of greatest activity is between the ages of thirty and forty, when the worker has acquired all the practical skills and has finished with the troublesome business of setting up home. After that, involvement diminishes. Among workers aged twenty to thirty, only a quarter are 'regular attenders' at meetings to discuss production: and more than half never show up at all, being short on experience or busy with their families.[15] But the new State enterprise law of 1987, providing for the election of brigade leaders, shop foremen and even department heads, could raise the level of interest. A hopeful sign was the number of young people elected in the first, experimental polls.

becomes a kind of second family, in which they feel at home and from which they expect a great deal. This includes taking care of workaday matters such as the provision of better bachelor quarters, crèches to help young mothers, sports grounds and holiday camps – particularly in the case of new enterprises. Managements often use these incentives to woo young skilled workers from other factories. And planners are concerned at the loss to the economy caused by the frequent changes of job.

Official language often blurs the distinction between social and economic needs. For example, when enterprises boast of their concern for young workers' welfare, they are concerned about raising labour productivity. And the rush to 'integrate' them with the least possible delay is simply a device to meet the urgent need for technicians at a time when the falling birth rate has cut the number coming into the pool.

But just as Soviet education aims at more than the mere acquisition of knowledge, so clearly it is supposed to take more than mere technical competence to make a good worker. From this mixture of technical and moral criteria is born an image of the worker that is typically Soviet.

Soviet experts hasten to insist that today's young workers do better than their predecessors,[16] thanks to higher technical qualifications and the disappearance of numerous manual jobs through automation.[17] This is supposed to make work more 'creative'[18] and change the worker's relationship with the job.[19] But all this is largely a matter of theory. In fact, automation is taking place very slowly, and industry cannot take proper advantage of it for the simple reason that it has to live with an antique infrastructure, which destroys many of the benefits.

The out-of-date design of industrial plants obliges many young workers to take jobs below the level for which they are qualified. This causes discontent among new arrivals. In general the number of workers satisfied with their jobs increases with their qualifications up to a certain level. But beyond this the reverse happens. Young people of university standard are the likeliest to feel dismayed, if not cruelly deceived, on their first contact with the working environment. More than ordinary workers, they expect to find 'creativity' and responsibility in their work, and consequently suffer more from the mindless routine and hidebound management.

Starting work is the young person's first contact with real life. Here he discovers that, to get on, strict standards of workmanship

Security guard: 'And you Misha – why are you going through the door?'
Workman: 'I don't have anything on me.'

and 'socially useful activity' are often less important than an ability to pull strings and make up to one's boss.[20] He sees what kind of tricks are used to cover up absence on 'unofficial' business.[21] He also learns that young newcomers are not always as welcome as they were led to expect; and that if they show keenness, they are regarded as trouble-makers. Witness the director of a collective farm who regularly discourages young people applying to work there, because 'they expect too much, always wanting new methods, a new life, a new culture, and expecting new houses and a new school'.[22]

On the other hand the young are more likely than their elders to be won over by the new legislation allowing more freedom to State enterprises, particularly in matters concerning welfare. It should be easier for work-collectives to meet young people's requirements now that they can put them through workers' councils. And the linking of pay to quality of output should lessen the frustration of seeing slackers earn nearly as much as good employees.

Another encouragement was the 1987 award of a pay increase, in some cases averaging 30–40 per cent over a number of years, in some very low pay levels such as those of surgeons, engineers and teachers. Finally in 1987 the law on private enterprise seemed to be exciting

'It's for a *komandirovka* [duty trip] to Sochi.'

the interest of young people. Many were quick to apply for loans with which to start co-operatives (restaurants, cafés, service centres,[g] etc.), hoping to escape the usual daily work round. But the process is likely to need time. Despite the enthusiasm, such forms of individual enterprise are still far from being understood by Soviet society.

Protectively educated in a system that represents Soviet society as the best possible, the young person arriving at his first job is suddenly faced with the system's inherent defects, to which he can see no answer. If, remembering all that he has been taught at school, he decides to 'shoulder his responsibilities', his workmates put him down as a 'stooge' or 'sucker', and that disillusions him even more. In this sense, to start work is indeed to come to maturity, but not always in the way promised by official speeches.

The system is almost scandalously easy-going, and the Soviet worker is not above giving it a touch of fantasy, like the use of business trips (*komandirovka*). Every day, as part of this magic game, trains and planes carry thousands of people of all kinds and seniorities to different parts of the country. Besides providing a welcome break with routine (and even occasionally serving a genuine official need), such trips enable one to bring home 'deficit' goods. They can also serve romantic purposes. By 1987 the wholesale abuse of *komandirovka* so worried economists that offices and enterprises were ordered to clamp down on it.

It is also amazingly easy to change jobs – and what better way to put 4,000 kilometres between oneself and a monotonous job or, for that matter, a troublesome wife? The law makes it simple for most people. Only Party members and some key personnel (in research centres for example) require their employers' agreement. Normally it is sufficient simply to give notice, which the employer must accept. Two weeks later the worker receives any pay that is owed to him and is handed back his work-book with the entry 'left for personal reasons'. He then has a whole month in which to deliver it to a new employer.

The vast migrations of these 'birds of passage' cause serious damage to the economy, which has a hard job maintaining an adequate labour-force. In the mid-1980s the cost of the annual turnover reached billions of roubles, and affected the majority of skilled workers under twenty-five. Only a minority of the migrants arrive at their new factories with the required qualifications. The rest must be trained on the job. Hardly have they become productive than they are off, and everything has to begin again from scratch.

There are many explanations for this phenomenon: traditional Russian restlessness; a constant hankering for somewhere better; inevitable disillusionment with first jobs; the attraction of a legal means of protest; dissatisfaction with living conditions (particularly accommodation); and the possibility of exploring one's vast homeland cheaply. Between Leningrad and Tashkent, say, there can be any number of detours. Such migrations allow one to 'enrich oneself as a person' and sample a variety of jobs – as had the taxi-driver (ex-wrestler and ex-furniture restorer) who asked us how he could now get a job as a stunt-man in the film studios.

All this raises a moral question. Should not Soviet society unequivocally condemn what C. Khaltchanko of the Volgograd region called the 'new Oblomovs'[g] – adherents of an 'alien philosophy' of giving the least and grabbing the most?

Not necessarily, says the sociologist Bestushev-Lada. Young people are entitled to time in which to absorb culture and exchange ideas, both very laudable aims. This new attitude of the young, and the incomprehending reaction of older people to it, are symptoms of the generation gap. If, from such motives, graduates and diploma-holders take jobs as street-sweepers, lift-attendants, caretakers, truck-drivers and so on, they deserve our respect. Nor is their choice incompatible with social reality in view of the current imbalance between better educational levels and the knowledge needed for many available jobs. Somebody has to do these lowly jobs, for which there is no longer a pool of uneducated and illiterate citizens such as existed in the 1920s.

According to Bestushev-Lada's criterion, if a young graduate 'drops out' from purely self-indulgent motives, he can be called a 'new Oblomov'. But if his aim is to gain culturally, it is better to be a simple mechanic or porter, at home with society and interested in all that it has to offer, than a doctor who resents having to treat patients or a teacher who hates school.[23]

But there can be quite other reasons for the young specialist turning down work for which he is qualified. 'When you first begin, you can't imagine how you're ever going to get your own home,' wrote a teacher in Briansk. 'Then there are problems with growing children, ageing parents. At the factory it's just as bad. So you wonder if it's not better to get a job that makes no demands on you, and gives you more free time.'

The 1970s incomes policy made pay differentials almost meaningless. Moves have been made to adjust this. But it is still possible for a doorman working two or three hours in the evening to earn as much as a scientist working all day. 'I have a friend who used to be a research worker,' says the teacher just quoted. 'Now he drives a taxi, and tells me he comes home without a care in his head. And let's not talk about those women who just sit at home sewing and earn more than a university professor.'[24]

Many job applicants keep their diplomas a secret for fear that employers will refuse to accept them for manual work. The fact that a railway-station porter can earn up to 300 roubles a month, and a young university lecturer not more than 180, might help to explain this.[25] But there are also young people with diplomas who are work-shy for almost any kind of job that means getting their hands dirty. And that is a new development too. Seeing their growing number, some older people would like to make them subject to the same rule as doctors, who cease to be qualified if they fail to practise after a time.[26] If not, they say, the way is open to 'parasitism'.

Apart from better pay, a university lecturer taking an unskilled job may also gain access to side benefits. A cartoon in *Krokodil* shows a shop manager inspecting the credentials of his salesmen: two doctors of science, three engineers and a bevy of teachers. Shop work is especially good for kick-backs, as well as obtaining 'deficit' goods that can be swopped for others in short supply. The government can pass as many laws as it likes, but as long as there's a system of permanent semi-shortage, anomalies of income will remain.

In 1986–7 there was much discussion about a new law on 'unearned incomes', a catch-all device ostensibly aimed at ending the 'parallel economy'. 'Bravo,' cried a reader of *Sobesednik*, 'but first tell us how to live on our pay alone.' Many of the prosecutions brought under the new law were both senseless and cruel. Semyon Ivachenko, a tenth-grade Rostov schoolboy, wrote, after seeing his father sent to prison for selling rabbit-skins:

> I see how our neighbours live, and I remember how five years ago we lived in a communal flat.[8] One neighbour's rooms had curtains stamped 'State property'. The other's larder was never short of food. The explanation was simple. The first one worked in a hospital, the second in a canteen. My parents saw what was going on. But what could they do? Go to the militia? One day my mother said to my father: 'If you ask me, we're the only people in this house to live on our pay alone.' That's how it happened that later, when we had a flat of our own, my father, a biologist, began this business with rabbits in the evening.[27]

About the same time there was a lively debate about 'overwork' and lack of free time. 'When I left the institute I took this job in a garage,' explained one reader. 'It doesn't even give me time to read a good book. On my days off I try to catch up on the week's lost sleep. With the qualifications I have, I shouldn't have any difficulty finding a job with fewer responsibilities. But then the State would get less than it gave to train me.'

'How to balance work and leisure? The question's not easy; but if we don't find an answer we shall get more and more people like A.M. of Moscow [another newspaper reader] who says he's going to leave industry and find a place in a quiet little workshop,' wrote Alexander Kouzmin, twenty-two, of Barnaoul. 'Some readers complain about poor work. But, mightn't it be that the workers don't get proper rest?' wrote L. Vassilieva of Leningrad. 'Every evening I get home at eight and do the housework. It's only after that I have time to be with my husband. Where can we spend this time? Go to the museums? They're open till six. Or perhaps the theatre? There's no late performance. Make a round of the cafés? They close at eight.'[28]

Young people are discovering that work is not the only thing in life. They see work and leisure quite differently from their parents. 'Free time can be as important as roubles. If a worker finishes early, he should be able to choose whether to stay on for more pay, or pack up and go home. Most men would probably go for the first (any extra comes in handy if you have a family to feed), and women the second,' said I. Filippova, a doctor, of Volgograd.

But you can always find an original. Like the young engineer, Gennadi Preosour, whose declaration of independence started a nationwide debate. Gennadi decided to work only two days a week, for which he received very little pay but enough. In return, he had five free days in which to do some reading, take some exercise, and go looking for 'deficit' goods. He thought this was closer to the communist ideal than obsessively working from morning to night. Unfriendly readers accused him of being 'un-Soviet', because he saw work from a purely selfish standpoint. But many others took his side and vowed that they too would devote their time to something beside their jobs.[29]

Young workers regularly complain about the shortage of accommodation. Some go on living with their parents, but most have jobs far away. The problem is worst in development zones and new towns, where the young form the majority of the population, and there is nearly always a delay between putting up housing and bringing in amenities.

Single workers complain bitterly about the hostels they are expected to live in, unless they find two or three friends and together can get hold of a flat. These outdated institutions are noisy, regimented and, with their rigid 'house rules' – about visitors, tidiness, 'hygiene inspections', etc. – totally unsuited to modern life.

Young couples come off worst, since most young workers' housing is designed for bachelors. Newly married pairs must often go on living in separate dormitories, without any relaxation of the rules. As visitors must be out by eleven, and inmates often sleep several to a room, the frustrations of married life can be imagined. Some hostels now accept couples, but none babies – which causes many young couples to begin married life with an abortion.

Work on the land can still hardly be called popular. But the rural exodus has been checked for the moment, and there are even cases of young people returning. Since the mid-1970s big investments have gone into improving rural life with running water, natural gas, asphalted roads and other amenities. There have also been efforts to improve housing and provide villages with better levels of schooling, medical care for families and Houses and Parks of Culture.

Again, the main target is the young, whom it is necessary to keep on the land for the sake of the economy. Success varies from region to region. Prosperous *kolkhozes* can rejuvenate the countryside, as they do in the Baltic republics, where collective farmers have a standard of living that townspeople envy. But in the heart of Russia, particularly the non-black earth regions, often depressingly called 'no-prospect zones', farms are too poor to afford these seductive operations.*

Some regions are experimenting with the consolidation of villages. In this way it is possible to install better facilities more cheaply, and prevent a handful of young couples becoming isolated in villages full of old people. There have been protests at the break with traditional village culture. But the young welcome it.

The problems of the countryside are no longer what they were in the 1970s, however. The main problem today is to find work for young specialists. This is within the realm of possibility in the case of boys. Mechanization, though still lacking to a certain extent, means more technical jobs, which are better paid. But women must be content to work with the livestock, at difficult hours and in dirty conditions, or even fall back on poorly paid seasonal work. Their underprivileged position is made harder still by their 'double day', because after the farm work comes the housework, with a vegetable plot and generally some household animals (chicken or pigs) to look after as well.

Not so long ago, as we mentioned earlier, boys would use military service as a way to escape from the land, where there were not enough jobs to make use of their improved educational standards. This left the girls short of husbands. Now that more boys are returning, thanks to more rewarding jobs, it is the girls who are going away and leaving the boys with the problem of finding a bride. And getting a town girl to come and live in the village can take some persuasion.

In the early 1980s the authorities tried the experiment of building apartment blocks in villages. These incongruous constructions were rejected by the elderly, who refused to leave their homely wooden *isbas*.[8] Nor was there much more enthusiasm for them on the part of the young, who much preferred the traditional design of village house, with relatively spacious rooms, a garden and back-yard. Some of these apartment blocks have never been occupied. The present trend is to encourage young couples to build their own homes, in the old style, with a cash advance for labour and materials and the grant

*In Central Asia the opposite is happening. Because young people refuse to leave the villages, factories in the cities are starved of labour. So it has become necessary to start a programme of rural factory-building.

of a plot of land. The attraction is considerable, and many now decide that country life is better, if only for the living space.

So keeping youth on the land is no longer so much a question of material living conditions (which in the better farms and villages can be made quite tolerable) but rather of status, i.e., of ending traces of the *kolkhoznik's* second-class citizenship, signified by the quality of jobs and amenities. As one letter put it, 'When at last you can visit the House of Culture in shoes, not gum-boots, and women can expect decent jobs, young couples will give us the development of agriculture we've been promised for decades.'[30]

One of the big myths of Soviet work philosophy is the 'educative' value of construction and farming projects undertaken by huge brigades of student workers. The most spectacular has been the building of the 3,000-kilometre railway known as the BAM[g] across Soviet East Asia. The young people threw themselves into the heavy construction work with all the zeal of early pioneers, confident that they were fulfilling to the utmost their duty as young communists. Before the BAM it was the opening up of the 'virgin lands' in Kazakhstan, and before that the building of the great hydro-electric dams.

But these youth projects are as far from having been triumphs of education as they have of economics. In none did the volunteers' undoubted early enthusiasm make up for their lack of skill and experience – and even enthusiasm is liable to succumb to the shock of reality in inhospitable regions and the face of a frequently cool welcome by regular workers.[31]

Student vacation work is similarly counter-productive. Organized in so-called 'third semesters', it is supposed to be a way of bringing students and workers together. But it is also used, with indifferent results, to fill out the labour-force. It is no mere chance that student work brigades (SSO[g]) are usually sent to construction sites or *kolkhozes* – areas perenially short of labour because the work is so unappealing. And there, as they hang about waiting for trucks and material that fail to arrive, or in sodden fields waiting to be told how to lift potatoes, official propaganda continues to describe their good fortune at being able to learn from 'socially useful' labour. As part of the *perestroika* there have been moves to make these excursions more attractive, by locating them in the students' own region or seeing that the locality gets some benefit from what the young people have learned in the course of their studies.[32] But any benefit remains essentially ideological, as does that of the 'manual work' sessions retained for schoolchildren under the reform of secondary education (see chapter 3).

'For over twenty-seven years the SSO organization has helped to complete 300,000 projects, worth 25,000 million roubles – equivalent to building twenty-five middle-sized towns,' declared *Sobesednik* in 1986.[33] The classic photograph shows a group of young people in yellow-khaki army vests, with the letters SSO and rows of other badges from earlier 'semesters' clearly in view, singing round a camp-fire with guitars. Beside it in the newspaper is a picture of the same young people hard at work, bringing in the harvest or unloading bricks.*

But, for all the brave words across the idyllic posters – 'Everyone to the Potatoes' – displayed in university corridors, the evidence on these so-called 'third semesters' is scarcely different from another form of 'voluntary work', the *subbotnik* (see chapter 7).

Sometimes students' vacation work is made the subject of a contract, generally with a *kolkhoz*. This specifies either a regular schedule of so many days' work per year, or else a specific task, such as harvesting a given number of hectares of crops. But this system is not really very 'educational' either.

First, the work allocated to a whole institute nearly always ends up on the shoulders of its 'unattached' members, because 'this one is on a duty trip, another has a sick relative, and a third cannot do physical work'. Secondly, the system is misused by local Party chiefs, who are quite capable of mobilizing a whole research institute for unskilled work that could be done more effectively by ordinary workers. Thus in Vladivostok the work of an entire research institute is brought to a stop, while the scientists working under Professor V. Vasovski spend two precious weeks grubbing dirt and stones from the city's tram-lines.[34]

'At the start of each school year, tenth-grade pupils in our town receive a work task,' wrote Igor Nevdachov, a Komsomol member and pupil of the Lenin School of Przevalsk in Kirghizia. So Igor went off to harvest potatoes, knowing that students must do their bit for the regional economy. But he learnt more than he had bargained for

---

*Vacation brigade work is also a chance to earn holiday money and for the 'socially active' student to strengthen the positive aspect of one's *karakteristika*.[8] To judge by the number of students, including girls, who sport their SSO uniform when they get back to their universities and institutes, this holiday work is indeed a matter of pride for some.

'and not only about potatoes'. What he discovered was not 'the community of labour' but muddle, idleness and wasted effort.[35] A similar discovery awaited twenty-two pupils of School Number 171 in Novosibirsk. One year they went to harvest cabbages; the following year they were sent to a vegetable distribution centre. On their first day at the centre they were struck by a pestilential smell coming from a mountain of decomposing green matter. When they examined it more closely, they found that it consisted of cabbages from the market-garden *kolkhoz* where they had worked the year before.[36]

Teachers and students would willingly participate in the life of the economy, particularly at harvest time, if the work was really useful; if it was not a way of letting factory and *kolkhoz* directors cover up their administrative mistakes, and did not distract students from their studies. 'The student's first task is to study. Does it make sense for doctors to lose the equivalent of a whole year of study on "third semesters" that have no relevance to their future work?' asked *Komsomolskaya Pravda*.[37] Among those who receive the students' 'help', there is no shortage of questions either – as a newspaper reader explained in a letter from his *kolkhoz*: 'During the 1950s we had students come to help with the potato harvest. It meant following the tractor and picking up the potatoes by hand. Today it can all be done mechanically, yet they still send us student brigades. But now I understand why. It's simpler to put the students into a bus than to look after the machines.'

He described in detail the wasteful process of assembling a convoy of thirty to forty buses for the thirty-to-fifty kilometre drive, keeping buses and drivers in idleness most of the day, having the students start work about 11 am then break for lunch, and work just two more hours in the afternoon before returning to the buses for the journey back to town. 'So the vegetables they pick are worth their weight in gold.'[38]

# 6

# The Drones

*Failure to instil a 'work-ethic' — public apathy and private initiative —*
*the black market — prostitution — individual rackets — fishery poaching*
*— antiques smuggling — professional gambling — race-course betting —*
*corruption in government ministries — the Moscow 'stores' trial —*
*Party corruption — police bribery — burglary — crimes of violence — the*
*drugs underworld*

At the launch of the *perestroika*, the Party sought to inspire the masses
with a vision of the year 2000, when the shops would be full of
desirable goods on which to spend well-earned pay. To this end the
Central Committee and the Supreme Soviet approved practical measures to revolutionize production, and to generate a spirit of social
responsibility such as had not existed since the nostalgically re-
membered early years of the Revolution. There were new laws that
permitted a range of one-man businesses, others allowing the election
of shop-floor and factory managers, and yet others (it was promised)
to encourage young people to put forward new ideas about production and management. In subtle ways people were exhorted to show
the kind of consideration and good manners that are supposed to be
the mark of a modern society.

But the immediate results were disappointing. Though the first
year of the *perestroika* saw a 4 per cent growth in national income
(double the rate for the preceding decade) for the consumer and
ordinary citizen, everything was much as before.

On 25 April *Komsomolskaya Pravda* published readers' letters in
answer to the question, 'What changes have you seen around you in
the past year?' Nearly all began with the same sentence, 'I have
noticed no changes whatever.' 'Lots of things have changed when
you listen to the radio, read the papers or watch television,' wrote an
anonymous reader from the Kirov region. 'But all around me and at
work, everything seems just the same.'

Next day another newspaper, *Sovietskaya Kultura*, published a selection of letters about everyday life. Many of these also began with the
same sentence — in this case with the words 'I don't understand . . .'

'I don't understand why there are so many locked doors,' wrote

'I warned you it was uneatable.'

one reader, 'in offices, hospitals, stations, shops. Who are those don't-care-less employees who, with half a dozen entrances available, oblige visitors to crowd before a single narrow door in the snow and rain?'

'I don't understand the queues,' wrote another. 'Why are there never enough cashiers or sales assistants? Why, even in the banks, when you go to pay the light or rent bill, are you forced to stand for hours, waiting patiently for your money to be taken?'

'I don't understand the secret military regime in our hotels,' wrote a third. 'Why must we face such a barrage of humiliations, and from so many staff: administrators, passport checkers, receptionists, clerks – not to mention key-ladies, forever alert to attend to your television, and your morals? You are followed, mistrusted and treated so rudely that you want to break something.'

'I don't understand,' wrote a Leningrad reader, 'why in the Gostini Dvor [department store] the broad backs of sales girls are always turned towards you; why one has to put up with humiliating stares, nerve-racking shouts, the unswerving disinclination to answer you politely, let alone smile.'

*Ogonek* magazine went even further.

> It will be difficult to count on the great changes intended for us without a significant change in our way of life. Look at Moscow's new districts. The buildings are boxes, the shops are boxes, the pharmacies are boxes, the libraries are boxes. The latest ones look as though they've been through an earthquake. And to get to shops and buses you have to pick your way along muddy sheep-tracks, because someone couldn't be bothered to extend the asphalt.

In the land of the model worker, the most copious examples of 'negative work' are called *brak*: the botched, unusable product, in industry, transport or for personal consumption. In 1980 a friend of one of the authors explained why her saucepans had no handles: 'It's nothing special. They weren't properly fixed, so I took them off, I don't want litres of scalding water all over me.' In 1988 things were hardly better. Even in the buildings reserved for foreigners, and therefore 'privileged', tenants paid Mayfair or Fifth Avenue rents for flats where it was necessary to put basins beneath leaks in the plumbing, to go for whole days, or weeks, without hot water because of minor breakdowns or annual 'prophylactic repairs', to put up with everything rickety and cracked.

Hardly surprising, then, that Soviet citizens should have to hunt high and low through the few shops that sell building materials – not everyone can have connections with factories and lorry-drivers – in order to be able to face winter in apartments that are poorly insulated or badly assembled, to repair the cracks that appear even before the first tenant moves in, to find the means of refixing everything that hangs by a single nail. (Knowing the exchange value of the smallest item, building workers pocket whatever they can.)

At the end of 1986 the woman director of a shop in Murmansk showed television viewers a consignment of shoes received the day before, of which not one pair was sellable; women's shoes with heels so high that no normal person could have taken two steps in them without falling, sandals with straps devoid of fasteners, shoes

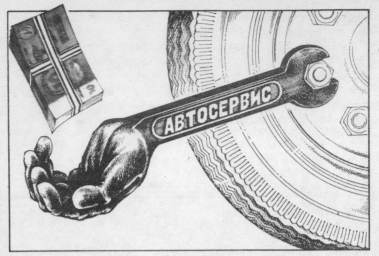

Car service.

with openings so small that no foot could ever have slipped into them.

Of course, light industry is the industrial economy's poor relation. But *brak* does not spare heavy industry either. Railway wagons without couplings and travelling cranes that cannot move above the factory assembly-line – these exist too.

At the end of 1986 the establishment of a quality-control commission, Gospromika, was considered one of the most important economic reforms. It was to be totally independent of enterprises, and would function on the model of the commission that inspects the output of enterprises working for defence. But when it began work in January 1987, it quickly forfeited any enthusiasm by workers, and directors too, even if they happened to condemn the system that obliged them to produce *brak*. As one of them put it, 'I know that what I produce is fit only for the scrap-heap. But with the machinery I have, it's an achievement to turn out anything. Up to now my workers have drawn bonuses that give them enough to live on. It's the most I can do.'

In theory everyone is for a system that would link pay to quality of output and halt the production of useless, even dangerous, goods (like short-circuiting television sets, which caused several hundred fires in Moscow and Leningrad in the winter of 1986–7). But the work of inspection is complicated by the social consequences of applying it too rigorously; in some factories there have even been work stoppages over loss of pay when the commission refused to pass their output.

In such circumstances it is hardly surprising that ordinary citizens in search of scarce goods, or the means with which to buy them, should turn to the black market. In a country of eternal 'deficits', there is almost nothing that cannot be obtained from the 'parallel economy'. Services range from running up a dress (illegal unless the seamstress is a 'registered entrepreneur' and paying full tax) to decorating a private apartment, in State time and often with State materials. Goods range from the caviare flogged for dollars by hotel staff, to expensive foreign cars acquired from foreign diplomats by means of faked accidents and 'write-offs'.

One day a reporter from *Komsomolskaya Pravda* visited the black market in Arkhangelsk, where some 'speculators' had just been detained in a swoop by the militia. One had come all the way from Baku. On the way, in Leningrad, he had bought a consignment of trendy, privately made shirts and was selling them at a profit of 70 roubles each by sticking on foreign labels. (If they had had Soviet labels, nobody would have bought them.) Another, a 27-year-old woman, was on pregnancy leave. She had managed to buy five pairs of running-shoes for forty roubles a pair in the Soviet–Finnish border town of Vyborg and was selling them in Arkhangelsk for one and a half times the original price. A third, also a woman, had come from Estonia to visit her Arkhangelsk cousin with two suitcases. These contained: '192 decorated plastic bags, 7 pairs of tights, 6 children's T-shirts, 2 pairs of children's trousers, 2 pairs of jeans, an assortment of gloves, a variety of coloured shampoos, and 25 bottles of cleansing lotion'. The plastic bags, costing only sixty kopecks in Tallin, were selling for up to three roubles.

Other bestselling items in the Arkhangelsk black market were Japanese watches, foreign sun-glasses and freshly printed copies of Mikhail Bulgakov's *The Master and Margarita*. (Speculators buy up editions of the classics as soon as they come on sale, confident of selling at a hefty profit because of their scarcity.)

And all this was happening in a narrow space that had been fenced off like a sheep-pen and was packed with people, while some sparse bushes near by were being used as changing rooms.[1]

Fake foreign labels are a regular part of the speculator's stock-in-trade. Using this device, in 1985 three Latvians, led by 29-year-old Ulmas Tabaks, decided to set up a 'firm' buying Soviet-made jeans and T-shirts and selling them as imports. The new 'Tabaks' line had to be sold on the black market, or no one would have taken the 'imports' for real. In this way the goods were an instant hit. The same garments with Soviet labels from the local (Latvia) factory were left nowhere. Such was the entrepreneurs' success that they decided to put their business on a more 'industrial' basis. Still working out of a garage, they engaged a 'staff' of employees to smuggle stock whole-sale from the State factory, switch the labels, bring it in for relabelling, and market the finished products.

One might have expected the local militia to spot so much unusual activity, yet they remained strangely blind. The reason came to light at the subsequent trial, when it transpired that one of the trio had had a contact in the Riga OBKhSS[g] – the head of the 'Campaign Against Speculation' Department.

Interviewed by the press shortly before the trial, satisfied customers testified to the high quality of the 'Tabaks' product. They said that the labels, unlike those of the State-produced goods, did not run as soon as they were put into the wash. But this did not save the entrepreneurs from receiving sentences of five years each.[2]

In Moscow young speculators are constantly having to move their pitch. At one time it was near the flower-stall outside the Gorky Park Metro station. Then, in the summer of 1986, they set up business on a patch of dusty earth in the Smolensk Triangle, immediately oppo-site the Ministry of Foreign Affairs. In this spectacular location the speculators could conveniently buy jeans and T-shirts off foreign tourists from the nearby Belgrade hotel and resell them at a profit to Soviet customers coming up from the Kievski railway station. After about 6 pm the main business became prostitution, mainly with foreign tourists for currency or drugs. The moral eyesore remained for several months, for the simple reason that it lay on the border between two police districts, neither of which wanted to take re-sponsibility. Eventually the scandal became too great; the area was cleared, and the 'traders' moved back to a place near Gorky Park. But by 1987 the young prostitutes were back on the beat, waiting for late-night guests as they returned to the hotel.


With the advent of *glasnost*, prostitution, which had always existed under police toleration, became a permitted newspaper topic. One of the first stories published was about Lisa Tamarina, a prostitute working in Moscow's fashionable Arbat restaurant, until she was picked up and given two and a half years for possession of drugs. She told the court she had turned to the trade in order to earn foreign currency with which to satisfy her addiction.[3] Foreign currency is the only payment with professional prostitutes, whereas 'amateurs' commonly ask for payment in kind: mostly clothing and luxuries, to sell or for their own use. Professionals want more substantial things: a *dacha*, a car or a foreign husband. In 1986 *Moskovski Komsomolyets* gave some 'typical' prices paid by prostitutes as: 20,000 Japanese yen for boots; 100 US dollars for sandals; and 500 French francs for a swimming costume.

The dream of every professional prostitute is to marry a foreigner – not in order to live abroad (prostitutes find visas hard to come by) but to acquire the right to hold foreign currency. The marriage is strictly commercial, and the husband disappears as soon as the couple have visited the notary's office to fill out a currency declaration after the wedding. In 1987 the price of a husband was 5,000 US dollars. At this rate, *Moskovski Komsomolyets* calculated, 'the wife-to-be must sleep with approximately fifty foreigners in order to afford one.'[4] (The newspaper, belonging to the Moscow youth organization, was warning young girls about the pitfalls of the 'good life'. But to judge from the number of solicitations afterwards, it also told hundreds what they had been missing.)

Part of the professional prostitute's earnings must go on bribes for doormen and hotel staff, and sometimes for taxi-drivers who bring clients. There is also a domestic side to the business. The lower end serves Soviet clients in the vicinity of some Moscow railway and Metro stations. The upper end is more bizarre. In 1988 the newspaper *Komsomolyets Kirgizii* (27 January) carried a letter from a Kirghiz called Oulbekov about his three-year association with Moscow prostitutes, one of whom was said to be in films, and a female ministry official. In 1981 he went to Moscow to a seminar and stayed at the Rossiya Hotel. 'Those who have stayed in the capital should know what kind of people stay at the Rossiya.' In the lobby he saw a film actress giving autographs during a film festival, and gave her his notebook. She raised her eyebrows in surprise, looked him over carefully and, giving him her autographed picture, asked him to wait for her until she finished. They drove off in her new white Zhiguli to the Prague restaurant, where she was welcomed as a steady customer.

When they arrived at her place, 'an expensive three-room apartment', at 1 am she uncovered a full-length nude portrait of herself. 'Now I realize it was a well-planned tactic.' She began smoking a long cigarette, asked him about himself, whether he was married and so on, and learned that he was in the fur trade. Next evening she came home with a plane ticket for him to return to Frunze (the Kirghiz capital) in the morning. He must forget his seminar, and she would buy his family presents while he went and came back with furs. Oulbekov saw her for the next three years. 'I committed a number of crimes and kept digging into the state's pocket.' To acquire furs and make trips he also became the lover of the woman in a ministry. 'I gave her 1,200 roubles to get me a good post. Now I realize she took the money for letting me stay at her place for a whole week. All these people I've been talking about are respected people, movie stars,' he told the newspaper. 'Some of them even go out to the subways [to hustle].'[5]

The militia (and it may safely be supposed the KGB) collude with prostitutes, who supply them with information. This can lead to bizarre situations, as when in 1986 a group of volunteer police auxiliaries (*druzhiniki*[8]) attempted to arrest a prostitute in Moscow. According to a Soviet reporter, she pressed her bag – 'the same colour as her green eyes' – to her breast, saying, 'Do you want to make trouble for yourselves boys?' Assuming that she worked for the police, the *druzhiniki* let her go. In fact, she worked for no one but herself.[6]

In 1987 the standard bribe to Intourist hotel doormen was 15 roubles. But at least one girl, Olga Yakonka, managed to by-pass the system by installing herself in the Mezhdunarodnaya, the leading Moscow businessmen's hotel.[7] Another found her clients among the audience at the Bolshoi theatre.

A Moscow girl called Blokha ('the Flea') is reputed to have earned more than 100,000 roubles in five years: forty years' pay at average legal wage levels. Similar earnings are possible at the fashionable Black Sea holiday resorts frequented by foreigners and Party members. A Soviet witness describes meeting a woman who was showing her fifteen-year-old daughter the ropes in the Zhemchuzhina hotel in Sochi. 'If she goes for the big-time, she can retire at twenty-five,' the mother told him.[8]

*Sovietskaya Estonia* reported an attempt to blackmail a prostitute in the Baltic republic, involving a payment of 10,000 roubles in cash. It quoted an article shortly before in *Literaturnaya Gazeta*, describing

Militia officer, letting prostitute go free: 'What could I do?
There's no law against it.'

prostitutes' grievances about the bribes they had to pay and a proposal
by some of them that their profession be legalized, in return for a 40
per cent tax on their earnings, payable in hard currency.[9]

Another city to come in for publicity has been Minsk, where,
according to *Sovietskaya Belorussiya*, Nina G. and a group of girl-
friends used to make a good living by picking up foreign tourists at
the Yubileini restaurant and taking them back to Nina's flat. The
girls charged twenty-five roubles 'plus coffee and tea extra' in whatever currency the guests happened to be carrying. They were eventually arrested and charged with keeping a 'den of thieves' (the word
'brothel' has no legal status), causing the newspaper to observe that
'in their mania for material possessions' the girls had 'forgotten their
destinies to be beloved wives and mothers'.[10]

But in 1986 Nina and her friends were not the only scandal in
Minsk. According to *Komsomolskaya Pravda*, other 'painted girls'
were making the city's Intourist hotel a veritable 'hot-bed':

> There was a time when they used to conceal their business, and, if
> caught, swear not to do it again. But today they exchange nods with

doormen and greet the militia like old friends. They know, and are known by, everyone in the hotel – in the bars and in the restaurant. Indeed, so persistently do they pester foreign guests that some of these have had to ask Intourist officials for protection from their attentions.[11]

Until June 1987 prostitution could not be punished as such, because in the perfect Soviet state it did not officially exist. Newspapers were obliged to call prostitutes 'business women' or occasionally 'courtesans'. They could be arrested if they had no job, but this eventuality could be avoided by buying a 'cover' job. In the end the only way was to charge them with illegal currency dealing. *Komsomolskaya Pravda* concluded, 'This disgraceful "business" still goes on – mainly because we allow it to. For years we pretended not to notice anything. We should be ashamed of having kept silent.'

From the 'hot-beds of vice' in Moscow and Minsk, it is 1,500 miles south to the Caspian and 5,000 east to the rivers and lakes of the Pacific seaboard, where hundreds of thousands of Soviet citizens derive a quite different form of 'parallel income', at the expense of the State fisheries. Poachers take whole sturgeon and salmon, mainly for black or red caviare.

State fisheries obtain this by netting the females, extracting the eggs by pressure on the roe, and then returning the fish to the water. But the poachers are generally incapable of distinguishing the sexes, and in their haste catch and kill both male and female indiscriminately. They rip out the eggs, salt them in pans, and rush the caviare and whatever they can preserve of the fish as quickly as possible to the nearest black market. The loss to the ecology and the State is enormous. In Sakhalin Island in 1985 poachers took an estimated 750,000 roubles' worth of fish. Among those found to have made poaching a regular business were a senior engineer, an army captain, a female member of the Korsakov School of Art and an old lady. The island's chief fishery inspector would show visitors a collection of stones thrown through his window, and inspectors describe how they had been 'chased with axes and hunted with guns'.[12]

Some poachers' stories of how they came by their 'catch' would excite admiration even in western Ireland. Caught spearing salmon with pitch-forks, three farm-hands from the Sokholovski State Farm explained: 'On peacefully fording the Mali Takoi river, we were attacked by huge salmon as big as sharks and forced to fight them off. As a result, we not only saved our lives but collected a whole barrelful of caviare.' Or so it was reported in the satirical weekly *Krokodil*.[13]

As an incentive to catch poachers in the early morning mist, inspectors receive 30 per cent of the value of the confiscated catch – until the accumulated 'bonus' exceeds five months' pay. Beyond that the inspector loses interest, and may well turn to a little poaching himself.

One day a team of fishery inspectors came on another group, off-duty and with 11,000 roubles' worth of poached fish. Not batting an eyelid, the junior inspector leading the second party explained away their 390 salmon, two nets, two inflatable boats and a lorry as confiscated goods. 'We are on patrol, Comrade Inspector!' he was reported to have exclaimed on being challenged. 'The poachers gave us the slip, but we bagged their fish and nets.' The story was not believed.[14]

In July 1986 *Sovietskaya Rossiya* reported from the north Caucasus that illegal black caviare was 'spilling across the whole of southern Russia' and 'home-smoked fish being delivered direct to apartment blocks'. A 'water militia' had been set up to help fishery inspectors, but such measures were merely symbolic.

Two months earlier a sergeant in the water militia had been caught in an ambulance with caviare poached from the Caspian fishing ground at Agrakhanski bay.

> A search of the vehicle revealed 346 kilograms of black caviare and twenty-one sturgeon. Nearly half the caviare was inedible. The haul was traced to a skilfully camouflaged poachers' depot, with a full supply of nets, explosives and equipment. The poachers were slitting open the sturgeon, removing the caviare and throwing the fish to wild boar. The caviare was conserved on the spot. The gang had destroyed 240–50 female sturgeon and nearly the same number of male fish – some weighing 100 kilos.

At the site of another sturgeon 'massacre', the militia found forty huge fish heads – and four poachers. 'And guess who led them? A fishery inspector!'[15]

The Soviet claim that crime by Soviet citizens is encouraged by foreigners can hardly be contested, particularly in the case of antiques. Every Soviet city has 'commission shops' where Soviet citizens may bring objects to be sold at a commission of 7 per cent. (Private buying and selling is officially forbidden.) Most of the stock is junk, expensively priced in a country impoverished by war and revolution. But sometimes there are items of real value. There are also a few official antique shops for hard-currency customers. Privately acquired antiques may not be exported without a permit, but regularly are – often in diplomats' luggage.

But for real profit the antique seller needs professional smuggling – like that brought to light in 1986, when a Soviet citizen and a foreigner were arrested in connection with antique musical instruments.

On 8 February a Thomas d'Oriya was arrested at Sheremetyevo airport with a Galliano violin worth 200,000 roubles. At the trial he was accused of attempting to export it for Sergei Dyachenko, a music teacher at the Moscow Conservatory. D'Oriya, a translator at the Progress State publishing house, was said to have brought in cheap violins from America, declaring them as valuable instruments on his immigration customs form. On leaving, he would take out antiques. In 1984 the ruse proved successful and a Santa Serafin violin was sold in the United States for 40,000 dollars. But in 1986 the customs inspector called over an expert who recognized the substitution. According to the prosecution, Dyachenko had successfully smuggled out four other violins, partly with the help of a foreign student. An 'entire underground' was said to have been used to get the money back to the Soviet Union, using a friend in New York, a contact in Israel and relatives of Dyachenko in Sukhumi. In all, the music teacher was said to have received 160,000 roubles.

Dyachenko was given seven years and d'Oriya three and a half – causing *Sovietskaya Rossiya* to observe that the violins had been 'paid for with the labour of Russian serfdom' and that a new law, enacted after d'Oriya's arrest, concerning the tracing of 'movable' historic valuables in private ownership had come 'very late in the day'.[16]

In another case the Soviet tanker carrying Second Officer Ivan Brunovsky began for some reason to deviate from its course. It was then discovered that a box forming part of its navigating equipment had been stuffed with four Orders of Lenin, three Orders of the Red Star, one Order of Glory and other medals. Brunovsky was taking them abroad to sell to foreign collectors. As if this were not shameful enough for the son of a veteran of the Great Patriotic War, the officer, on an earlier trip homeward, had smuggled aboard 150 car radios, 'and even two cars, under the guise of necessary spare parts.'

This discovery was just one in a series involving smuggling by ships' crews and passengers on routes between the Soviet Union and Finland. And where foreigners were involved, there was always a Soviet contact waiting for the smuggler at the Russian end.

In 1986 a Finn, Palo Yarmo, was accused of trying to bring in twenty-one copies of pornographic material in the bottom of a biscuit tin; another Finn, Valye Savolainen, was accused of carrying four 'anti-Soviet' video-cassettes; and Zalma Nieminena, yet another Finn, of having 1,450 dollars in a flower-pot. According to *Ogonek*, many of the Finns who make short visits to the Estonian port of Tallin for a few days 'do not come to listen to the opera or wander round the streets of the old quarter. They leave the ancient capital of Estonia much lighter – without their heavy suitcases.'

In November 1986 the Finnish newspaper *Helsingin Sanomat* reported that a large 'contraband organization' had been operating for the past four years in the Finnish port of Pori. The organizers were alleged to have offered unemployed Finns a free holiday in the USSR, a hundred roubles pocket-money and a night out in a restaurant – all in return for taking in Western goods to sell and bringing out items with a price in the West. Among the Western goods were jeans, running-shoes, radios, watches, video-recorders, cassettes and motor spares; and among the things wanted from the Soviet Union were caviare, paintings and antiques.

*Ogonek* further accused a former Estonian Soviet citizen, whom it named as A. Perinauska, of running a marriage business. This business was said to provide Soviet nationals with foreign wives at 6,000 dollars 'per spouse', including legal aid with subsequent divorces.

Surprisingly, in a country where 'unearned incomes' are illegal and the average monthly wage is less than 200 roubles, the Soviet Union has a regular big-time gambling community. The police are said to know 300 big-timers.[17] But since, in most of the fifteen republics, gambling is only an 'offence' and not a 'crime', the maximum penalty the law can impose is a fine of fifty roubles. It is therefore necessary to charge gamblers on other grounds.

The sums that change hands can be colossal. The press reported the case of a man called Brodsky who had made a fortune from a clandestine jeans factory. In a single evening Brodsky lost 380,000 roubles at the Sandunov baths, a Moscow gambling haunt with access to nearby apartments and hotel rooms. He managed to scrape together 300,000 in cash, but had to steal to obtain the balance. He was caught and given a long prison sentence.[18] Another professional gambler, known as 'Lucky', was found to have kept an exercise book in which he entered his wins and losses, 'items that ran into six digits'.[19]

These big-time players are all black marketeers, as secretive about how they spend their money as about how they get it. To make use of their wealth, they must resort to such time-honoured devices as *dachas* bought under pseudonyms and yachts registered in the names of clubs. But in case of trouble, there are no easy bolt holes. The Soviet borders are too tightly guarded, and for non-payment of debts or the use of marked cards the retribution of the gambling community is reputedly pitiless.

Dostoevskian dramas also occur at a humbler level. Dzhabrail Kandokhov and his friend Kushkov, a thirty-year-old construction worker, were gambling partners in the small town of Narktal in the Kabardino Balkarski, an autonomous republic in the north Caucasus. One day in 1986, having lost all he possessed (including an advance of money on his home) in a card game, Kushkov decided that his only recourse was to steal from his more successful partner. While Kandukhov was out of the room, telephoning his wife to say he would be home soon, Kushkov took 500 roubles from his partner's pocket. When Kandukhov later discovered the theft, he demanded not only the return of the money but also a 'fine' in return for not telling their friends.

Shortly afterwards four card-players, including Kushkov and Kandukhov, gathered for a game in another apartment. But before they could begin, Kushkov had to produce the money to repay his debt. Acting on a sudden impulse, he got up and left the apartment, and went to Kandukhov's home. And there, with an axe, he blindly killed Kandukhov's wife and eighteen-month-old daughter, before taking 500 roubles and returning calmly to the game.

After Kushkov had been tried for murder and sentenced to death, a meeting of the Party *raikom*[g] rapped local officials for allowing gambling to go on virtually under their noses. Kushkov and his friends had not confined their games to private apartments, said the *raikom*; they had also gambled openly – in shops, on building sites and on collective farms. 'Even now the card-players have not taken cover. And it is not only in Narktal that teenagers are being drawn into this dangerous pursuit.'[20]

★

One day in 1986 an *Izvestia* reporter, dressed in the uniform of a GAI (traffic police) inspector, complete with metal badge and white baton, stood in Moscow's Yaroslavl Street and flagged down drivers for minor infringements of traffic rules. When he asked to see their driving licences, he was astounded to find how many were handed to him with discreetly folded notes of three or five roubles inside. It was no different in other parts of Moscow. Afterwards a GAI major told him:

> *You* saw only three- or five-rouble notes; but often inspectors are offered *twenty*-fives. Imagine a new inspector repeatedly offered money each day. The first time he refuses, and the second, and the third. But what about the twentieth or the hundredth time? The weak ones break down and pocket the money. And then by degrees they develop a liking for such 'presents' and start demanding them.[21]

GAI statistics show reported cases of extortion and bribery as roughly equal. Inspectors are most open to corruption in Moscow, Uzbekistan, Georgia, Kirghizia, Tadzhikstan and the Trans-Caucasus. According to *Izvestia*, in 1984 alone 'thousands' of people were dismissed from the GAI and hundreds put on trial. In 1985 the figure was said to have dropped,[22] but in 1987 there were no further statistics. Even bribes of twenty-five roubles are certainly not the limit. In 1987 a driver breathalyzed after crossing a white line was persuaded to pay 300 roubles in order to keep his licence.[23]

But corruption in the traffic police is a minor affair compared with rackets in the food trade. At the time of the 1986 Moscow 'stores' trial, involving top managers of the city's biggest department stores (Novo-Arbatski, GUM and Gastronom Number 1), V. Olenik, a senior official investigating crimes in the Moscow trade network, gave an interview to *Izvestia*. He described how fifteen managers and Trade Directorate officials had taken over a million roubles in bribes from subordinates, and paid out three-quarters of this sum in bribes to their own colleagues and overseers. At the start of the inquiry, OBKhSS inspectors made 'control' purchases. In one day they were cheated 156 times out of 193, 'and that in some of the most reputable shops in the city'. The chief forms of cheating involved overcharging, tampering with the scales or selling low-grade produce at the price of better quality.

Over the years people with no experience had been appointed shop directors through knowing the right people – for example, a jockey's assistant, V. Tulchinsky, who had been made Director of

'Her hand is getting heavier and heavier.'

Shop Number 6 in the Sovietski district and 'had served his sponsors loyally'. Modern-day Potemkin, villages had been organized along the routes used by Party bosses, so that if one of them were to drop in on a shop, he would find everything in order, with a fair choice of goods, satisfied customers and polite assistants.

Certainly there had been reports about corruption from customers, but it was always the Main Trade Directorate (Glavtorg) that dealt with them – and the directors of Glavtorg were themselves on trial.

Illustrating the system of protection in the trade, Olenik described how Ambartsumyan, director of a Moscow fruit and vegetable warehouse, had for ten years kept an account book in which he meth-odically entered details of 'gifts' to officials. 'Four times a year, on the eve of public holidays, hampers with delicacies were sent to officials of District Party and Executive Committees, the Trade Direc-torate, the Trade Ministry, and the OBKhSS itself.' Similar gifts had been made by trade officials to their superiors: 'a regular tribute', a kind of advance. They always achieved their purpose. Pressure was put on investigators to drop inquiries, and the investigators had had to appeal to high Party sources for help.

Despite the trial, little had changed within the trade system, said the investigator. 'If this vicious protection racket is not replaced by responsible business methods, we shall be back where we started.' [24]

In 1986 four senior officials of the Ministry of Foreign Trade re-ceived fifteen years each for taking bribes from foreign business-men. In this case Western influence was blamed. At the trial, one of them, named Likov, told how, on visits abroad, 'foreigners literally guessed what our wishes were. It needed only one nod at a chosen object for it to be immediately wrapped up and delivered by the shop to our hotel room.' According to the men's lawyer, it was 'like Aladdin's cave': into their rooms poured 'lawn-mowers, stereo-systems, massage and sauna equipment, medicines, bathroom taps, heated car-seats, radar-detection gadgets, and goodness knows what.' In their eagerness to conclude contracts, the four officials caused the Soviet government to lose millions. For example, pre-fabricated houses were bought at an excessively high price, and because the contract was not studied carefully enough, 'some settlements ended up without baths'. (The Soviet government was eventually paid 11 million roubles in compensation.)

At the trial the prosecutor demanded the death sentence for Likov, 'the most persistent of the bribe-takers'. But the judge gave him fifteen years like the three others. [25]

An increase in the ownership of material goods, which began in the Brezhnev period, has led to an increase in house crime. One of the first things a visitor notices in Soviet cities is that all ground-floor windows have iron grilles. Burglaries of apartments are now an everyday occurrence; and many blocks have an entrance security lock that can be opened only by knowing the code.

The militia divide burglars into two types: the 'artist on tour' (*gastroler*) and the 'local' (*zemlyak*). The *gastroler* is usually a dapper type who burgles a flat, then hops on a plane to the next city. The *zemlyak* operates from home. The average burglar, of either type, is young, presentable and educated. Only one in four burglaries is committed by a gang, and the crime is nearly always committed in daytime, when people are out at work. Doors and locks are often so weak that only a shove is needed to force them. Shoddy workmanship is said to make new housing districts particularly easy game. And apartment blocks of eighteen and twenty-two storeys discourage watchful neighbourliness.

One *zemlyak* burglar, a petite woman called Svetlana Rud, would ring people's doorbells, holding a box of chocolates or a bunch of flowers, and pretend to be looking for friends. If the door was answered, she would say she had mistaken the address. If not, she would force it with a small jemmy carried in her handbag. Inside she would fill one of the owner's suitcases with jewellery, perfume, clothes, crystal and anything else of interest, then frequently get a local resident to help her carry it to a taxi. When finally caught she had burgled 128 flats in two years.

A well-known *gastroler* began his tour in Novokuznyetsk and, leaving behind a trail of empty flats, flew to Novosibirsk, Lvov, Dnepropetrovsk, Minsk, Kiev and Leningrad. According to the police, this 'Gentleman Jim' was always well dressed, carried a brief-case, and whenever possible would select a good book ('such as *Shakespeare's Sonnets*') from the shelves of the apartments he was robbing. A man of principle, he kept regular working hours, from ten to six.[26]

Crimes of violence, at least for gain, remain relatively rare in the Soviet Union. In Moscow and other cities it is still usually possible to walk at night through ill-lit streets without the fear of mugging that exists in many Western cities. The violent type of criminal is typically a drunk who in a fit of anger kills the person nearest to him (often his wife) with the closest thing to hand. This makes the work of Number 38 Petrov Street (Moscow police headquarters) a sinecure compared to that of Scotland Yard. But there are exceptions. The British correspondent Martin Walker reports the case of Soviet friends whose son was mugged and murdered, and their apartment rifled with the help of his stolen key. Such crimes have grown with the drugs problem, particularly in provincial towns that are less heavily policed than the big cities.

One such provincial town is Orenburg. Its street maps show a district called Podmaychni as an empty circle. In the words of a

Soviet reporter, it is 'just a blob – the streets are not even lit'. In 1986 taxi-drivers were refusing to take passengers into Podmaychni, which is known locally as 'Shanghai' on account of the drugs trade. One night a group of four addicts murdered a militia captain who had gone there to meet them. One of the gang was shot dead, and the others arrested, including a seventeen-year-old girl who described how she had struck the officer on the head with a hammer. She and her family of four had been living on her grandmother's pension and selling *samogon* in exchange for potatoes.[27]

The militia are worried by the increasingly low age level among Soviet criminals. In 1987 one theft in every five, one assault in every three, and every second car theft were the work of minors. But they can be signally relaxed about a more vicious form of crime. 'We are confident about tomorrow,' wrote a Soviet newspaper reader, referring to Mr Gorbachev's reforms. 'But what about this evening?' What he was talking about was rape.

The taboo on discussing the subject was broken by the publication in *Sovietskaya Kultura* of angry letters received after the newspaper carried a story about a rapist receiving a ludicrously light sentence because of the character reference supplied by his enterprise.

On her way home one evening, a woman student had accepted a ride in a passing car. The driver had taken her to the woods, raped her, and made off. At the police station, she was able to describe some unusual ornaments dangling from the car's rear-view mirror. But the militia showed no hurry to follow the case up. Finally the girl's father took it on himself to do so. After searching the streets of the town where they lived, he found the car and brought the owner to court. But the man received only three years, because of the character reference and the fact that he was the father of small children.

The most revealing letter to reach *Sovietskaya Kultura* was from a militia lieutenant. The police were far from treating rapes as priority cases, he wrote. 'As a militia officer I am well aware that we are not expected to go to any great lengths to solve such cases. Our top priority is the theft of State property, and thefts from people's homes are priority number 10.'[28]

The fastest growing category is now that of crimes resulting from the use or possession of drugs. In one of the worst-affected cities, Alma-Ata, in 1986 over half the burglaries and other types of theft were related to narcotics, which were also the cause of two particularly grisly murders. In one, two young men stabbed a drugs dealer who was behind with repayment of a 3,000-rouble debt for four kilos of hashish. In the other, two junkies killed and dismembered a young woman student.[29]

'A gramme of opium is worth a gramme of gold on the black market,' observed Ernst Barasov, the Kazakhstan Deputy Interior Minister. The republic authorities had just uncovered a drugs connection between Kazakhstan and Leningrad. Raw narcotics were bought from locals with vodka, then passed to a conductor on the Alma-Ata–Leningrad express. In other cases drug-pushers were taking advantage of the local labour shortage to get temporary farm work near hemp and poppy plantations. When they had picked enough hemp and poppy heads, they would vanish without waiting for their wages. Despite stricter control over employment, said Barasov, drug-pushers were still coming to the wild hemp valleys of Kazakhstan from all over the Soviet Union: 'Frunze, Dnepropetrovsk, Irkutsk, Togliatti'. Asked why it was not possible to destroy the wild-hemp fields, the Minister said there were 'hundreds of thousands of hectares' of pasture land where, even if the hemp were destroyed with chemicals, it would quickly return – and the herbicides would kill the pastures.[30]

During 'Operation Opium', an attempted clean-up in Uzbekistan, a worker on a State farm near Kokand was found with 19,000 roubles in his car and one and a half kilos of opium in his refrigerator. The militia explained how the system worked:

> Somebody supplies his 'man' in the region with a large sum of money – say 50,000 roubles. The middle-man then visits an acquaintance working on a collective farm, offers him money, and says trustingly, 'Sow your plot with poppies and harvest them in May. Here's an advance.' In the spring he comes and collects them.[31]

Higher up the ladder, the big dealers, 'looking every bit like decent citizens', command a network of transport and distributors. 'Nobody would think that body-guards sleep by their beds, or that hundreds of thousands of roubles are kept under their floorboards,' commented a reporter. In 1986, arrests included the head doctor of a hospital,[32] and a sports coach using his team's bus for distribution.

Meanwhile the drugs wave has given the cities a new criminal terminology. Among the gangs it is the boss (*pakhan*) who prepares the drugs and the 'quick one' (*shustrilo*) who acquires the raw materials. Ordinary gang members are 'boot boys' (*shesterki*) and those on whom their concoctions are tried out are 'rabbits' (*kroliki*).

# 7

# Bureaucracy or Democracy?

*Party membership – organization – 'democratic' voting – role of Komsomol – school and student politics – politics of young industrial workers – bureaucracy in Komsomol – 1987 Congress – arrival of Gorbachev – multi-candidate factory elections – constitutional changes – Moscow under Yeltsin*

There are only two kinds of political status in the Soviet Union: Party and non-Party. But membership of the Party is not a matter of simple personal choice. The candidate must be chosen by existing members and go through a period of probation before receiving his 'card'. The choice falls on those who 'participate actively in production and the life of society'.[1]

Hard as it may be to enter, the Party is even more dangerous to leave. Voluntary departure amounts to civic suicide, and expulsion to a ball and chain for life. Only important political figures can hope to be rehabilitated and readmitted to the top ranks. This consideration counts heavily in refusals to join.

Then there is the exacting role demanded of members. In campaigns against alcoholism or for better discipline, it is they who must set the example: one 'bad conduct' can mean a reprimand or even expulsion. In addition to attending meetings of the 'primary organization', or basic cell, the member must 'volunteer' for a variety of socially useful activities. And, of course, he must never miss a *subbotnik*:[g] one of those Saturdays of 'voluntary' work when intellectuals who scarcely know one end of a broom from the other are mobilized to clean up the city.

Its role of social searchlight entitles the Party cell to involve itself freely in members' private lives. For example, in certain professional circles, especially the army, divorce is heavily frowned on; and the importance attached to an unblemished private life can lead to sordid tit-for-tats. A former Party member described one such experience:

> Our plans for divorce came apart when my wife demanded possession of our flat and custody of our daughter. Soon afterwards an anonymous letter arrived at the university, saying that I had assaulted her and was

collaborating without permission in various publications. Obviously my wife was the source of this letter. But I refused both to submit to her blackmail and to appear before my cell committee to lay bare my private life. I left the Party, and my academic career was finished.

Following this episode, Vladimir, a brilliant research scientist, was unable to get even a teaching job at a secondary school. He was barred from the offices of newspapers and magazines and now scrapes a living by doing translations.

Before expulsion, which must be approved by a series of tribunals as a safeguard against personal vindictiveness, there are various lesser sanctions. One is the entering of a so-called 'restriction' in the delinquent member's Party record – a bar to certain types of promotion that follows the person wherever he goes. Such inquisitorial and disciplinary consequences help to explain a net decline (nearly a halving in some major centres) in the number of Party members active in the intelligentsia, particularly senior specialists and artists.[2] They also explain why, for reasons of efficiency, it has become necessary to open administrative functions more widely to non-Party people.

On 1 January 1986 the Party had just over 19 million members. Of these, 45 per cent were workers, 11.8 per cent collective farmers and 43.2 per cent 'employees', i.e., white-collar workers. The years between 1981 and 1985 saw a significant increase in size, with 1.5 million new members. This has led to a rejuvenation, since four-fifths of the new members are young people, It also means the Party must adapt to a new professional structure (22 per cent of the newcomers are economic specialists) and to the increased representation of women, who have moved in twenty years from a fifth to a quarter of the membership.[3]

In this time, the distribution pattern across the country has not greatly changed. One republic retains a higher proportion of Party members than the rest: the Russian Federation (52 per cent of the population, 61 per cent of Party membership). There is also a high proportion of Georgians and Armenians, but very few Balts. Jews, as one of the official 'nationalities', account for twice as many members in the higher ranks of the Party as they do in the population at large – a reflection of their high level of education and concentration in towns and cities. But any deductions as to future distribution become risky in the case of Central Asia, where fertility has meant a large population increase; the children concerned have yet to reach an age at which they could enter massively into the Party.

Internal organization is on the classic Soviet pyramid pattern. At the bottom is the cell (*pervitchnaya partoriganisatsya*), headed by one person and consisting of three primary units of between three and thirty members. These are based on work-places or, in the case of non-active members, on places of residence. Cells are then grouped in sections (*tsekhovaya organisatsya*) with a strength upward of a hundred people, headed by a Secretary and small Bureau.

Sections are grouped in Party organizations (*partinaya organisatsya*), generally with a minimum of 500 members, directed by a Secretary and Party Committee, each of whose members is responsible for a specific sector of activity, for example 'Propaganda'. This is the first level at which the Secretary, and sometimes his two assistants, are paid professionals. Above it the Party is structured geographically, always with the same pattern, of a Bureau grouped round a First Secretary, first at the *rayon*[g] level, then that of *oblast*, then republic, and finally Union.

Political participation, in the widest sense, is open to any member of the country's 2.5 million work collectives; or 3.9 million basic trade union groups; or 1,100 voluntary organizations, ranging from the 3-million strong 'Knowledge' (*Znanie*) scientific association to the almost universal membership, through trade unions and other bodies, of the Red Cross and Red Crescent. But for most people practical politics is limited to voting, obligatorily, in elections.

This need no longer be just a formality. In the 1987 elections to regional and local councils, 56.7 per cent of those elected were non-Party. For the first time there were lists with more than one candidate (albeit for less than 1 per cent of seats), and newspapers published the names of candidates, including Party candidates, obtaining less than the necessary 50 per cent of votes. Over 32 per cent of those elected were under thirty; 20.7 per cent were Komsomol members; and 49.4 per cent were women.* Nevertheless, as long as the majority of seats at every level is held by nominees of the Party, there can be no decision by any assembly – local, regional, republican or higher – without the Party's prior approval.

For young people the chief forum of political activity is the League

---

*Membership of the Supreme Soviet included 71.5 per cent Party members. 22 per cent of the deputies were under thirty; 15 per cent Komsomol members; and 32.8 per cent women. Decisions approved by the June 1987 plenum of the Central Committee suggested that the process of 'democratization', cautiously begun at local level, could be extended to the next Supreme Soviet elections in 1989, and to those for the parliament of the Russian Federation in 1990.[4]

of Young Communists, better known simply as the Komsomol, the most senior of three youth organizations.

The first, for seven- to ten-year-olds, is the Young Octobrists, whose star-shaped badge carries a picture of the chubby infant Lenin. Organized by the Komsomol, Young Octobrists take simple vows of honesty and truth that echo those of Baden-Powell's Wolf Cubs.

The second organization, the Pioneers, is for those aged ten to fourteen. This is supposed to produce 'convinced fighters for the Communist Party cause', with a 'love of labour and knowledge' and 'imbued with the spirit of communist consciousness and morality'. But despite these formidable words, it is very much a 'fun' organization; and Pioneer palaces, in every town and city, provide a roof for all kinds of hobby from aeroplane-modelling to amateur theatricals. Each summer Pioneer camps take some 25 million children off their parents' hands, and give them a breath of rural or seaside adventure. Nearly every Soviet child joins the Pioneers, who are also under Komsomol direction.

The Komsomol is a much more serious body. Entry is less automatic, and its wide age-bracket, fourteen to twenty-eight, permits an organization that is in many ways a junior replica of the Party. Entry is through one of the primary Komsomol organizations, of which there are nearly half a million at places of work or study. Each local organization has the right to elect representatives to the hierarchy above, with a Committee or Bureau elected to run day-to-day activities at every level.

At the apex is a Congress, meeting, like that of the Party, every five years and electing a Central Committee, which is supposed to meet every six months. This in turn elects a Bureau and Secretariat (and a First Secretary) to direct work between meetings. There are three Komsomol publishing houses; a national daily newspaper, *Komsomolskaya Pravda* (a lighter and brighter product than the Party's *Pravda*); and more than 200 local papers, including the lively and much quoted *Moskovski Komsomolyets*.

Seven out of ten young people join the Komsomol but only a fraction are politically active; and often these have a less simplistic faith than was the case in the past, when surveys indicated that 84 per cent of the young believed socialism to be the only philosophy capable of giving the people social and political rights. In 1987 more than a quarter of 1,260 Komsomol Committee Secretaries thought that their colleagues had joined the Komsomol to further their careers. A survey at the time of the Twenty-seventh Party Congress showed that 70 per cent did not expect the problem of housing to be settled by the year 2000, as the Congress had indicated. And when *Komsomolskaya Pravda* invited contributions on the theme, 'What I Would Say to the Twentieth Komsomol Congress' (held the next year), 30 per cent were apparently so critical that the writers dared not sign them.[5]

Students in the Komsomol can follow political education courses in 'social faculties' and 'young speakers' schools' or join 'agitation' campaigns and attend 'lectures'. Often these gatherings are a means to test both the student's political knowledge and his ability to instruct others – by organizing a debate, running an agitation campaign, holding or giving a lecture.

Young industrial workers and collective farmers take part in similar educational meetings. For them, the Komsomol is centred on their work-place, where its task is to 'insert' the young worker into the collective, and look after his rights and political education. Here a member's socio-political activity increases with his qualifications.[6] The lowering of the age level in some factories has created a new situation in which the young form a majority in the work collective.[7] The Komsomol is thus expected to play a bigger role in the organization of work, the improvement of production and the achievement of profitability.


A lot has happened since the Komsomol was founded, in the first flush of the Revolution in 1917. For a year or so, it remained a non-political body, giving social and cultural help to young workers and the children of workers. At its first Congress in 1918, it was still possible to have a long debate about whether it was necessary to include the word 'communist' in its name. But then young Bolsheviks acquired controlling positions.

Later it became the spearhead of every big movement: industrialization, eradication of illiteracy, resistance to the German occupation, opening up the virgin lands, development of new zones, work on the BAM. Glorious pages, particularly in the Second World War, alternate with dark passages. In the late 1920s the Komsomol distinguished itself by hounding down peasants during collectivization, and subsequently by persecuting religious believers and 'disreputable elements'. But, wanting to re-endow it with its spearhead role, and calling for a return to the spirit of the past, the Twentieth Congress in 1987 passed in silence over these times.

Today, as before, the Komsomol has two key tasks: to provide a reserve of recruitment for the Party (70 per cent of Party members are from the Komsomol) and to ensure the political education of young people from fourteen to twenty-eight.* It is also expected to contribute to the economic life of the country, and, when needed, plenty of zealous young Komsomolists can always be found on the farms.[8]

But the awkward truth, demonstrated at its Twentieth Congress, is that the Komsomol is one of the most bureaucratic organizations in the Soviet Union. 'And nothing is harder to reform than a young bureaucrat,' says the political commentator Alexander Bovin. As for aiding the restructuring of the economy and 'educating' the young, it is simply falling down.

In 1987, following eighteen months of intensive propaganda about new working methods, improved economic efficiency and all the goals of the *perestroika*, the Donetz region Party Bureau inquired into the state of political education among working-class youth in the region – an inquiry of particular interest, since the region's workers included 630,000 Komsomol members and a high proportion of other young people. The inquiry was conducted in fifty enterprises, large and small, regardless of performance record. The findings caused a shock through the country. The majority of young workers had totally failed to follow the meaning of current slogans, and had no clear idea of their place and role in the reform of the economy. It was found that 90 per cent could not give the precise meaning of such conceptual key-words as 'self-financing' and 'self-profitable', which were at the heart of the reforms about which there was so much discussion. And this when they worked in enterprises that were supposed to be observing these new standards.[9]

The findings provoked a host of editorials about the need to lift political education, pre-eminently the responsibility of the Komsomol, out of the rut of theoretical argument and high-flown speeches; the Komsomol should come down to earth and talk sensibly with young people. The Komsomol thus became deeply embroiled in a nationwide argument about 'formalism' – the Party catch-phrase for the use of time-worn clichés that by the mid-1980s had come close to sapping all meaning from Soviet political life, like a kind of ideological AIDS.

*As membership of the Party can begin at eighteen, and one cannot belong to both organizations (except as a paid organizer), politically active Komsomol members must choose between the two.

Komsomol formalists are accused of pursuing a 'cult of paper', complemented by the ritual of meetings that end in hot air. Debates before the Twentieth Congress touched the heart of the problem. 'Tear up your papers. Come out of your offices. Look about you. Life has changed. And so has the duty of the Komsomol,' cried one critic.[10]

A young woman called Olga wrote:

> I have been in the Komsomol since I was fourteen. My husband is a member of the *apparat*.[g] When I ask him why he comes home so late, his answer is nearly always, 'Papers.' Often he works all night on them. Komsomol officers are buried by paperwork. Before working in the *apparat*, my husband was happy doing a whole lot of interesting things at his school. Today I can't remember when I last saw a book in his hand.[11]

But when it came to the Congress, nothing was done. Nor was the Bureau prepared to take action on an equally serious problem raised by delegates on all sides. This was the question of membership. For years the prestige of the Komsomol was related to the steady increase in its numbers: in 1918, 21,000; in 1950, 10.5 million; in 1986, 40 million. Wanting to get rid of the huge burden of those who joined simply because it was easier than to refuse, many Komsomol members sought a change in the age and conditions of entry.

Oleg M. of Kiev wrote:

> I'll tell you how I became a Komsomolist. At the end of the tenth grade, when I'd decided that nothing would make me join, I took the entrance exam for Tekhnikum Number 4 at Zhitomir. There were three of us. We'd been on the booze. But, coming back to the hostel, we ran into a Komsomol official. He knew quite well where we stood, but he virtually forced me to fill out an application form. So you can imagine what kind of Komsomolist I am.[12]

Stanislav Sekan of Tashkent worked in a factory and was told that all he had to do to be admitted was to pay his subscription (generally a few kopecks a month, according to wages) when asked by the factory committee. 'I made an experiment. I didn't pay it for a whole year; and nobody said a word.'[13] Sergei Garchin, a committee member in Krasnoyarsk *rayon*, was enrolled on the spot when he came before the military commission for call-up.[14]

Yet in pre-Congress debates, speaker after speaker protested at mixing the chaff with the grain. 'We must raise entry to sixteen and make fourteen to sixteen a trial period,' declared Ekaterina Goussenko, a student in Kursk. 'Joining just so as to be like everyone is simply not wanted,' said Alexei Yakovlev, Second Secretary of a section in Leninsk.

At present, choosing not to enter the Komsomol makes a child an exception. It frequently happens with religious families, like Natasha's. 'Of course, it sets me apart,' she said. 'But it doesn't throw me. All these keen Komsomol types, I just don't believe they're real.' But her small brother, who had just refused to enter the Pioneers, was less happy. 'The priest told us not to join, but my friends seem to have a lot of fun there.'

'In our university, we had a survey with the question, "Would you leave the Komsomol if there were no bad consequences?"' wrote Larissa S. of Moscow in *Sobesednik*.

> Nearly all of us answered 'Yes'. We had joined at fourteen. All we knew about it was the heroic history of the Komsomol in the Great Patriotic War and the civil war. But what unites us with the Komsomol today? Ideals? They're the same as those of all Soviet citizens. No one [in the Komsomol] bothers much about the problems of our institute. The last word is always with the dean or the *raikom*. It's time we protested at all the nonsense that goes on, the silly political tests. I have no real friends in the Komsomol. No one is obliged to stay a member, but there's always a scandal if you leave. I don't want a scandal and I'm not looking for problems.[15]

In the same issue of *Sobesednik*, Alexandrov of Tashkent told how he had been expelled from the Komsomol at school for joining 'what was then called an "informal group"'.* At his institute he had re-joined and seen the organization with new eyes: 'There's too much dead wood in this millions-strong army. It should limit itself to worthier members. I'd be quite happy to leave myself if necessary.'

Though Komsomol *apparatchiks* pay lip-service to the campaign against formalism (a *perestroika* catchword), they may not always realize that young people could take them at their word. Witness the row at a school in Semipalatinsk, described in a letter to the press by sixteen tenth-grade pupils.[16] Encouraged by *perestroika* and *glasnost*, they had started, in the Komsomol, to criticize the school reform, only to be slapped down by their Komsomol group leader (*staroste*). It was 'absolutely unthinkable' for the Komsomol to support pupils against their teachers, they were told. But the students took a different

---

*Unofficial group or association for the pursuit of almost any kind of interest, ranging from political to artistic – in this case possibly a rock-music group.

view. It was the 'first Komsomol meeting worthy of the name', and everyone had taken part. They were astounded at the officials' reaction. Wasn't the idea to fight formalism and get young people involved? But now that they were taking the slogans seriously, there were howls of protest. The head of the school hit back. The pupils' letter was 'rubbish'; he failed to understand how a newspaper could publish it. The discussion had been quickly settled, because 'in any case, the last word is with me'.*

On 2 September 1986, leading newspapers published an account of the debates in the pre-Congress plenum of the Komsomol Central Committee, something that had previously been reserved for 'informed circles'.

Otherwise the famous Congress served only to demonstrate the extent of the Komsomol's ossification. True, there were some vigorous interventions. But the bold decisions needed to regenerate the organization – like changing the entry rules and reducing the membership – were not taken. Even the proposal for a 'Law on Youth', demanded by many delegates as a safeguard for the rights of young people in society, was quietly pigeonholed by the Bureau, despite being unambiguously supported in a speech by Gorbachev. Asked about it at a closing press conference, the First Secretary Mironenko could only say that membership was a delicate subject on which there could be no precipitate decision, and that a group of young lawyers would be meeting 'to draw up proposals in legal terms'. A year later the project was still under discussion with no sign of any draft.

The Komsomol shares the task of youth's political education with one other institution: school. 'Political and moral culture begins, above all, with knowledge,' says *Komsomolskaya Pravda*.[17] And school is the obvious place to impart this, not through strict political instruction but rather in a politicized atmosphere diffused through teaching the usual subjects, such as history.

In the ninth and tenth grades, history teachers give so-called 'social lessons' (*obchestvovedenie*) for two hours each week. But their combination of a little sociology, a little philosophy (dialectical and histor-

*By a decision of the Bureau in September 1987, there ceased to be two separate Komsomol organizations in schools, one for pupils and one for young teachers. By instituting a single organization, it was hoped to bring the two sides together so that they could 'exchange viewpoints and experiences'.

ical materialism), a little law and a little economics is too much of mish-mash to evoke the interest of either pupils or staff. 'In any case, any idea of *interesting* the children is totally alien to the Ministry of Education, which is one of the most conservative in the country,' observed one Moscow secondary schoolteacher before it was put under new direction in the 1988 shake-up.

In higher education, first-year students receive a short course on the history of the Communist Party. Those in their second and third years have courses on Marxist philosophy and *politekonomia*, a mixture of politics and economics; and those in their fourth a course on 'scientific communism'. There is also a politically oriented course of psychology–pedagogy. Students who wish to specialize in one of these subjects can do so in the relevant faculty, under the eye of the 'chair of social science' that exists in every institute and university. Or they may enter a special faculty of 'philosophical science' as in Moscow State University.

Outside these institutions, young people's politics can also take the form of participating in 'grass roots' movements, such as the peace movement.[18] Or they can be called on to fulfil their internationalist duty by 'helping another nation to build its freedom'. In the 1980s this duty was very specific. Its name was Afghanistan.

In an article on political education, *Pravda* once reflected that its purpose was 'to supply an answer to all questions, in all spheres of life, and to follow the country's socio-economic-political development'.[19] The definition, though long-winded, is revealing. In the Soviet Union, defects in political education are regularly blamed for untoward events for which Westerners would clearly see a host of other reasons. An outstanding example was during the post-mortem on the 1986 Alma-Ata riots. Party investigations quickly produced the finding that young 'hooligans' and 'anti-social elements' were not the only ones involved in what had happened in the streets on those days. 'All-round excellent' students, honourable teachers, even Komsomol members had all taken part. Also in the dock was the Komsomol organization itself, for not having 'forged the characters of young internationalist communists'.

Under the headline 'A Bitter Lesson', *Komsomolskaya Pravda* saw the causes of the outbreak as a failure to carry out 'youth ideological work' and the 'enfeeblement of patriotic-internationalist education'. It cited a whole list of developments that should have served the organization as a warning: ethnic discrimination in student housing allocation; actions by the local militia protecting 'their own people';

the poor teaching of Russian in local schools; the survival of village clans in the city. 'Things can't be allowed to go on as before,' concluded the Komsomol's own newspaper.[20]

But this tendency to expect everything of the Komsomol so far as young people are concerned was vigorously criticized by delegates at the Twentieth Congress, who refused to be held responsible for society's inability to adapt to the needs of the new generation. If young people used the state lottery as a means to get rich, even using computers to work out 'lucky numbers', the Komsomol was blamed for failing to teach a healthy attitude towards money. It was expected to keep order in hostels,[21] to endow PTU students with a sense of responsibility towards their future enterprises,[22] to 'work on' young voters at election time,[23] to take part in the work of committees on youth questions,[24] and to defend the social interests of young people generally.[25] It was also held responsible for organizing leisure, preventing delinquency, and even assisting the militia to maintain law and order.[26] In all fairness, this was more than it could possibly bear alone.

The reform of the Party itself, though vastly more complex and fraught with uncertainties, offers a distinctly more promising prospect for Soviet youth than that of its official youth organization.

On arriving in power, Gorbachev immediately set out to create a new relationship between rulers and people. There was his early visit to the Likhachev truck factory, a school in the Moscow suburbs, a hospital – the first astonishing walk-abouts, during one of which a woman called, 'Be close to us!', and he, not without a touch of demagoguery, answered: 'How can I be closer than I am now!'

But everything depended on changing the Party rules. This had been on the agenda since Brezhnev set up a working group to study a possible revision at the Twenty-sixth Congress in 1981. Andropov took up the theme in his speech to the June 1983 plenum of the Central Committee. But it was necessary to wait for the Twenty-seventh Congress to know what the first changes would be – and for the January 1987 plenum (whose late assembly was thought to be due to resistance by part of the *apparat*) to approve them.

By the time the plenum met, the words 'democracy' and 'democratization' had been bandied about for some time. But now people heard from the lips of the First Secretary himself the first astounding mention of multi-candidate elections. Till then the Party

Idle bureaucrat, doing crossword: 'I've got it: *perestroika!*'

had always defended the system of single candidates with the argument that these emerged 'democratically' as a result of successive choices from below. This was generally eyewash; the elections were, in fact, merely ratifications.

Under the slogan 'Democracy will be in the Factories or Not at All', the first trial polls were held within weeks of the plenum. Up for election were brigade leaders, department heads and directors of enterprises. Filmed by television cameras brought in (with some difficulty) by *Komsomolskaya Pravda*, committees of workers in the Latvian R A Fg truck plant heard and questioned half a dozen candidates for the top management post. They finally selected two, to be voted on secretly by the whole work-force. Viewers were shown how the candidates campaigned, taking several weeks in which to familiarize themselves with the factory and its problems, and formulate their proposals for dealing with them. These were then presented to open meetings and in face-to-face talks with work brigades. Though the campaign itself was real enough, the participation and enthusiasm of the work-force were distinctly uneven. Several shop-floors never even bothered to hear the candidates, while others followed the process intently at every step.

At the same time multi-candidate elections were held across the country, for *kolkhoz* directors (whose appointment had always been elective in theory but was in fact a rubber-stamped Party choice), shop managers, chief engineers and – more cautiously and only at primary levels – members of the Party *apparat* and Komsomol First Secretaries.

Another step towards democracy was, as already noted, the June 1987 elections for local and regional councillors, republic deputies and lay magistrates. The results, including an increase in the number of non-Party candidates successfully standing, could be taken as evidence of Gorbachev's intention to involve the whole population in political life, at least locally and regionally (perhaps reserving Party members for key posts).

Another noteworthy feature was the publicity given to cases in which candidates, particularly unopposed Party nominees, failed to get the minimum 50 per cent of the poll required for election, a requirement that can often benefit small communities by obliging their representatives to be active on local issues. Of particular note was the unprecedented failure of a Party candidate, a woman, to get re-elected to a district seat in Moscow's large Gagarin *rayon*.[27]

The elections were preceded by a remarkable speech by Yeltsin. In it the then First Secretary of the Moscow Party laid into the so-called 'wedding generals' (*svadebnye generaly*) ★ who encumber all levels of Soviet political life, especially the Supreme Soviet. It had become the custom, said Yeltsin, to elect anyone who 'counted' locally: the head of the *kolkhoz*, the head of the militia, the director of the principal factory, the rector of the university. But these people were not necessarily interested in the work of a deputy, since they already had demanding jobs in their departments or enterprises. And, clinging to

★Allusion to the custom of inviting a general to the wedding feast in order to lend lustre.

their seats, they blocked the way to others from one election to the next.

A much more substantial advance came in July 1988, when a special Party conference approved major changes in the political system. Among its decisions, in spite of the resistance of conservatives, were plans to:

- establish an executive-style presidency;
- limit Party executives to a maximum of ten years in office;
- transfer numerous, unspecified administrative responsibilities from the Party to popularly elected councils.

Most notable was a decision to enlarge the functions of the Supreme Soviet. After increasing its membership to 2,250, with 750 representatives from central Party bodies such as women's and professional organizations, this would choose a permanent standing commission of 400 to 450, or 'streamlined Supreme Soviet', to legislate on day-to-day affairs.

One aim of the move was to give non-Party citizens a visible role in the process of reconstruction. Time would show whether this would happen, and whether, as Gorbachev suggested, a move was afoot to separate the powers of the Party and the State.

Nothing was said to indicate any intention of allowing a multiparty system, as opposed to giving a 'constructive' role to approved non-Party groups. But the unprecedented openness of the conference, in which delegates freely criticized leading personalities before a nationwide television audience, seemed the surest guarantee that now there could be no going back on *glasnost*, and that, whatever the difficulties still facing it, the *perestroika* would proceed.

# 8

# Leisure

*Tradition of organized leisure — pursuits in order of popularity — absence of 'family' holidays — emphasis on 'cultural' recreation — actual free time — lack of facilities in the countryside and new towns — young people's cafés — new ideas in television — acceptance of discothèques — the 'disco under the bridge' — intervention by Komsomol — rock and the music scene — Soviet views on Western stars*

The Soviet constitution concerns itself not only with work but also with the question of free time. Article 46 guarantees access to 'culture' and Article 40 the right to rest. But the use of leisure is not for the citizen alone to decide. Leisure affects the individual's 'equilibrium', and therefore all of society's.

Free time is defined as that which permits a person to develop creative instincts, to put his or her 'life forces' to the test, to acquire initiative. Personal pleasure scarcely comes into the question. 'Education' is all. Perhaps this is a relic of a distant past when every moment of life was ritualized. Today it adds up to an ingrained fear of any kind of spontaneous activity, an unquestioning conviction that leisure must be *organized*, that otherwise people would find nothing better to do after work than sit watching television. At the same time, there is no leisure industry in the Western sense, no range of commercial alternatives from which to choose how to spend a day or an evening.

Young people must be given the correct pursuits for their age group, and provided with an 'education in leisure' that will enable them, when grown up, to spend their free time 'positively'. To this end, the State offers an impressive network of facilities: art and music schools, clubs, libraries, Houses and Palaces of Youth, special theatres, camps and so on [1] — all intended to further the process of education and, in the case of children, to help parents who may not know how to further the process of development.[2]

The system works well enough — up to a point. The needs of the very young are well taken care of. Where it breaks down is at the onset of adolescence, when the young person looks for a way of escape, discovers vastly different needs, and develops faster than the capacity of the system to cope. It is then likely to break down under the face of two obstacles whose social causes are little analysed and whose consequences are described in the next chapter: alcoholism and delinquency.


For as long as most Soviet citizens can remember, the arrangement of holidays has been the responsibility of work organizations. Time has not altered the system, which began in the 1920s. As a result, husbands and wives, even when working in the same enterprise, tend to take holidays separately. To the astonishment of most foreigners, the notion of 'family holidays' remains quite strange to most Russians – though moves are now being made to encourage them as part of the campaign to cut the divorce rate (see chapter 2).

The system is justified on two grounds. The first is that people should be able to spend their holidays as they like. Many men want nothing better than to spend the whole day fishing or tramping in the country with a rucksack, alone or with friends. Others just want to potter round their *dachas*. Women usually prefer a break by the sea or at some health resort. And for everyone living in small, crowded apartments, it is a relief to get away from the family.

The second is that in a country where buying a train or plane ticket can mean queuing for hours or days, and where individual rooms in the better hotels are nearly all reserved for foreigners, it is easier to travel in organized groups. Consequently, many people have entirely lost the habit of going anywhere alone, and factories even organize coach parties for local mushroom-picking excursions.

Organized holidays are generally obtained through a system of vouchers (*putiovki*). These are sold by trade unions at a price that bears no relation to the actual cost, and secure a place in the enterprise's holiday centre or a tourist hotel. For example, a two-week stay in a typical holiday centre costing 150 roubles is sold for fifty. This includes a shared room, meals (of decent quality according to most people), and access to clubs, services and other facilities. Vouchers can be swapped, and often change hands at high prices. The benefits provided, including stays in convalescent homes (*sanatoria*), holiday camps and 'expeditions' for children, take a large share of most enterprises' 'social funds', which are usually equivalent to 30 per cent of the workers' direct pay.

For shorter breaks, there are Houses of Leisure, maintained by most cities in leafy suburban 'leisure zones'. In Moscow every *rayon* has one. The authorities of Vilnius in Lithuania go further: factory

Students on vacation: 'We're off to work in the country.'
Prostitutes: 'We envy you, lucky girls. We're off to work in Sochi.'

and office workers there are allocated whole tracts of forest where they can build their own *dachas*.

But not every Soviet citizen takes an organized vacation. Less than one in four obtain places in holiday camps, hotels and other official establishments, including *sanatoria*.* From necessity or choice the rest take holidays at home, or at their *dachas*, or with relatives in the country, or make private arrangements. Those in this last group are known as 'wild ones' (*dikari*); among them are many family groups, for whom State establishments operating on the voucher system make no provision.

*Dikari* are often quite shamefully fleeced, sometimes being charged the full rent of a room for a bed on an open balcony. A 1986 survey in the Crimea, a favourite holiday haunt, showed that 60 per cent of those vacationing privately were bitterly dissatisfied with what they found: a widespread lack of washing and toilet facilities, poor-quality meals, ticket queues, jam-packed beaches, inferior entertainments, generally high prices and overcrowding. 'Visitors are treated as a burden – almost as a natural disaster,' commented *Sovietskaya Kultura*.[3]

*In 1985 some 28 million went to hotels and holiday camps, 5.1 million to Houses of Leisure and State-owned boarding-houses, and 3.9 million to State 'recreation centres'. Nearly 11 million were given places at convalescent homes and health-cure centres.

'I don't know what to write [for an essay on the theme "How I Spent Sunday"], our TV was out of order.'

Even for the handful who can afford to pay for better, life can be bitter too. In 1987 Soviet film director Stanislav Govorukhin took a holiday in Yalta, which had once been his favourite resort. But now he discovered that the good hotels were exclusively reserved for foreigners. For Soviet citizens, there were only ninety-six rooms, often 'with only the most basic facilities'. 'If a Russian does manage to get into an Intourist hotel, he suffers all kinds of humiliations,' wrote Govorukhin.

His entrance pass is a different colour from foreigners' passes, which means that he will be given service last of all, and that not all the facilities of the hotel are open to him.

Foreigners feel at ease in Yalta – they laugh, dance and enjoy themselves. But Russians humbly look on, and are afraid to go into cafés, restaurants and swimming pools. Of course, our government needs currency . . . to buy computers, medical equipment, clothing and perfumery. But isn't currency costing us too dear? When waiters, doormen and administrators wag their tails at foreigners, and are rude and rough to their compatriots, then the Soviet citizen looks like a slave, and a slave has the mentality of a slave.

Just think – we are allowing a class of slaves to be created before our very eyes.[4]*

★

*Following protests, a legal ruling in 1988 made all hotels open to everybody, but in practice hard-currency requirements left matters much as they were.

In 1982 sociologists questioned 698 citizens in the city of Kerch about how they spent their leisure time. They found that: 79.2 per cent regularly watched television; 53.3 per cent regularly read books; 25.9 per cent went for walks; 14.8 per cent visited or entertained friends; 14.6 per cent played sports or took similar exercise; 14.5 per cent played games such as chess, dominoes or cards; 8 per cent studied; 7.7 per cent went regularly to the cinema; 1.2 per cent listened regularly to the radio. This showed a marked decline in the popularity of 'cultural' pursuits, compared with the results of a survey taken seventeen years before in the statistically comparable city of Pskov.* Between the two surveys, a three-fold increase in television-watching had been accompanied by a 20 per cent decline in the number of people reading books, a 60 per cent drop in the number studying, a halving or more of the number regularly going to the cinema and, among men, a sharp drop in the number playing sports. In 1982 two-thirds of the men in Kerch did not know how to play football; 37 per cent could not ride a bicycle; 43.5 per cent hardly ever ventured into the countryside; and 72.4 per cent never attended sports events. The average citizen spent two-thirds of his or her spare-time indoors, usually in front of the television.

*See the following table:

| ACTIVITY | MEN | | WOMEN | |
|---|---|---|---|---|
| | Pskov (1965) | Kerch (1982) | Pskov (1965) | Kerch (1982) |
| Studying | 27.1 | 10.0 | 14.8 | 6.4 |
| Television | 39.7 | 81.9 | 26.3 | 77.1 |
| Radio | 29.1 | 1.9 | 19.1 | 0.5 |
| Newspapers | 62.3 | 46.6 | 29.1 | 12.9 |
| Books | 40.3 | 34.3 | 33.5 | 28.5 |
| Cinema | 15.3 | 9.7 | 14.1 | 6.2 |
| Theatre | 1.0 | 0.3 | 2.5 | 1.0 |
| Entertaining | 6.2 | 12.0 | 3.1 | 5.4 |
| Cafés, etc. | 20.4 | 0.7 | 9.9 | 0.3 |
| Sports | 28.9 | 22.7 | 11.5 | 24.9 |
| Walking | 21.2 | 27.5 | 14.1 | 24.7 |

An accompanying commentary by a social expert of the Academy of Sciences criticized local authorities for failing to set up community clubs and sports facilities. These should have been used to counter a negative effect of urbanization: 'the lack of contact between neighbours in blocks of flats'. Damningly, in a society priding itself on a 'collective' spirit, 45.3 per cent of the over-sixties and 45.5 per cent of single women were found to spend nearly all their free time alone.[5]

The word 'culture', which features so prominently in Soviet organized leisure programmes, has a special meaning in Russian. One of the strongest pejoratives in the whole language is 'uncultured' (*niekulturny*), meaning short of social graces, such as failing to give up one's overcoat on entering an office building. Its frequent use reflects the importance popularly given to culture in the higher sense.

It is not just a chronic shortage of theatres that causes box-offices to display regular 'sold out' signs. The queues for seats are the result of a culture hunger that the West hardly knows. Tickets are snatched up like the rarest consumer goods. The same happens with newly published books, including editions of the great Russian classics. Poetry recitals are crowded by people of all kinds and ages.

This thirst for culture is not confined to any particular age group or region. Obviously the young have different and more varied tastes, but culture, for them too, is written with a capital *C*. And when Russians complain of young people's lack of interest in reading, for example, one must set this against the findings of recent surveys. In 1987 one of these was aimed at discovering how many young people of school age 'hardly ever read a book'. The results would have delighted any Western educator: only 4 per cent of full secondary-cycle students, 5.4 per cent of technical students and 11.9 per cent of those in training for other blue-collar jobs.[6]

Provincial municipalities like Novosibirsk spend enormous sums to maintain or import first-class ballet companies, theatre productions and orchestras, putting their best-equipped buildings at their disposal. And the more prosperous kinds of collective farm proudly devote significant amounts of their social budget to bringing down, say, a singer from Moscow or Leningrad to give an operatic recital. Undeterred by any suggestion of paternalism, and without deference to popular taste, the policy in cultural matters is simply to give the public the best.

In Baltic and Caucasian cities the tendency is heightened by national considerations. People want to show that culture is not all concentrated in Moscow and Leningrad, and that they too have old (indeed perhaps older) civilizations than the Russian. Thus the triumph of overseas tours by Georgia's Rustaveli theatre echoes through the whole republic. Of interest also is the fact that two leading writers, Chingiz Aitmatov and Valentin Rasputin, continue to reside in the far corners of their provinces, Aitmatov in Kirghizia, Rasputin in Siberia, rather than in the 'literary' capital.

But enjoyment of the leisure opportunities so loudly proclaimed by official policy is often prevented by the time factor – particularly in the case of parents with young children, who in the dash between crèche and work-place must stop to queue for the family shopping. Another constraint is the necessity to book or queue to get into almost any restaurant, café, cinema or discothèque.

Then there are absurd regulations like Article 947 of the Moscow municipal code, which as late as 1987 still forbade 'unaccompanied' young people to be on the streets after 9 pm. In a letter to *Komsomolskaya Pravda* a group of youngsters argued that the city should follow Riga and lower the age to sixteen, the age at which one received a passport.

Finally there are the constraints imposed by one's pocket – and by the 'closed shop', as Mrs Kalinina, a divorced 32-year-old Muscovite, discovered. She wanted to learn to swim, but with a small daughter and only 150 roubles a month (which her enterprise refused her permission to supplement by teaching English), she could not afford the forty-five roubles for a three-month course of weekly lessons. So she tried tennis. 'Every day for two months I went to the courts to buy a season ticket. Each time I was told, "Too early, come again." Till one day I came and this time they said, "Sold out for the season." When I asked how this could be, all I received was a shrug of the shoulders and the advice to go and hit balls against a wall.'[7]

According to a survey taken in 1986, only six out of ten young people saw any real chance of developing their 'creative talents' and only half found their leisure to be of any cultural value. Two-thirds complained that they could not buy the books they wanted. And nearly as many had no chance of going regularly to the theatre. Major exhibitions and concerts in the large cities, and even quite modest functions in smaller towns, are rarely open to 'ordinary' citizens, who are also excluded from seeing the greater part of the country's museum collections on grounds of 'shortage of space' or because the public is 'not ready to appreciate' them. Things are worst in the development zones, where it is not uncommon to find a new town of half a million with only one cinema, and desperately poor shopping and sports facilities.

In 1986 *Sovietskaya Rossiya* published the result of an inquiry among young women at the giant Kamaz truck plant in the Volga region. From this it emerged that a typical worker, Zoulfira Gatoulina, spent between two and three hours of each day shopping because of the queues and the shortage of 'service centre' facilities. For example, there was a two-month wait for shoe-repairs. If there was any time left after doing their chores, the married women would spend it with their children. Single women could choose between choir practice and evening classes. Really there wasn't much. The public library was nothing to speak about, and the good books always out. Theatre performances and concerts were rare.*[8] Investigating the same problem in the countryside, another investigator asked youngsters, 'Why don't you go to the club?' He got dusty answers nearly everywhere, like, 'When they've paved and lit the streets, we can talk about it.' Or, 'What's the point of a new pair of shoes when you have to go dancing in gum-boots?'[9]

The lack of amenities affects both the countryside and the new towns almost equally, but for different reasons. What happens in the poorer rural areas is that the *kolkhoz* directors often refuse to devote part of their budget to building a House of Culture that will serve working people outside, and small enterprises cannot afford to maintain a club all by themselves – one of the arguments put forward for regrouping them under the Gosagropom programme.[8] In the new development zones it is rather a question of facilities falling behind housing construction.

In 1986 the northern gas-field town of Novi Urengoi experienced a wave of unrest and 'hooliganism', including the stabbing of a student by a factory worker. In a report on it, *Komsomolskaya Pravda* discovered an 'alarming situation' in which the town's population had become divided between 'them' and 'us': adults who had come only to make a fast rouble and bored teenagers looking for trouble.

The trouble was that 'from the very first brick, this was a "Ministerial" town – the Ministry [of Gas] decided everything'. Its only interest was the plan for gas extraction. There was only one disco, open

*Visiting the plant in March 1988, the authors were told that the facts had been exaggerated. Certainly amenities in the adjoining city of Brezhnev (now renamed Naberezhnie Chelni) had been improved following earlier criticism, but the landscape of huge housing blocks remained bleak and intimidating.

at weekends, and one cinema, open once a week, showing the same film every time. Of the two men in the stabbing, the worker, Isa Khamichev, had come to Novi Urengoi with a promise of being able to buy a car (normally needing several years' wait) and being put at the head of the list for a flat. The student, Roman Voinov, was earning holiday money on the tundra. Until they met, and saw each other as 'natural enemies', both had been 'basically good people', said the reporter; it was the 'unnatural social conditions' that were bad.[10]

The newspaper made no mention of alcohol, generally a factor in such incidents. But when another paper in the Tyumen gas fields printed a gushing piece about 'healthy recreation' in bars serving only fruit juice, the local militia chief told *Komsomolskaya Pravda* that production of *samogon* had gone up 1,400 per cent.[11]

Here and there local initiative helps to provide what is missing. In Novosibirsk a group of young teachers immediately seized on the 1987 law on private enterprise to open a 'leisure co-operative'. In Moscow there are non-official clubs, like the old-established (and recently rejuvenated) Anglers' Association, which holds festivals on the Moskva river and whose members can be seen shopping for tackle in the Taganka street-market at weekends.

The mid-1980s saw a wave of enthusiasm for restoring old buildings and monuments. In 1983–6 some 30,000 Muscovites gave 200 Sundays to the activity, which began when *Moskovski Komsomolyets* published an announcement inviting volunteers 'with a love of their capital and homeland, not just in words but in deeds' to come to the historic Kuzminki estate on Sunday. Among those who responded were 'factory and office workers, doctors, poets, soldiers and journalists'. By 1986 they had restored the Tsaritsyn ponds (described in Turgenev's novel *On the Eve*), the Serednikovo estate where Lermontov had lived, and a number of pavilions on the Kuskovo estate. The token sum paid them by the city was then given to the Peace Fund or the twenty-year-old All-Russian Fund for Historical Monument Protection (VOOPIK).[12]

In 1986 over 1,000 people took part in voluntary restoration work at the Chusev Museum. Others met weekly to restore the Donskoi monastery under the direction of volunteer museum staff. Moscow University history students gave their time to restore the tomb of Professor Granovski, the 'father' of Russian historical studies. Every weekend dozens of youngsters can be found restoring historic memorials in some fifty Moscow cemeteries. Similar groups meet in Leningrad, Yaroslavl, Andropov, Tallin, Kiev and other cities; while out in the countryside, volunteer groups spend weekends and holidays helping nature conservation – not without personal risk, as in the Ufa region, where student volunteers have been attacked and killed by poachers.[13]

All these groups are unofficial. The only help they receive from authorities is an occasional press announcement about where they meet and how to join.

On Moscow's Arbat street, elegantly restored as a pedestrian precinct, there are a number of cafés of the kind frequented by young people. In one of them, the Komsomol holds a 'youth arts forum', where well-known figures hold discussions about the cinema, rock music, poetry and similar topics.[14] But the rest of the scene is hardly as bright as this welcome initiative by the Komsomol suggests. The cafés just mentioned are constantly being closed 'for technical reasons' – and, of course, there are always queues. Even the waiters ridicule what they have to offer: fruit juices and ices, perhaps coffee if there has not been a hitch in supplies. They also complain of customers who spend a whole hour over a fruit juice, while others queue outside, making it impossible for the café to 'fulfill its plan'. In fact, several cafés have had to close for this very reason.[15]

The young have plenty to grouse about too, especially the queues and the poor quality of the music. 'There's decent music at the Metelitsa on Kalinin Prospect,' says Dima, a P T U pupil out for the evening with a classmate. 'But you can't get away for less than five roubles – three to get in and two for an ice or a drink.' So the two future metal-workers go traipsing round the Arbat, refusing to have any truck with the 'stupid' Komsomol clubs and the 'stupid' video saloon* – 'Nothing but the same silly films you can see anywhere in town.' And the cafés close at 9.45.[16]

The Komsomol gets roundly blamed for this state of affairs, being regularly accused of failing to come up with brighter alternatives, with the result that young people turn to activities outside its control. The idea of simply letting young people get together to enjoy themselves without supervision is painfully hard for the system to accept; indeed, to the official mind such gatherings are positively suspicious. So the Komsomol is expected to find new formulas. Hence the first

---

*A cross between a cinema and a video library, where one may book a video film and a booth in which to watch it.

appearance in the early 1980s of the Komsomol clubs and Komsomol cafés so despised by the young PTU students mentioned above. Sometimes the idea succeeds, when the organizer is given some rope or a group of young people set up the café themselves. But all too often when the Komsomol interferes the clientele vanishes.

This leaves the field open to people like Sania the barman, who serves alcoholic cocktails in his café in Khabarovsk. Sania's bar is (or was) a regular rendezvous point for traffickers in 'deficit' goods and Sania not above providing some 'small services' himself. He thus runs his own 'House of Culture', which is well known to the militia and the juvenile welfare squad. In 1987 the Khabarovsk Komsomol was trying to set up 'dry' discos, as were students of the local polytechnic. 'They're planning to hold one of these "dry" weddings,' says Sania sarcastically. But he's not in the least worried. Time is on his side. 'They'll always need people with my kind of ticket, we're indispensable. They close down my bar. Okay, so what? I've got plenty of calls to organize evenings at home – for *top* people.' [17]


At the 1986 Youth TV and Film Festival in Baku, *Komsomolskaya Pravda* found plenty to criticize – like a film called *How to Become a Millionaire*, about the life of a team of young coalminers. 'Why are there no real characters in it? Just a load of words. No wonder the kids are bored.' Nor did it spare television, of all the Soviet media still the most hidebound. 'Who in their senses would stop youngsters in the middle of a dance with damn-fool questions like: "What was the last book you read?" Or "What's your favourite picture in the Tretyakov Gallery?" – as happened in a broadcast from Kuibishev.' [18]

Since then things have improved a bit, thanks to new directors with talent and some guts. Among the better new programmes are *The World and Youth*, whose reporters and cameras go into the streets, schools and clubs, and get young people to talk freely about their worries and wants; and *Twelfth Floor*, which does the same with a studio audience. Then there are the so-called 'tele-bridges', in which youngsters talk 'live' with their counterparts in other Soviet cities, and even in America. These programmes show that Soviet television can be serious without preaching, and without boring the young with gloomy commentaries. But they are frequently accused, especially *Twelfth Floor*, of giving the floor to 'noise-mongers' and projecting a far from glittering picture of Soviet youth. [19]

Young people's rejection of 'official' clubs and the eternal supervision of the Komsomol make the formative role of the street all the more important. For want of any better place to meet in (their 'room' at home is often no more than a divan in the living-room, with a poster of a rock star above it), they take to staircases and courtyards with the time-honoured Russian trio 'a smoke, a bottle and a guitar'. Inevitably adults sneer about 'idle kids', their awful clothes, the girls with cigarettes stuck in their mouths, and say, 'Haven't you anything better to do?' [20]

Another kind of get-together, which first appeared in 1986, took the Moscow authorities unawares: motorbike meetings. On summer evenings almost a thousand riders would converge on the Luzniki Olympic complex, bike-mad boys and girls with only one thought: to ride about together without joining organized clubs. In any case, as *Nedelia* remarked, they had nowhere else to go, since dirt-tracks were reserved for sports groups, preferably promising performers (*perspektivni*), not simply amateurs.[21]

Their abrasive relations with the police began with complaints about waking up neighbourhoods with the noise of back-fires and, worse, their behaviour about town. Their idea of fun was to tear round the inner ring road at night or even through the Arbat pedestrian precinct in groups. Another kick was to taunt the militia whose Zhiguli patrol-cars were too slow to catch up with them. After descents on the city and races with the police had put a fair number in hospital, Moscow made it an offence to ride in groups on arterial roads – but with little effect. Mocking the police has become the Moscow rockers' favourite game. 'We enjoy a good laugh,' they told *Moskovski Komsomolyets*, 'especially with the G A I. A policeman stops us, so we pull up. But when he comes towards us full of confidence, our mates open their throttles, and he just has time to jump back on the pavement. Or else we steer towards him and pinch his baton and accelerate. He runs after us, and we die laughing.'[22] The article in *Nedelia* makes light of the matter, which received almost sensational treatment in many Moscow newspapers in 1987. Gangs of motorcyclists, all lights blazing as they raced through the city on a summer night, made a startling picture. Even smaller provincial towns were caught up in the 'informal group' movement of which the motorcycle rallies were merely one instance. With unaccustomed frankness, in August 1987 a Kazan newspaper devoted a whole page to reporting the unedifying activities of groups of young people in the city: their drunken parties, assignations in out-of-town *dachas*, group sex, the activities of young girls who commercialized their services.

The readers' reactions could have been those of Moscow in similar circumstances: indignation at the facts but also anger with those who pretended that 'it doesn't happen here'. The only difference was that in Moscow the hypocrites said, 'It only happens in the West,' whereas in provincial towns they said, 'It only happens in Moscow.' But there were thoughtful letters too, like that of the reader who wrote to say that 'these groups can have a lot of different aims; one mustn't confuse them. Some are just looking for friends with the same interests and never indulge in the games in your report.'[23]

'Informal groups' mushroomed in the mid- to late-1980s, especially in new working-class districts, where young people still say that they're the best remedy for loneliness[24] – unlike the official 'clubs', where newcomers are not always as welcome as they are supposed to be,[25] and activities are often little different from those offered elsewhere (in schools, Houses of Youth and so on). They are also perceived as a reaction against a world of over-organization.

If this proliferation is sometimes presented as one of the successes of the *perestroika*, it is also followed with anxiety by adults, to say nothing of the local militia. There are clubs for almost everything, for ecology and psychology, international affairs, gramophone-record collecting. Their names can be classic, like 'Confidence' or 'Society'; exotic, like 'Che Guevara' or 'Western Style'; or simply odd, like 'House of Aliens'. Those with a political bent are usually set up by adults. All this is because the young want to do something 'real', to make contact with one another as human beings, not learn handicrafts and collect stamps. Sometimes a sympathetic school will lay on a small party, on a pupil's birthday for example. But there are nearly always busybodies ('What business have schools running dances?') who seize on any pretext to stop them – generally with the argument that 'the kids always take drink along'.

What young people want is somewhere to meet. There doesn't have to be dancing, although that can be an important part of it. Hence the success of the first approved pop and folk-music evenings, when the audience could meet the performers afterwards, provided there was no rowdiness. But in the end the needs of the young could be met only by a Western import: and so the word 'disco' entered the Russian vocabulary.

The first Soviet discos, to give the name to nothing more than a record player and a room to dance in, appeared in students' clubs in the early 1980s. As their popularity spread, the first official reaction was to stamp on them as a symptom of empty-mindedness. Any kind of pretext was used to close them down. At Krasnoy Yufimsk, near Sverdlovsk, where the disco was set up in the House of Culture, it was suddenly found necessary to renew the drains: a five-month job, as these things go in the Soviet Union.

But, as time went on, the disco came to be accepted as a necessary evil, a demand that could no longer be resisted. Somebody then evolved a theory that because music was a 'good thing' in itself, discos would eventually lead the young to concerts of classical music.[26] So the best course was to help them to fulfil a social purpose – in the safe hands of the Komsomol.

The Komsomol's first ventures into the business quickly brought trouble on its head. If they succeeded, they were accused of leading young people astray and disturbing respectable neighbourhoods.[27] If they failed, they were accused of misusing funds. Today, however, many local Komsomol organizations run discos – and the job of disco 'organizer' is a 'social occupation' requiring formal training like any other kind of job in entertainment and the arts.[28] It is also noteworthy that, unlike cafés and restaurants, discos are excluded from the list of businesses open to 'unofficial' management under the 1987 law on private enterprise.

One need only visit a Soviet disco (not one of the 'disco-bars' in Intourist hotels, from which Soviet citizens are generally barred) to realize that such places are hardly dens of vice. Generally they consist of large, lugubrious, perfunctorily decorated halls, in which, as in all public places, smoking is forbidden, no alcohol is served, and the waitresses have all the charm of the imperious *babushkas* to be found in any Soviet factory canteen. The music blares out at full volume, but the selection strikes young Western visitors as poor and old fashioned. No chance of letting one's hair down or ruining one's health in nights of abandonment. At 10.45 the disc-jockey announces the last dance – and, as with cafés and restaurants, doors close at 11 pm.

An original, but short-lived, development in the mid-1980s was the so-called 'disco under the bridge'. Teenagers would gather under Moscow's Krymsky Bridge in the evening and dance. They had their star performers, a disc-jockey and even a 'Queen of Ceremonies', whose job was to get solitary kids on to the 'dance floor' – all good, unexceptionable fun. Passers-by would gather on the bridge above and jokingly throw down coins. But presently a different crowd started to gather, the atmosphere changed, there were too many people, and they threw down cigarettes. All this attracted the attention of the militia, who came and put an end to it.

'Why did one have to wait for the militia to take action? Why not the local Komsomol?' demanded the then prim and unreformed *Sobesednik*. But somewhere, even in the system itself, there must also have been some rebels – because about the same time the Soviet railways started a 'discotheque on wheels', with a non-alcoholic bar serving tea and candies, on the Moscow–Riga Latvia Express.[29]

So far as young people are concerned, the Soviet musical scene is in a state of confusion. There are still vast audiences for classical 'folk' artists, like Bulat Okujava, who are essentially poets singing their own verses to the haunting Russian guitar. But the audience for pop and rock is much wider. Since the early 1980s the authorities have had to live with rock and pop in full flood, to their obvious alarm. Thus, although there has always been an official 'soft spot' for John Lennon, reckoned to have been a victim of capitalist violence, it was not until 1986 that the first 'official' Beatles records appeared. The year 1987 saw the start of regular 'hit-parades' in *Komsomolskaya Pravda* and other youth newspapers. The first showed no great eclecticism, however. Top was Leontiev, followed by the Gay Dogs and three songs by Alla Pugacheva – all pretty *passé* for most Soviet youngsters.

For most Soviet musicians, in contrast to Western-style 'stars' like Pugacheva, music is still a second, 'amateur' occupation. The great Vysotsky was a simple actor at the Taganka theatre; the popular 'troubadour' Aleksandr Rosenbaum worked for years as a casualty doctor in a hospital in Leningrad; the Nikitins were scientists. Today's rock and pop groups include many scientists, engineers and teachers. Their records may have only a limited circulation but the pirated cassettes reach much further.

Kids who strike it lucky in the inevitable scramble for concert tickets frequently smuggle in tape-recorders and later exchange the cassettes for cash or goods on the black market. Some get a kick out of doing what is forbidden, but most would prefer to be able to buy what they want legally, instead of forking out seventy roubles for pirated recordings (up to 200 roubles in the case of some Western groups).

The chief villain behind the flourishing black market is the State-owned Melodia record company, which is continually criticized for its meagre output of classical as well as popular music, and for its stubborn refusal to pay any regard to popular taste. (In 1988 it was reported by the newspaper *Sotsialistitcheskaya Industria* to have 140 million roubles' worth of unsellable records on its shelves.[30]) In 1987 there was only one recording studio of any quality in Moscow, with two more under construction − one for Melodia and one for the film industry − though facilities were better in Leningrad, Riga and Tallin, the birth-places of Soviet rock in the 1960s.

In the early phase of the Soviet rock movement, Soviet performers were mostly content to copy leading American groups. But by the mid-1980s the movement had extended to include the whole rock spectrum and was trying to become more Soviet by addressing themes connected with the life of Soviet young people: boredom and loneliness, absence of horizons, the all-pervading pretence and inertia of the everyday world. At this juncture Soviet groups were given an unexpected opportunity: access to the radio and television, coverage of their activities by the press (including Party youth newspapers) and publication of the hit parades already mentioned. Developments in Leningrad were a case in point. At the start of the 1980s, there were just three rock groups in Lenkontsert (the Leningrad concert organization). By 1987 there were twenty-five, including six with professional status.

But this was in contrast to the generally shabby treatment of some outstanding amateur musicians. In January 1987 *Sovietskaya Kultura* carried an interview with Boris Grebenshchikov, the lead singer in one of the country's most popular rock groups, Aquarium. In it he described the group's fifteen-year existence and the problems of amateur status, which it still retains by choice.

At the time of its formation, Grebenshchikov had just graduated from Leningrad University and gone to work as a computer programmer. Eight years later, in 1980, having won national fame through the underground distribution of cassettes of their music, the group was invited to the Tblisi all-Union festival of popular music. 'Subsequently, a letter was sent reporting that we had played some kind of punk rock. I was expelled from the Komsomol and had to leave my job.'

Grebenshchikov then spent several years working as a night-watchman for a timber firm, till in 1986 he was accepted as a member of the Playwrights' Union in virtue of the fact that he composes music for the theatre. This meant at last that he no longer had to have an 'official' job.

'I want to listen to music that I like, but there isn't any, so I am filling a vacuum,' he told the reporter. 'We are not like those people who write music to order.' But he then went on to describe a recent

Lenkontsert concert in the Jubilee sports stadium. 'What happened was monstrous. We were given twenty-year-old equipment that emitted a constant background squeal or cut out completely. I personally had two electric shocks – it was a miracle I wasn't killed. Nobody could hear our lyrics, which were vital to the whole performance.'[31]

In time the authorities learned to turn an occasional deaf ear to music that was really 'way out'. Thus, at the famous 'unofficial' concert for the Chernobyl disaster fund, in Moscow's Olympic stadium, the youthful audience, heavily salted with guardians of public morals, heard not only established performers like Aleksandr Glasky and Pugacheva, but also – surrounded by strobe lights, wafts of smoke and an angry red glow to symbolize the burning reactor – hard-rock groups like Autograph and Kruiz (Cruise). But none of these groups was as far out as the West German rock group Modern Talking, which was all the rage with Soviet teenagers in 1986–7.

In 1986, as a daring concession, Soviet correspondents were for the first time allowed to interview popular groups abroad – provided that they inserted the necessary small note of political education. 'Do you sing songs about peace?' *Komsomolskaya Pravda*'s Bonn correspondent asked Dieter Bolen of Modern Talking. To which Bolen is reported to have replied diplomatically: 'For me, love songs and peace songs are the same. Because without peace, how can you speak about love?'

In the war of words over rock and pop, the young are more relaxed than their elders. They say they need a 'new kind of music' that allows them to 'speak straight from the heart', 'communicate instantly' and *participate*;[32] and that words matter less than rhythm. (Hence the large audience for Western songs, whose lyrics not many understand.) Fast rhythm is a mark, 'not of aggression, but of the faster pace of life'.[33]

Naïve, perhaps; but hardly less trite than some of the broadsides from the older camp: 'Worst of all, it's foreign music – rooted in an alien society. Everything about it makes it non-Soviet.'[34] Or the following from Yuri Sergeev at the 1987 Congress of the Union of Writers:

> I want to speak of the mass culture of filth, sex, murders and cruelty that has invaded the West by way of rock music . . . Metal rock is not

music but a bourgeois psychological movement. In our writing we must fight for heroes who are psychologically healthy and strong. Today's youth needs them like a draught of fresh air . . .

To which another writer, Viktor Rozov, replied:

What I've just listened to frightens me. How often haven't I heard 'Stop that! That's forbidden,' and 'Oh, that hair, those trousers.' But where will it all end? We have to ask ourselves why youth finds an escape in these groups. Many of them don't please me either. But we need to find new ways – not take refuge in forbidding everything. When the tango first arrived, and the fox-trot, the older generation shook its heads and said how awful, just as Yuri Sergeev here has done about youth today. But when the war came, we weren't short of volunteers to go to the front – and a lot of them didn't come back.

Since nothing in the Soviet view is neutral, rock music is blamed for all the sins of Soviet youth: not only its clothing and hair styles, but also its sexual precocity, its minimal work-ethic, its depoliticization, the rise in crime and the spread of drugs. The last straw for the older generation is the hard-rock 'metallists'. With their studded denims, chains and bracelets, they are more in evidence in the newspapers than on the streets. But their mere appearance can terrorize a suburban train. One evening in 1987 the authors saw a group drinking from a bottle in the Metro, which was enough to call down a whole body of police, though it turned out that the bottle contained only water.

In October 1986 a shocked reader complained to *Sovietskaya Rossiya* that officer cadets at an officers' school at Tyumen were regularly reading the West German rock magazine *Bravo* – a pernicious publication aimed at the 'bourgeois upper-crust' and 'glorifying the values of the consumer society'.[35] (In an accompanying comment the paper let slip that after it had published an article on 'heavy metal' it had been asked by the militia for the addresses of the fans it had interviewed, 'in order that measures could be taken'. But it did not say if it had given them.) Few things could better illustrate the *angst* of the older generation than this alarm at the thought that the alien rock culture might infect the Soviet officer corps – the citadel of patriotism and socialist values.

In October 1986 a group of heavy-metal fans fell in with a Tass correspondent, Vladimir Kulikov. They wore the usual chains, medallions, studded gloves and other *metallist* paraphernalia. One of them had paid fifteen roubles (about fifteen pounds) for the cover of the

West German rock magazine *Metal Hammer*. On learning that Kuli-kov was a journalist, they invited him to their 'bunker' late one night. He was led through holes in fences, across courtyards, and finally down into a dark basement festooned with pipes and wiring. This was their 'den'. When he asked why they 'freaked out' nightly in this dismal warren, one of them, Charlie, told him it was their only refuge; nobody knew what might happen to them next. 'The militia can clear us out any time and confiscate all our tapes. It wouldn't be the first time it's happened.' Another, called 'The Brick', who was training as a construction worker, delivered some well-chosen words about the Komsomol: 'Either they make out they're activists, but do nothing, or else they speak so beautifully and cor-rectly that it sends you to sleep. It's all just show.' [36]

Much trouble is taken to try and present Soviet rock as indigenous and not a slavish imitation of Western music. Foreign students at Moscow's Pushkin Institute are sometimes given a talk on the subject. The official line appears in the following appreciation of the music of David Bowie, Boy George, Madonna and others:

> Boy George admits that he perceived the future as an endless queue in search of work, and he tries to 'escape from reality' in his works. He was captivated by the anarchistic, nihilistic style of 'punk'. The Sex Pistols worked on the axiom 'learn a couple of chords and use them to get on society's nerves'; they contrived to look ugly, and they sang hymns to primitive instincts such as cruelty, brute force and a thirst for profits. In this way they became integral parts of the society they were supposed to be spurning.
>
> Hatred typifies the works of another rock idol – D. Bowie. However much he may change his style and appearance, he is driving home one point – a person is alone; he hates others and takes vengeance on them. When answering the question 'Why is your music so aggressive?' he inadvertently exposed all the falsity [*izhivost*] of his bourgeois morals: 'I detest all that stuff about love, peace and spiritual unity. It's all fake, flaccid and stifling.'
>
> Madonna, a rock singer popular among teenagers, promises to teach her audience how to become porn queens.
>
> The answer to the question 'Why is rock music so cruel, ugly and inhuman?' should be sought in the social and political climate of those countries where it has appeared and grown strong.

Unemployment is one reason. 'It forces you to hate and suspect yesterday's friend, seeing him as a competitor.' It humiliates young people and makes them cruel – and 'the majority of young musicians are forced to serve the golden calf rather than music. Their main aim in life is simply to get rich.'[37]


In 1987 the authorities thought to respond to the unofficial rock wave by organizing a 'rock laboratory' in the Gorbunov House of Culture, near Moscow's Kurski railway station. The event consisted of three heavy-metal programmes, approved in advance by the organizing 'artistic council'. But the reporters sent to cover it for *Komsomolskaya Pravda* came back 'shocked and alarmed'. They hardly knew which was worse: the audience of young people who tore their clothes and made Satanic signs (imitating goats' heads) or a group called Chudo-Yudo, who blew up condoms on the stage and swore at each other. Another group, more respectably, merely smashed chairs.

Wrote the *Moskovski Komsomolyets* team: 'The artistic council may have approved a set programme for all these groups. But the audience never saw it. What they got was an hysterical and hooliganistic eulogy of perversion and senseless indecency.' Most alarmingly, nobody in authority intervened to stop it. 'The trust that had been shown in these young musicians was reduced within fifteen minutes to an all-permissive, licentious farce. Can "games" with condoms and foul language ever possibly be justified in the name of a search for new forms of expression?'

Allowing rock-music fans to give public support to groups of their choice was part of the democratic changes now taking place in Soviet society, the writers conceded. But there were limits. Russian rock groups shamelessly plagiarized Western groups, the only difference being that they sang in Russian.

> They copy everything: aggressive behaviour on stage, the waving of microphones, the daubing of black crosses on their faces, the wearing of masses of metal trinkets on their leather jackets. We are not demanding that the rock-laboratory be closed. But events have shown that it is time to stop and appraise the situation.[38]

However, this did not prevent the holding of another rock concert, this time at an army camp in Samarkand, when 'informal groups' were allowed to decorate the auditorium. For eight days 15,000 young people followed what the Uzbekistan Komsomol newspaper called a 'great event'. This normally stern journal even gave the floor to a number of fans, one of whom declared, 'We want a rock *festival* at Samarkand, otherwise we shall turn to drugs.' Another went to the heart of the problem: 'From kindergarten on, they fill our heads with formulas, quotations, little pills for all life's possible circumstances. They've taught us to whisper, to look behind our backs. They've not stopped protecting us, wanting the best for us. They've accustomed us to insipidity, timidity, mental complexes. We've had enough.'[39]

# 9

# 'Negative Leisure'

*Vodka consumption – campaign against alcoholism – deaths from substitutes – sobriety societies – alcohol and young people – youth and narcotics – drug therapy – sex – development of street gangs – gang violence – 1986 Lyuberi 'scare'*

The healthy activities so tirelessly preached by the Party are matched by a range of quite opposite tendencies that, in the Party's for once expressive terminology, are called 'negative leisure'. In its most concrete form, negative leisure continues to be enjoyed by the litre.

By late 1987 the consumption of vodka, which had supposedly been halved during the first year of the 1985 campaign against alcoholism, was estimated to be back to at least 70 per cent of the original, thanks to a rising tide of home-distilled *samogon*. Even at its moment of sharpest impact, it is doubtful whether the law restricting sales cut anywhere as deep as the authorities hoped and pretended.

In 1986 a citizen named Vladivarov thought to test the situation by driving round Moscow's inner ring-road. Twenty times during the fifty-minute drive he was hailed by people at the kerbside. Three wanted lifts – the rest wanted vodka, which was being openly peddled by taxi-drivers. The first, a smartly dressed young man, said simply, 'Help me, brother,' and held up his little finger, 'obviously standard language for wanting a bottle'. (The word 'vodka' could have meant trouble with the police.) A youth asked for a 'hair of the dog'. A student offered fourteen roubles, 'all that's left of my grant', for the means to drown his sorrow at losing his girlfriend. A seventeen-year-old boy said he needed it for his dad. There was also a 'flirtatious young woman' and 'two grim-looking men' who said they were depressed. When Vladivarov suggested that they drink tea instead, they almost struck him.

Other drivers were selling vodka under the very noses of the police near the Park Kultury Metro station, 'so perhaps some officials have an interest in seeing that everything stays as it was'.[1]

And if citizens craved for a nip on the Moscow ring-road, how much more so in the frozen Siberian wastes. Deep in the taiga is the village of Gutara, where, except for a small plane bringing food and supplies ('everything from bricks to matches'), the only means of approach is by horse. The 250 villagers, belonging to a tiny nation called Tofars, live by hunting and reindeer-herding. In 1986 this idyll was marred by only one thing. As soon as the hum of the plane was heard, everyone rushed to the village store. After queuing to get their bottles of vodka, they would go to their homes and be happy for an hour or two. Then they would crawl out into the streets, dead drunk. In the words of a Soviet journalist who made the hazardous horseback ride, they become 'a transformed people, malicious, thirsting for fights – and armed'.

In one fight, which arose because someone had not filled a glass to the rim, one Tofar stabbed another with his knife. The wounded man was taken to the medical clinic, which was in the charge of a junior doctor who was himself undergoing a cure for alcoholism, and died. Another man shot himself during a hangover, and a third was burned to death after falling, drunk, into his camp-fire. Two hunters, also drunk, were lured out of their snow shelter by imaginary voices. One froze to death in a snow-drift, the other drowned in a hole in the ice.

Shortly after the inauguration of the anti-alcohol campaign, the conscientious head of the village council, called Vera Bobkina, called a meeting to discuss the matter, and a reluctant majority of the Tofars agreed to restrict vodka sales to weekends. Almost immediately, Gutara experienced its first theft in twenty-years. The village store was broken into, and several crates of vodka taken. 'Everyone must have known who was responsible,' said the journalist. The building was repaired, and the following Monday the store resumed weekday sales of the indispensable spirit. Seeing what was afoot, the scandalized Bobkina rushed to the scene to 'save' her fellow-villagers from perdition – and was herself saved from lynching only by the timely appearance of her hunter husband.

When some weeks later the magazine Smena telephoned to learn the sequel, it was told that Comrade Bobkina was 'no longer chairman'.[2]

According to a study in the mid-1980s, 65–75 per cent of Soviet alcoholics fall victim to 'immoderate' drinking before they are twenty, an age when addiction and damage to health both proceed rapidly. Three-quarters learn to drink at thirteen to fourteen. This overall description now includes girls, of whom an increasing number admit to beginning in their early teens, and doctors are concerned at the number of abnormal children born to alcoholic mothers. Young people with drink problems frequently write to newspapers as their 'last resort', asking for help – evidence, perhaps, that the official machinery for guidance and help is inadequate.

In dealing with alcoholism, as with sex and marital problems, the tendency is to look to the doctor, rather than to the sociologist or psychologist, on the assumption that what makes an alcoholic is the fact of drinking. Recovery is achieved when the patient gives up drinking. Most of the time treatment is based on revulsion and severance cures. These can be made compulsory on pain of losing one's job or having to pay a fine (which may help to explain a high percentage of successful cures). Other forms of treatment call for help from the family or work collective, so that the 'patient' does not feel isolated and decide to take a 'nip' to boost his morale. There are also therapies calling for changes of job and life-style, while for the problem of alcoholism generally there are calls to improve leisure and raise the general level of culture.

Of course, the problem of national alcoholism is not just Russian. It is found among populations across the whole of northern Europe above a certain degree of latitude. But in Russia alcohol has for centuries been a folk remedy for almost everything, from tooth-ache and sprained ankles to heart-ache and melancholia. And it was none other than Prince Vladimir, the founder of Ukrainian and Russian Orthodoxy, who rejected Islam in favour of Christianity on the practical ground that total abstinence was incompatible with a cold climate.

Gorbachev's law of 1985 restricted sales of vodka to only a few hours each day, and practically banned all kinds of alcohol from cafés and restaurants.\* Despite its unpopularity, it achieved one important result. There was no longer the widespread drinking at work that had been the cause of huge economic losses and frequent industrial accidents. It also cleared everyday drunkenness on the streets, though within a year it was again not uncommon to encounter individuals whose upright position depended only on an iron will, and the knowledge that sobriety is defined by the militia as the ability to remain on one's feet.

But the institution of near-Prohibition had negative consequences.

\*Drinks may be served in restaurants after 2 pm, but in practice are available only in the more expensive ones. As a result of unrest, the opening hours of 'wine-shops' were slightly relaxed in 1987, and in 1988 some breweries were reopened.

too. Hardened drinkers were sent in search of frequently dangerous substitutes, such as industrial alcohol – and young ones after drugs and *samogon*.* So much for the shouts of victory based on the fall in the *sales* of alcohol. People drink differently, and often more than before. In the first six months of 1986 the militia detained 4.2 million drunks, of whom 6.5 per cent were adolescents, a higher percentage than in the previous year.[3] At the same time the officer in charge of a Moscow 'sobering up' station recorded an increase of up to 60 per cent in the number of workers from eight local factories brought in to him after arriving drunk at their places of work.[4] In 1985, when the law was introduced, accidental poisoning deaths in Moscow rose by 30 per cent (Minsk reported a five-fold increase.) And in the first quarter of 1986, the Ministry of the Interior reported fourteen cases of group poisoning involving a hundred deaths, the worst cases being in Moscow, Kazakhstan, the Ukraine, the Krasnoyarsk region and the northerly Tyumen *oblast*.

– In Bukhara three people died after drinking 'unidentified spirits' at a wedding party.

– In Dankov three workers died after drinking stolen methanol.

– In Chimkent three died from a similar cause.

– In Chapaevsk, in the Kuibishev region, three members of a family died at a wedding breakfast and the bridegroom the day after, also after drinking industrial spirits.[5]

– In July two traffic policemen and three drivers died in a village near Stavropol after mistaking a jar of anti-freeze for *samogon*.[6]

– In August five workers died from drinking ethylene glycol stolen (despite warnings from their works sobriety society) from a chemical factory near Rostov.[7]

– In September fifteen people died in Kaunas after drinking anti-freeze that they thought was a green liqueur.[8]

Among generally less lethal substitutes for regular spirits are alcohol-based perfumes. Others include air-fresheners, cockroach poison and extracts of tooth-paste and boot polish (see page 70). The demand for perfumes has led to their being rationed and subjected to stiff price increases. In 1986 the manager of a shop in Kuibishev had to call the militia after delivery of a consignment of cheap eau-de-Cologne. Customers demanded that it be sold by the carton, and

*In 1987 one-third of those arrested for the illegal making of *samogon* were in higher education.

'Chanel No. 5?'

when sales staff limited them to two bottles each there was almost a riot.[9]

In 1985 returns from the Checherski district of Gomel *oblast* showed a doubling of demand for window-cleaning liquids. There was also a widespread move into glue-sniffing. 'When delivery of BF glue comes in, we have to fight them off,' a Moscow hardware store told reporters.

As complaints about the wine-shop queues and severity of the 1985 law began mounting, the overlooked question 'Who suffers most?' was poignantly answered by an anonymous woman in a letter to *Sovietskaya Kultura*.

> I am one of the people who regularly join those queues, though I would much rather be at home with my children. What is it that drives me there? I will tell you. My husband has been drinking for a long time. I daren't tell you what happens when he comes home and doesn't find a bottle in the place. He threatens to murder me and the children, and he's not joking.
>
> So I stand in the queues. Because if there's a bottle at home he'll drink it and roll over and go to sleep, like he always does when he's drunk, and leave us in peace.[10]

In 1986 the Soviet press came out with a rash of alcoholic horror stories. 'In my own village dozens of people have committed suicide because of it,' wrote N. Petrenko, a vineyard agronomist. 'Three young family men have hanged themselves here,' wrote a collective farmer in Zaporozhskaya *oblast*. 'Three more were killed in a motorbike accident. Another drank himself to death.' A grandmother with three orphaned grandchildren in the Kirovskaya *oblast* told how her son grew so desperate at his wife's drinking that he killed her with a crowbar and hanged himself. A Moscow reader recalled that in his native village more than a hundred had died of drink in living memory. 'In the Novoshmakov children's home only two out of ninety-six are orphans; the rest are the children of alcoholics,' wrote V. Lebedev from Akademgorodok.[11] The liberal sociologist Bestusev-Lada wrote: 'Whatever people say about the nightmare of drunkenness, the reality is much worse. The effects on our health, and particularly our genetic fund, can only be compared with the plagues of past centuries.'

To carry the anti-alcohol campaign forward, the authorities devised a number of gimmicks. One of these was the 'dry wedding'. Party officials, directors of factories, heads of collective farms and the like were required to set an example by giving their sons or daughters a well-publicized send-off at which the strongest potion was milk or grape juice. But since this was not always popular with the couple or prospective in-laws, it was sometimes necessary to offer inducements – and arrangements for these could go awry.

Thus, when Andrei Antonovich and his fiancée, Irina, applied to marry, the groom's father, a quarry worker, laid in five crates of vodka 'to celebrate in style'. But since the parents on both sides had only two-room flats, the married couple would have nowhere to live. By chance the town council was just then urgently in need of a non-alcoholic wedding such as everyone else seemed to be having; and the municipal culture department was given the job of fixing it.

It did not have to look far; for Irina's father was director of the local *dom kulturi*.[g] The only trouble was the loud objections of her mother. To silence these the council promised the young couple a one-room flat in the quarry settlement. But now it was the people of the settlement who protested. Everyone knew that S. Strunnikova, an unmarried worker, had just been refused a place on the waiting list for a flat, though she had worked at the quarry for thirteen years. Strunnikova complained to her trade union, which ordered an inspector to investigate.

His window on the world.

The 'non-alcoholic wedding' duly went ahead; but, because of the union's intervention, all that the couple got out of it in the end was a colour television-set that had been intended for a kindergarten.[12]

Another gimmick was the setting up of so-called 'sobriety societies'. Only five names are needed to register this kind of association, and by 1986 the movement's Moscow co-ordinating body claimed the existence of thousands throughout the country. To Western ears their aims immediately suggest those of 'Alcoholics Anonymous'. But in an interview with a magazine, Nikolai Chernykh, Deputy Chairman of the All-Union Voluntary Sobriety's Central Council, denied any similarity: 'Alcoholics Anonymous clubs are self-help organizations, whereas our societies aim to propagate a sober way of life not only among their members but throughout the whole of the working masses.' Another 'fundamental difference from foreign A A clubs' was that sobriety societies' members had to be 'worthy and respected both at work and at home'. But this did not stop Chernykh criticizing some local societies for 'formalism' and superficial campaigning (*kampaneishchina*). To boost their numbers some were admitting drinkers (*lyudi vipivayushchi*), and even *forcing* people to join.[13]

In February 1987 the national medical journal *Meditsinskaya Gazeta* reported an investigation into the giving of alcohol to very small children. A group of five-year-olds in Voroshilovgrad kindergarten group had been asked what kinds of drinks (*mapitki*) they could name. Eighty-five per cent mentioned vodka and wine before anything else, and twenty-eight in the group (kindergarten groups are rarely more than thirty) already knew what alcoholic drinks tasted like. Most of the children had not liked spirits, but eleven had found brandy 'tasty', champagne 'sweet' and dry wine 'nice'.

A fuller account of the practice appeared in an article in *Selskaya Zhizn*. 'I have been investigating sick, backward and "problem" children for over a quarter of a century,' wrote the head of the scientific section of the Russian Federation Pedagogical Society, 'and have often found that many of them, even first-graders (six- to seven-year-olds), already know what wine is like. They are given it not only by their "loving" parents but also by those who are supposed to bring wisdom to the family – their grandparents.' A teacher had asked a class of eleven-year-olds how they spent their birthdays. 'One described how she had drunk champagne, another wine and a third liqueur.' On another occasion, while testing the ability of a backward eight-year-old girl to compare different objects, the writer had held up a picture of an empty glass and another of a glass of tea and asked what the difference was. 'In the second one there's *samogon*!' she had said brightly. In a rather more tragic incident a seven-year-old boy died of poisoning after his parents gave him half a tumbler of vodka – wanting to laugh when he was tipsy.[14]


In the mid-1960s a group of men aged between twenty and forty were spotted lying naked on a hillside facing the town of Petropavlovsk. But so innocent were the authorities in those days that they did not know what to make of these so-called 'hedonists', and promptly released them. Had they inquired more closely they would have stumbled on what was to become one of the country's biggest problems – drug taking.[15]

By the early 1970s, according to Soviet journalist and writer Zorii Balayan, anyone with an ounce of medical knowledge must have realized that drug abuse had become widespread. He himself started gathering material for an article on the subject. When he had what he needed, he went to the offices of the Pacific coast newspaper

*Kamchatskaya Pravda*. But, says Balayan, the editor simply shrugged his shoulders. Drugs were a forbidden subject, and only shortly before the Ministry of Health had stated categorically that 'drug-taking is not a serious problem'. 'We were kidding ourselves, and still are,' Balayan said. 'It's time to stop pretending that drug-users come only from backward or broken families. Over half the drug-takers questioned in recent surveys turned out to be from well-off backgrounds – a far cry from communal flats.'

In most republics, the law on drugs is harsh and clear. Article 44 of the criminal code of the Russian Federation, dating from the Revolution, forbids the use of drugs without a doctor's prescription. Article 16 prescribes penalties for their misuse. The same republic's 'family code' provides for the withdrawal of addicts' rights as parents. More recent legislation (late 1986) makes the preparation, acquisition, carrying or distribution of drugs with intent to sell punishable with up to ten years' imprisonment (three if the drugs are for the offender's own use). Encouraging another person to use drugs (even, for example, offering a 'smoke' to a friend) can mean five years, the same penalty as for organizing a ring.

Another, all-Union law, introduced in 1987, provides for the compulsory treatment of teenage addicts in special Preventative Education Treatment (PET) centres run by the militia. Fourteen- to eighteen-year-olds who evade treatment in ordinary narcological establishments can be sent to these centres, which incorporate special schools and PTUs, for six months to two years of cure and 're-education'. Those completing the course are given qualification certificates and found jobs in a PET work organization. Absconders are liable to a year's imprisonment.

However, severance cures for drug addiction are scarcely more successful than those for alcoholics. Only one in fifty of those taking treatment do so voluntarily. Interviewed in 1987 by *Izvestia*, a Lieutenant-General Panikin of the Ministry of the Interior admitted that 'the treatment of drug addicts is a problem for the entire world' and that 'in our country only one addict in six leads a normal life after treatment'.[16]

Serioza N., a young ex-addict in Moscow, raised another point:

> I was treated successfully. It was all done anonymously. But under 'diagnosis' in my discharge paper they wrote 'narcotic addiction'. No hope of a job after *that*, or of going back to one's old school. I know plenty of addicts who refuse to do anything about themselves because they're afraid of carrying these handicaps for the rest of their lives.[17]

In January 1987 the Soviet Interior Minister, Alexander Vlasov, said there were 46,000 diagnosed drug addicts in the Soviet Union, of whom 80 per cent were under thirty. He divided supplies into those coming from narcotics-growing areas, where 30,000 illegal poppy plantations and 100,000 hectares of wild hemp had recently been destroyed, and those emanating from medical stores as a result of theft or false prescriptions. Vlasov let drop that the head doctor of Isaklin hospital, near Kuybyshev, had recently been caught after stealing 22,000 ampoules.[18] At a humbler level, a nurse was found to have kept 150 ampoules of morphia returned by the relatives of patients who had died.[19]

According to the Ministry's Criminal Investigation Directorate, home-grown hemp and poppies accounted for four-fifths of the illegal drugs, and pharmaceutical leakages for the rest. 'So far nobody knows what to do with the fields of wild hemp growing over vast territories,' its deputy-head, Gennadi Alekseev, confided. 'Over the past quarter-century the area has increased by 2,500 per cent.' In the case of pharmaceuticals, the major worry was not thefts from pharmacies but doctors who made out false prescriptions or switched ampoules of weak drugs for strong ones, which they then sold. Asked if the Soviet police might not benefit from the advice of Western police forces with experience of the drug problem, Alekseev answered curtly, 'We are well enough informed about the experience of Western police forces – it does not suit us.'[20]

In view of the custom in the Brezhnev period to sweep every problem under the carpet, it is perhaps not surprising that any mention of drug abuse should have been so long suppressed. It first came into the open with the publication in 1986 of Chengis Aitmatov's novel *Plakha* (*The Executioner's Block*; see page 182). Shortly afterwards the Director of the narcotics division of the Health Ministry, Vladimir Yegforov, was asked 'Why has the problem only now been brought to light? Is it a new problem for us?' Yegforov gave the evasive answer that drugs had been used in some regions of the Soviet Union, in particular Central Asia, for centuries. But, 'according to sociologists, the main cause of drug abuse is social immaturity'. Asked how the Ministry intended to deal with the problem in the future, Yegforov replied blandly: 'Of course, the most effective measure is to educate the rising generation in the spirit of the socialist way of life.'[21]

Perhaps Yegforov was thinking of a 29-year old addict interviewed by the evening newspaper *Vechernaya Moskva* under the name Olga

Konopoleva. Olga told the paper's reporter that she came from a well-off family.

> I lived in the city-centre in Herzen Street and studied at an English-language *spets-schkoly*. My grandfather worked in the Ministry of the Interior; my mother and father are both engineers. As you can see – we were well enough situated. But then in the early 1970s we had to move to another neighbourhood. It was about the time the hippies started appearing in Moscow, and I joined them. In the evening we hung around on the 'Patch' in front of the Bolshoi or else in the Tube, which is what we called the subway by the National Hotel. An older friend asked if I'd like to try a 'shot', and I agreed. At fifteen you're curious about everything.

So in the open stairwell of an apartment block on Pushkin Street the friend injected her with three cubic centimetres of morphine. Olga became hooked and 'seemed to turn into another person – I was "born again",' she said. And, of course, she was not alone. 'There were boys and girls from so-called well-to-do society among us; sons of famous musicians and performers, for example. Something drove even *them* out of their nice comfortable apartments into the stairwells, down to the 'Patch' and into the Tube.'[22]

In January 1987 the education newspaper *Uchitelskaya Gazeta* devoted two half-pages to a poster warning children against accepting drugs. Teachers were asked to cut it out and show it to pupils from the fourth grade (ten-years-old) upwards. Entitled 'Beware the White Clouds', the text and picture described a young addict suffering withdrawal symptoms. One picture showed him in convulsions, thinking he was being eaten alive by worms. Older children were called on to help younger ones. 'Some silly boys have learned to poison themselves with furniture polish and insecticides.' There was also a warning not to accept cigarettes that might contain narcotics or packets of powder to keep 'for friends'. 'You little cat's-paw. Just one gram found in your home, one packet in your pocket, means arrest and prison . . . There is no way of escape.'[23]

A few weeks before this a group of specialists studying the problem for the Ministry of Health had found that some 6 per cent of sixteen- to eighteen-year-olds had in one way or another used 'substances producing narcotic effects'. But only one-sixth of these had used real drugs. The rest had 'poisoned themselves with chemical preparations' such as medicines and glue.[24]

'Nevertheless we are very concerned,' said Kira Agafonova, head of the Schools Directorate of the Ministry of Education. 'Drug-taking in school has become more frequent lately.' And she singled out areas of special concern, such as Odessa and parts of Central Asia.[25] The Ministry also admitted that there were 'serious short-comings in the campaign against juvenile drug-taking'. *Uchitelskaya Gazeta* said there were no books on teenage addictions, and no really reliable statistics. The returns received by the Schools Directorate were in nearly every case identically superficial. Either officials were 'too lazy to count' or they preferred to keep the figures secret.

In February 1986 the Ministry was supposed to have sent every school a list of 'recommendations' concerning the juvenile drugs problem and a description of the measures being taken to combat it. Among these was the printing of a number of books by the 'Education' publishing house. But when *Uchitelskaya Gazeta* asked the publishers about this, it was told that the only book envisaged might not be ready before 1989.

The newspaper then telephoned a number of schools to find out how the list of recommendations was being followed. The first head-mistress it called said she had never received it. Asked if she knew what action to take in cases of 'toxicomania' such as glue-sniffing, she said she had no idea. The second headmistress to be telephoned said the list was hanging on the wall next to her desk, but when she was asked about a recommendation on glue-sniffing, she had difficulty in locating it. In all the schools telephoned, not one teacher had actually read the recommendations.[26]

Another problem of the authorities is the increase, often related to drugs, of physical violence. Towards the end of 1986 a Soviet journalist waiting for the train at the Moscow suburban railway station of Peredelkino heard sounds of a fight. A local resident explained that this was the usual Saturday punch-up between Peredelkino and nearby Solntsevo motorbike gangs. Then, just as the train approached, a blood-smeared youth was chased on to the railway track and killed by the locomotive before the writer's eyes.

The event caused him to investigate two vastly more callous incidents. He found that in another suburban community a teenager had stopped a thirty-year-old woman on her way home from the city and tormented her for an hour with his knife before finally killing her.

She screamed for help and begged him to spare her life. Her cries were so terrible that, according to neighbours, a German shepherd dog strained at its leash like a mad thing. But the boy knew that nobody would come out and that the dog would not be let loose. He knew that nobody would attempt to interfere – even though everyone was listening.

In the second incident a youth killed two people simply to steal their fur hats. 'He could have taken the hats – one made of musk-rat, the other of rabbit fur – without murdering anyone, but he had to finish the job properly.' The reporter was so stunned by the sense-lessness of the second crime that he went to interview the boy in prison. Was he a maniac, he wondered? But no, not at all. 'That is the terrible thing. What struck me most about him was his ordin-ary behaviour. He just had the usual scared look of an everyday petty hooligan.'

Where had this terrible wave of motiveless and unjustified cruelty come from, the journalist wondered? And the conclusion he reached was little short of startling, even in the context of Gorbachev's *glas-nost*.

Senseless violence came not from the 'moral infantilism' that every-one was talking about, but from a positive desire to act against society. And this in turn was caused by

the endless eulogizing of our achievements, the endless overstating of what does not need to be overstated, eternal incantations about the bound-less worthiness of Soviet man.

All this falsity and exaggeration, these back-slapping lies and endless assurances that people in our country are always comrades and brothers, and that if anything happens everyone will offer a helping hand, have simply cultivated an atmosphere of cynicism, an almost open trampling underfoot of all moral laws.[27]

Soviet law defines hooliganism as 'the conscious commission of acts that seriously disturb public order and manifest an evident disrespect for society' – a description that can be used to cover almost any activity in public of which the authorities disapprove. A similarly special meaning is given to 'delinquency'. This has come to mean primarily offences against property, and particularly State property.*

According to sociologists, the greatest risk of delinquency occurs

*Despite an increase in burglaries (see page 109), offences against private property are in the minority, and receive a much lower degree of attention by the police. With regard to government property, the public makes its own distinction. As if theft of this were not really stealing, people often speak loosely of 'acquiring' goods that belong to the State.

at fifteen to seventeen,[28] chiefly among boys. Very often it is brack-eted with alcoholism and, nowadays, drugs – a convenient way of avoiding analysis of its real causes. Of course, when the moment comes, alcohol and drugs can make a young person jump the barriers that usually hold him back. But what drives young people to drink or drugs in the first place?

Soviet readers are warned against the facile attribution of de-linquency to a disturbed family life. Naturally, the absence of a father's hand can be partly responsible, and often a teacher–parent meeting is enough to check delinquency in a school. But it does not follow that fathers always set a good example, e.g., the father who buys his son a moped and steals petrol from his enterprise to fill it up.[29] It is also recognized that delinquency can be caused by parents' over-affection.[30]

The education system also comes in for criticism – schools that over-stress purely scholastic education,[31] as well as inexpertly staffed youth centres.

The favourite explanation is more frequently political. 'There is a popular fallacy that shows of indiscipline are due to adolescence . . . [but] the problem at this age is not one of growing up, or the faults of society in the larger sense, but one of the individual's failure to submit to collective life.'[32] Not only is society right to refuse to question its own rectitude, but the struggle against hooliganism is made the duty of every citizen, not just of the apparatus of the State.[33]

The fight against delinquency has produced a wide range of theories about the treatment of delinquents. Most give priority to separating them from others of their age group who are liable to contamination.[34] Young people coming before the courts are sent to special camps, where they are supposed to receive a normal education but in prison-like conditions. As in the case of adults, there are 'normal' and 'hard' camps. (In 1987, as a postscript to the film *Pum-bum*, about the life of delinquents and criminals, Moscow audiences were shown pictures of boys in a 'normal' camp – with shaven heads, in grey prison clothes, sitting in a grim classroom.)

But this method of treatment is increasingly criticized by penal reformists, who point out that camps, no less than prisons, breed criminal friendships and create future recidivists. (As with *internats*, the difficulty of finding an alternative is the lack of properly qualified staff.[35])

In other respects the law on minors can sometimes be quite liberal. It permits local experiments, such as allowing offenders to work on the land, or even to sublimate their violence in boxing classes.[36] Younger offenders can be put under the supervision of a woman inspector who is supposed to see that they go straight and lead a normal life.[37] In some places there are even teams of experts to help delinquents' families with problems beyond their means.

Like other countries, the Soviet Union looks for ways to protect society from the dangerous individual but also, particularly if the offender is young, to give him a chance to lead a normal life while paying his debt. This old dream is supposed to be realized in so-called 'Makarenko' colonies, based on collective living and the restoration in each child of a sense of responsibility. But the dream is rarely achieved in reality, due to difficulties similar to those in homes for abandoned children (see chapter 2).

In 1987 *Moskovski Komsomolyets* described life in a 'special PTU' for girls at Pokrov, in the country north of Moscow. The girls, aged from fourteen to eighteen, learn garment-making in a workshop in the grounds of a former convent. On the principle 'keep them occupied', the woman director tries to integrate her 'pupils' with the life of the locality. But she has to achieve a difficult co-existence between girls of all kinds of backgrounds: those who have broken with their families and come to Pokrov voluntarily, abandoned girls, girls expelled from school because of pregnancy, petty delinquents and prostitutes. Moreover their social reintegration is often defeated by the attitude of enterprises, which, when they discover where they got their educational diplomas, generally refuse to take them on.[38]

What looks like a much more successful venture is the result of private initiative. This is a naval training-camp founded on 'Outward Bound' lines by a former sailor and construction engineer, Captain Fred Yusfin, on the banks of the huge Bratsk hydro-electric reservoir in Siberia. Since 1968 the Varyag camp (named after a famous Russian cruiser) has become home to nearly 8,000 former delinquents. Life in the camp is said to be based on independence and trust. There is a minimal staff of grown-ups: the Captain himself, a doctor, a radio operator and two cooks, plus some junior officers seconded from naval schools who act as instructors. There is a good deal of manual work, helping in the galley, cleaning, preparation of skiffs and so on, but no coercion or mindless drill. The worst punishment a boy can receive is public disgrace and expulsion.

Yufsin, with no pedagogical training, faced deep suspicion when he started the venture, but its worth is now officially recognized. In 1987 he told a reporter:

Seamanship means excitement, its value is to develop initiative.

Today's feminization is not only due to most teachers being women. Society encourages qualities typical of girls. There are fewer opportunities for boys to show themselves. The fortunate ones are those who have a talent for sport, music or science. But what about the rest? I felt I should help boys like that.[39]

In February 1987 Western newspaper readers were given yet another new word to add to their nascent Russian vocabulary. A group of Jewish activists had gathered in Moscow's Arbat Street to demonstrate for the release of the imprisoned refusenik Josef Begun, and were set on by a crowd of young toughs. In the mêlée blows were rained on the demonstrators and on Western television crews whom the former had invited to be present. The Foreign Ministry later suggested sheepishly that the young toughs had been 'unofficial vigilantes', but reporters preferred to call them *lyuberi*. The name comes from the industrial town of Lyubertsi, south-east of Moscow. In the mid-1980s Lyubertsi teenagers, generally dressed in baggy tartan trousers, white shirts and narrow black ties, were frequently seen coming into Moscow to pick fights with other youth groups. The chief targets were break-dance fans (*breikeri*), 'fanatics' (*fanati*), heavy-metal fans (*metallisti*) and new-wave fans (*volna*).

To most Muscovites they were simply young louts. But the *lyuberi* projected a more romantic picture of themselves. 'We've been going to Moscow for ten to fifteen years,' said one. 'But we don't beat up just anyone, the way people seem to think – only ones we disapprove of. Do *you* approve of the ones who go about with rivets and chains [heavy-metal fans] or with paint all over their faces [punks]? They're a national disgrace!'[40]

In due course the *lyuberi* were subjected to some investigative journalism by *Ogonek*. This alleged that in their self-appointed mission to rid Moscow of punks, 'hippies' and others, they had founded a Masonic-like organization called 'The Office' (Kontora), divided into sections, each headed by an 'elder'. Members of the Office would come into Moscow by the 7 am train from Lyubertsi and split into groups to hunt for victims. According to the magazine, the *lyuberi* did not drink, smoke or take drugs. Their passion was body-building in home-made gymnasia beneath Lyubertsi's apartment blocks.

An *Ogonek* reporter, who claimed to have been beaten up during his inquiries, went to look at one of these 'underground' gymnasia in the centre of the town. There he was told he had been watched from the moment he left the train. Though he failed to obtain an interview with an Office boss, he claimed to have discovered the truth about the organization. This was that while sixteen- and seventeen-year-old *lyuberi* were encouraged to believe in their 'simple right to beat people up', the bosses, in their late twenties, were more interested in loot. Victims were not attacked because they were morally offensive but in order to relieve them of 'attributes of an alien way of life': leather bracelets, metal-studded jeans, jackets, football scarves, etc., which were then sold at a good profit.[41]

In a rival article the weekly *Sobesednik* said the *lyuberi* beat up 'anyone they happened to set eyes on', preferably solitary victims when the odds were three to one. They went to Moscow to kidnap the prettiest girls and take them back to Lyubertsi. It dismissed reports of the Office as 'sensationalism'. The reason the *lyuberi* beat up Muscovites was that they felt Moscow despised them: Moscow was 'chic' whereas Lyubertsi was a provincial town where you could not even buy a decent sausage.[42]

In February 1987 sheets began to appear on Moscow school and PTU notice-boards that promised a major confrontation with the *lyuberi*. Thus typically: 'On 22 February, PTU Number 13 will go to Park Kulturi to put down the "Lyuberites". PTUs Numbers 1, 139, 197, 82, 39, 51, 3, 11 and 37 are joining us. We shall defend Moscow!' Another announced: 'We, the Moscow *metallists*, declare war on the "Lyuberites" throughout the city.' Despite the juvenile wording, the emotions aroused by the notices seem to have convinced a senior police officer, Major-General Viktor Goncharov, that it was 'only with the greatest difficulty that we managed to prevent a clash'.

Goncharov blamed the Soviet press for sensationally stoking passions. The militia had found that the 'myth' of the terrible Lyuberites was based simply on rumour and exaggeration. Two 'terrible Lyuberites', photographed stripped to the waist and flexing their muscles, had turned out to be 'good lads and Komsomol members' who had been told that the picture was for an article about sports clubs. This irresponsible reporting had created a 'difficult situation' in the capital, where young Muscovites were uniting to fight this so-called foe. In fact, only 1.6 per cent of Moscow crimes were committed by Lyuberites, who were more concerned with physical training in their fifty-six 'gymnasia' than with beating up people.[43]

Some people might think that 1.6 per cent of Moscow's crimes was quite a high proportion. In any case the bland picture presented by the police was rudely contradicted when, in November 1987, one of the authors happened to be in Lyubertsi on the day of the funeral of a prominent 23-year-old member of a Lyuberite gang, called Vanya.

Vanya had died, horribly, in a gang fight. Some said he had been stabbed in the groin with a stiletto; others that he had been wounded with the sharp end of a crowbar as he lay pinioned in the back of a car. But the mortician had done a professional job. The wounds on his meagre body in the traditional open coffin were covered by an over-large double-breasted suit, and his whitened face wore the studied frown of a 23-year-old tough.

It was immediately clear that this was no ordinary funeral. The ice-covered track leading to the out-of-town cemetery was punctuated at every yard by splashes of red – carnations dropped deliberately behind the cortège. Inside the cemetery gates, beyond the long row of cars, was a five-piece brass band of middle-aged men who, between sounding brief funeral dirges, returned their instruments to their coats to protect them from the cold.

At least six of Lyubertsi's criminal gangs were present, to judge from the knots that formed round their leaders – the latter dressed in such a studied imitation of the Chicago styles of the 1920s as to make one wonder if this could really be the Soviet Union in 1987. There were the well-worn borsalino hats pulled hard over the eyes, the shabby camel-hair coats, the high-heeled white leather brogues. Associates who could not muster the whole outfit had at least achieved the dangling cigarette, the up-turned collars and the *sotto voce* sentences dropped from the corner of the mouth. They numbered perhaps a hundred, the remaining fifty 'mourners' being either women members of the dead man's family or instantly recognizable camera-armed plain-clothes police.

The coffin had been placed on a red carpet, Vanya's parents were half-kneeling, half-lying on the ground beside it, talking to their son as if he were still alive, and occasionally reaching out to touch the cold body. There was no ceremony save the appearance after about half an hour of a table laden with vodka (not *samogon*, but real Moskovskaya in green-labelled bottles), from which the family filled the glasses of guests to wish the young man on his way. Then, as the thin winter sun dipped down, and the temperature dropped to twenty below zero, they lifted the coffin into the brick-lined vault that had been opened in the frozen earth.

# Living with the System

'To understand the present and prepare for the future, we must know our past — all of it, both its triumphs and its mistakes,' declared a young actress appearing in Mikhail Shatrov's *The Dictatorship of Conscience* (see page 26).

Generations of young people have been systematically kept ignorant of the darker pages of Soviet history. Schools gave them the version of the moment, while parents who were witnesses or victims generally kept silent. And just as recent history was doctored to hide the worst excesses of Stalinism, so the distant past was either abolished or adapted to glorify the Revolution. 'Perhaps they're at last going to admit that it didn't all begin in 1917,' exploded Yuri, a lecturer at Moscow University in the changing climate of 1988.

The Russians as a nation have been more cut off from their history than other Soviet peoples, who have been encouraged to take an interest in their cultural past. This is partly to avoid accusations of national chauvinism, identified as a Tsarist phenomenon, and also because the promotion of Russian culture could look like encouragement of a nationalist revival. The irony is that while non-Russians feel that Russian culture is dominating (because of the imposition of the Russian language), young Russians, on the contrary, feel 'decultured'.

Hence the latter-day craze for collecting icons, antiques, bits of china and pieces of old furniture. Gone are the days when grandchildren waited for grandma to breathe her last so as to be able to exchange her wedding icon for a pair of jeans. Nowadays it is quite the thing to have visitors admire a piece of silver, some Sèvres or jewellery from 'the old days', dropping hints that it is 'all that remains from the family shipwreck'.

Increasingly, young parents take care to preserve family objects for their children, even to collect the simplest mementoes of the past – like the father who, on the birth of his son, started collecting postcards of surviving corners of old Moscow.

The poorly known pre-Revolutionary past is now idealized as something quite other than the time of injustice and obscurantism that people were taught about at school. It has become a time of gentleness, when people were more cultured, more polite and had more time to think. To restore the link, one can turn to religion with its deep cultural and historical connotations – or one can embrace the lapidary passion that unites archaeologists and voluntary restorers (see chapter 8).

A feeling for the continuum of human existence underlies the concern of young people for the environment. For years Soviet society has lived on the principle that Progress is Good and that Man must tame Nature. Today one finds a profound admiration for those of the older generation, generally writers or scientists, who have dared to contradict this, leading the fight against destructive development projects. In the same good cause young enthusiasts join clubs and scour woods and meadows with chemical monitors, or march vigilantly through the countryside with the 'little red book of protected species' in their hands.

And, of course, they have inherited an older generation's addiction to the great outdoors, to camping, canoeing, skiing, fishing and, to a lesser extent, hunting, which leads them to invade the stations, packs on their backs, from the first fine weekend of every new year.

But official theory on the making of a socially responsible citizen is more complicated. 'Insertion into society', to use the almost religious phrase denoting the arrival of the citizen within the system, presupposes his possession of two singularly Soviet characteristics: *obraz zhizni* (which we describe below) and 'personality'. Without good marks in both, the postulant cannot become a productive member of the collective, or part of that healthy majority for whom, according to surveys, 'material values and personal freedom count less than an interesting job, a happy family life, and friendships' (though pay becomes more important in proportion to disillusionment with the job and with an increase in family commitments).[1]

There is no exact English equivalent of *obraz zhizni*. The nearest non-Russian word is the German *weltanschauung*, sometimes awkwardly translated as 'world outlook' or 'philosophy of life'. The many works devoted to the subject stress a contrast between the socialist 'philosophy', which is supposed to embrace the whole of life – intellectual, social, cultural and 'work' life – and the capitalist concept of a 'standard of living'. The latter is seen as betraying a pre-emptive flight from the contradictions of the capitalist system, in which the inevitable inequality of wealth reduces any philosophy to purely material dimensions.[2,3]

The task of creating a correct *obraz zhizni* rests with teachers.[4] But the Party plays the same supervisory role as with the development of social awareness at school.[5] A correct *obraz zhizni* ensures obedience to a whole series of virtuous concepts, regarded as typically socialist, such as collectivism, humanism and democracy – the last, according to Bestushev-Lada, 'presupposes a faith in socialist man'.[6]

The notion of 'personality' involves the same optimism. But, unlike *obraz zhizni*, responsibility for its formation extends beyond the educational process to the individual's capacity for self-teaching.[7]

The main obstacle to the development of a good *obraz zhizni* and 'personality' is formalism. Formalism must be eradicated or it leads to anti-social behaviour. To prevent it, there has to be a dialogue, both at a school and at work, between students and workers and those in authority. Dialogue encourages a young person to 'take on his responsibilities'. When, after years of learning to do this, the individual is ready to take his place in the work collective, the process of socialization has finally succeeded.

In practice there is no end of obstacles to this famous 'insertion' into society.

For many years, Soviet society was true to its great concept of social mobility. This consisted of improving one's skills and, with them, the opportunity to serve one's country in a more prestigious and better-paid post,[8] whereas capitalist mobility was a 'vertical' process, enabling the worker to leave the exploited class for the exploiting one. In those days the young person saw the great doors open in front of him, no matter where he came from, provided only that he had courage and was socially active and involved.

Soviet teaching still insists on the fundamental difference in social mobility between the two systems. But since the early 1970s all the evidence is that social mobility, in terms of access to study and job opportunities, has been in regression – or at least in stagnation, if one takes account of population changes.[9]

This may explain what could be seen as a compensating phenomenon: a big increase in geographical mobility. This is something that particularly affects the young, just when the theoretical purpose of all their education, insertion into the work collective, is about to be realized.

The number of people annually changing jobs is of the order of 25 million (nearly one in every five of the working population). A substantial number are single young men, with those aged between twenty-one and twenty-four being the most restless of all, largely because of disillusionment with first jobs.[10] This kind of migration now exceeds that from the country to the cities.[11] But it does include one economically positive factor: a steady movement of young people to development zones, in search of new horizons, adventure, promotion or better pay.

It takes just a shrug to cut oneself free from one's background, or forget a romantic disappointment. As we explained in chapter 5, some of the young migrants become regular 'birds of passage', leaving job after job as soon as their purpose is served or they encounter the next disappointment[12] – at great cost to the economy. They also tend to move out of regions in serious need of manpower (including most European zones) to those with a surplus, such as the South and Central Asia, with their high birth rates. Migrants of this type seldom go to regions in need, like Siberia. And since there is no longer any question of controlling these movements by force, as happened in the past, the authorities must rely on incentives.[13]

Migrants newly arriving in strange cities encounter a problem new to the Soviet Union: loneliness. There are young women, happy enough at their daily work, who spend long evenings in solitude;[14] single mothers, lost in the company of young people who pay scant attention to them;[15] and youngsters who have had to change school or home, leaving all their friends behind.[16] The last are often neglected by the very people supposed to look after their welfare. Witness the case, reported in the press, of a young girl living alone in a tiny apartment resembling a garbage dump. Neither the militia nor the Komsomol, nor even her school (which knew she was without friends or parents) had done so much as come near her.[17]

The real blame for this desperate kind of loneliness lies with the huge, impersonal apartment blocks. These lack facilities for adolescents, who are past the age for swings and see-saws.

For a long time the authorities left it to voluntary good-neighbourliness to solve the problem.[18] Then some cities started 'S O S Solitude'

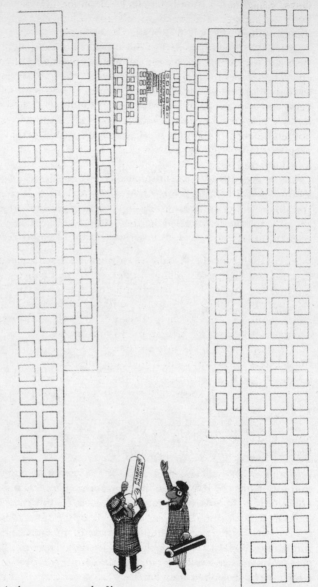

'And where is the sports complex?'
'In perspective.'

clubs, which had a round-the-clock telephone number, with some-body on hand for the lonely to talk to, to help take their mind off things without the help of a bottle.[19]

After 1985, mainly as part of the anti-alcohol campaign, the accent switched to keeping an eye on the whole community living in each apartment block, especially adolescents.[20] (In a block in Moscow, activists enrolled sixty-eight Party members, 180 Komsomol mem-bers, and a number of other people, including a chess-master, to build a playground, start a chess club, and set up a workshop for household repairs. Within weeks they were said to have won the support of every young person in the block.[21]) But the problem of loneliness remains.

On 10 April 1986 *Komsomolskaya Pravda* published a letter from a Krasnodar P T U student called Andrei: 'Although I have friends, I am alone. I have nobody in whom I can confide.' Within a month 32,548 more letters landed in the newspaper's mail-box from all over the country.

– Nikolai (Arkangelsk) said his mother had been an alcoholic, and he himself a teenage drinker and thief, till he met a nice girl and they got married. Now he was happy and doing his military service.[22]

– Natasha (Odessa) had no one with whom to share her feelings; and her mother was no help, because 'she's the one at home who decides everything. Please help me to find friends.'[23]

– Maxim (Moscow), just finishing P T U, couldn't understand these letters. *He* always had something interesting to do, like fixing up an old car with lessons from a local workshop. It was all too easy to sit on your hands and wait for somebody to come and take care of you.[24]

– Julia (Kharkov) had been studying at School Number 3 in Cher-nobyl and had lost all her friends in the evacuation. 'I'm very sad. Please help me to find them again.'[25]

Young people can also 'feel empty'. They want to 'fight for some-thing, but get the impression that everything has been done'. Such youngsters tend to withdraw into themselves. All they want is to settle down comfortably with a small family.[26] But then they dis-cover that this requires a certain amount of financial independence and cannot be done without the help of their parents. (These com-plex sentiments are well portrayed in the film *Is It Easy to be Young?* of which we have spoken elsewhere.)

*

Loneliness – the absence of anyone near in whom to confide – is clearly a factor behind the number of youthful suicides. Although no overall figures have been published, these had become sufficiently frequent to prompt a number of articles in the press in 1986. Suicides were the commonest cause of early death after heart disease, cancer and traffic accidents, confided Professor Aina Anbrumova, Director of a centre for the 'study and prevention of extreme situations', in a 1987 interview with *Argumenti i Fakti*.[27] She blamed the increased stress of living, the impersonality of life in cities (especially for students from the country) and the psychological pressures caused by new fashions, such as 'drink, sexual permissivenesss, rock music and drugs'.

According to Anbrumova, one suicide in every three succeeds, and most are by young people between sixteen and twenty. Survivors are treated in special hospitals, often with the help of hypnosis therapy and autotraining.[28] There are also twenty-three centres for psychological consultation in Moscow, including eight for students and two for adolescents. Similar centres operate in Riga and Dniepropetrovsk. In 1987 there were plans for others in Leningrad, Rostov-on-Don and Murmansk.[29] Moscow also has a 'crisis unit' and a confidential telephone line (not unlike that of the SOS Loneliness groups and the West's Samaritans), in this case permanently manned by psychotherapists.

The motives for young suicides look ordinary enough:

– Oleg I., sixteen, was rescued after cutting his wrists over a girl.

– Olga D., nineteen, took 150 tranquillizers after a row with her parents. She is now an invalid.

– Igor M., twenty, tried to kill himself after poor examination results.

But there is more to each of these cases than first appears. Oleg had been ordered to appear before his teachers' council for pursuing the girl on whom he had a crush. Olga's parents had ordered their daughter to be home by ten every evening, and stormed if she came in late. One day, during one of these scenes, her father had called her a prostitute. And Igor had come to Moscow from Gomel and was having trouble with his fourth-year studies. He had been told by the faculty council to change his career plans. Each time it was a case of the last straw, said *Komsomolskaya Pravda*, which accused those responsible of gross insensitivity towards young people's feelings. The newspaper asked:

What grown person would want to parade his private affairs in front of a teachers' council, as Oleg had to? If Olga had been only four years older, would her parents have dared to use such cruel words? Since one is citizen enough to be given a passport at sixteen, might not one then deserve to be treated as such?

Young people who tried to commit suicide very rarely wanted to die; they only wanted to shout, 'Look how unhappy I am.' Sadly, not all got away with it.[30]

But none of this compares with the disturbing situation that exists in the Central Asian republics, particularly for girls in rural areas. In Tadjikstan in 1986 there were forty cases of self-immolation by young women and girls, in nearly every case at home, with parents and family present in the same house.

The phenomenon caused *Komsomolskaya Pravda* to contrast the official picture of Tadjikstan as a republic 'resounding with achievements', where statistics showed numerous women in higher education and political posts, with the reality. Tadjikstan had the fewest hospitals, schools and kindergartens, as well as the highest birth and infant mortality rates, of almost any republic. The newspaper continued: 'It is shameful to go out without a headscarf. Forbidden to go to the cinema. Shameful to be seen with a boy. Forbidden to disobey one's parents. Shameful to go and study. Shameful to marry without the consent of one's parents.'[31] While the press was lauding progress, said *Komsomolskaya Pravda*, girls who wanted to be allowed to study and marry the man they loved were the victims of a continuing secret war. Forced marriages were cited as the the cause of frequent suicides in the neighbouring republic of Turkmenia; and, in all, more than 200 young women committed suicide by burning themselves in Central Asia in 1984–7 for the same reason. In 1987 *Trud* reported how five Turkmenian brides-to-be had killed themselves in protest against being sold for *kalim* – all in one district (Khalach) in Chardzhouski *oblast*. The mothers of four of the girls were sentenced to long prison terms. One father of twelve children, including two daughters, told *Trud* that he had sold his first daughter for 11,000 roubles and soon hoped to find a buyer for the next one. 'I fed them, clothed them and brought them up – who will repay these expenditures?' He would not be able to pay *kalim* for his ten sons if he had not received it for his daughters.[32]

A few months later *Komsomolskaya Pravda* received a letter from an Uzbek woman from Babkent whose husband thought she was not a virgin when married. The Uzbek custom is to show the bridegroom's parents a blood-stained sheet after the wedding night, and in this case it was not stained. The young husband took his bride to court, demanding to know the name of her previous lover. But when she insisted that she was indeed a virgin, both the court and the local Party sided with her husband, despite a doctor's testimony. According to the newspaper, there were often such cases, ending in self-immolation by a disgraced bride.

In the mid-1960s the Soviet press (led by the Latvian newspaper *Rigas Balss*) began to publish 'lonely hearts' columns in which young adults, frequently under thirty, looked for a partner. Following success by *Rigas Balss*, the idea was copied by papers in Moscow, Kiev and other large cities. Most of the letters, whatever the quests or descriptions of their writers, were evidence of a longing for security and a wish to start a respectable, peaceful home. 'I am twenty-two, with a three-month-old son,' ran one not untypical letter. 'We need the strong arms of a man. One man has abandoned us, but we think not all are like that.' But by 1987 there were complaints that these columns had turned into a market for marriages of convenience (generally for the sake of permits to reside in a big city). Witness 'Pavel', a resident of Saratov, looking for 'a female companion with an apartment in Moscow' and claiming to be '29-years-old, six foot tall, an actor, with higher education, a GAZ-24 [Volga] car and a *dacha*'. In the same issue of Moscow's Khimskinski district newspaper another advertiser (a woman) sought a car-owning companion, and a man sought a woman with a private plot.

Hand in hand with loneliness goes boredom – at its worst in the country, where one may feel less alone than in the city, but where the *ennui* is terrible, and even with friends there is nothing to do. 'You look at the mirror and see yourself getting older. You ask, "Where is life leading?", and you don't know.'[33]

Such are the reflections that for years caused young people to leave the villages, where 'leisure' was limited to emptying a bottle as fast as possible, the Saturday night fling in a weed-filled square pretentiously called Park of Culture or an evening listening to a raucous gramophone in the sinister local called the Youth Club. But ironically those who fled to the cities became the new rootless ones, complaining of the loneliness of impersonal suburbs.

The same kind of *ennui* – nothing to do, nowhere to meet, and no friends – is shared by the new towns. But in this case it has not been ignored. In 1987 villages and new towns were promised priority in the creation of sports grounds and cultural centres.

A more hopeful example of today's rural scene is 'Enbek' *sovk-hoz*,[g] formed in the late 1970s by the amalgamation of three 'dead-end' villages in the north Caucasus. In 1986 fifteen new houses were built, all now occupied by young people, who, thanks to the mechanization of agriculture, have found jobs as specialists. 'Leisure is no more difficult here than it was in town,' one of them told *Pravda*.[34] But the problem is to find qualified jobs for the women, for example by mechanizing work with the animals (see chapter 5).

Despite the urge of the Party to be everywhere, and its certainty as to the place awaiting the young in society, it is not always simple for young people to find this place. Indeed, their attempts to do so are often chaotic. There are those who think the young should be allowed to learn from their mistakes, rather than cling to their parents' coat-tails; others that it is necessary to counter the infection of bourgeois habits; and others that the whole system of education is at fault – in the family, the school and also in the Komsomol, which they accuse of neglecting urgent questions of day-to-day life in its conceited preoccupation with 'greater things'.[35]

'Bourgeois contagion' is a convenient formula with which to explain almost any bad behaviour – like the 'vulgarity' of young girls who smoke in public, eye passers-by or, supreme shame, get ticked off by strangers.[36] In retaliation, the young people concerned may opt for an 'interesting' life-style. 'We decided to be romantic, to go off into the country, wander through the streets at night, visit other cities, celebrate birthdays with a bottle of champagne at the railway station.' (In this instance, the beautiful adventure was terminated by the participants being expelled from their student hostel.[37])

Many young people escape the boredom of model behaviour by becoming what they call 'two-faces'. At school they are obedient pupils, model Komsomol members; at home, dutiful sons and daughters. But outside they are members of a gang, with leaders and nicknames, smoking and drinking, unconditional admirers of everything non-Soviet, from hard-rock music to 'super-fashionable clothes' – 'all bought on the black market, not just unashamedly but with pride in being "smart" '. Fifteen-year-old Tatiana wrote:

I lead a double life: one life at school and at home, the other in the street. I like 'hooligans' and 'tough guys'. I can switch roles to match the company. With my teachers and classmates, I'm an intelligent, serious girl. At home, though I don't understand my parents, I try to be an attentive, loving daughter. What do I like? Well, smoking, laughing, listening to Western music, especially hard rock.[38]

Her letter to *Sobesednik* prompted scores of others, including ones from readers who recognized themselves in Tatiana. Like Galina of Arkhangelsk, who wrote: 'It's because I like playing different roles that people like me.'[39]

Another newspaper, *Komsomolskaya Pravda*, printed a letter from a group of sixteen-year-olds at School Number 10 in Belgorod, which described in detail their life as 'two-faces'.[40] The letter caused an outcry, not only from the school but also from the local Party branch and Komsomol organization (which threw out one of the signatories' applications to join).[41] But in the end the 'two-faces' get more public sympathy than another unprincipled community – the 'pragmatists'.

The pragmatists' one desire is to join the system and get all they can out of it; for example by 'making a good marriage' and then, when the time comes, divorcing the partner who has ceased to be useful.[42] Some younger pragmatists even regret having parents who are too honest.[43]

With the pragmatists must be bracketed Russia's 'gilded youth', the 'youngsters who don't need to queue'. With their all-powerful papas, all they need is a touch on the right sleeve to secure a place in one of the 'posh' institutes or a voucher for one of the best holiday resorts. A phone call opens the most tightly locked doors for them, or gets them out of the militia station after a bust-up. Such was one Maxim Tarassevsky, a tenth-grade pupil who, to the astonishment of his local Party headquarters, asked to be admitted to the Komsomol without being able to answer a single question put by the Committee. Maxim was told to come back for a second interview, but he didn't need to. 'Dad' stepped in to fix things.[44]

And yet there are plenty of young people who reject the shabby compromises in vogue with their elders: like the doctor's daughter who, during her own medical training, on discovering how hospital staff demand payment for nearly every small service for patients, was not afraid to be called a fool for refusing to do the same.[45] Or the young hairdresser who refused to join in the 'humiliating' practice of fellow-workers who insisted on a tip before making customers' appointments.[46]

One other way in which the young co-exist with the system is neither a deception nor a demonstration but a denial of its values all the same. This is through a frenzy of consumption that bears no relation to the spending of Western consumers in times of economic boom. It is simply a means of compensation, rejection by the young of the older generation's submission to a system of semi-shortage – and, in the case of foreign goods, with their aura of wealth and 'interesting relationships', a means of passing, however imaginatively, beyond encircling frontiers.

Nobody is deceived. The phenomenon receives endless inquisitions among educators, Party officials and sociologists, who have even coined a word for it: '*veshism*' from the word *vesh*, meaning 'thing'.

The Party responds with stereotyped phrases that serve as a condemnation while evading the causes. *Veshism* is 'copying the petit-bourgeois life-style, forgetting true values, adopting a passive attitude'. Parents are accused of allowing their children to spend more while students than they will ever earn in their first jobs.[47] Nor is the ideological war ever far distant. Doesn't the CIA-backed Radio Liberty proudly announce that most of its listeners are young people? And is it not the dream of the West to turn Soviet youth into an apolitical mass, concerned only with material things?[48] So that already a horrified grandmother can return from a trip to the West to hear her small granddaughter's first question: 'Is it true that the shops over there are full of lovely gear, and without any queues?'[49]

One of the most glaring shortages is in a field with which the government has sought to characterize the advance of Soviet technology – that of personal computers. The Russian pavilion at Moscow's Exhibition of Economic Achievements has a whole corner for them. Children come to play computer games, and adults to sit at machines that promise to transform their lives. But actually to buy a personal computer (at three times Western prices) is another matter, as Mrs S. Belyaeva explained. 'My husband and I decided it was time to have one in the family,' she told *Komsomolskaya Pravda*. 'After all, why live behind the times? The papers say there will soon be a computer in every home.'

They decided on the much publicized BK-0010 and Belyaeva went to the local 'Elektronika' shop. When she got there, she could not see any computers. She therefore went to the supervisor, and the following conversation took place.

'I want to buy a personal computer.'

'We sell them only to people living in Moscow.'

'Yes, yes – but I am from Moscow.'

'Then fill in a card for the waiting list.'

Balyaeva continued: 'Since I was buying a computer, I decided I should speak to a specialist, and approached a consultant, a nice girl with a box of computer manuals.' The following then took place:

'I've read that in addition to computers using FOCAL there are computers using BASIC.'

'You should read less.'

'Why?'

'Because there aren't any, and there won't be any.'

'But computers do sometimes come on sale?'

'No.'

'But surely *some* computers are available?'

'No, none.'

But, being a serious buyer, Belyaeva decided she should at least try to see the BK-0010 brochure. 'The girl fished around in her box and told me she had nothing.' So she went to the manager, a woman. On the wall was a large poster saying, 'BK-0010 – The Computer for the Home'.

> At last I cheered up. But all that happened was that I was advised to go to the firm's warehouse, where there was a consultant from the factory.
>
> I knocked for a long time and at last a young man appeared. When I told him I'd come from the shop, he said that they hadn't been giving consultations for a long time. However, in the end he went and found two brochures and handed them out through the barred window.

When she got home, having left her umbrella as security for the return of the brochures, Mrs Belyaeva was consoled by her husband, who told her that another electronics shop, Radio-Technika, was said to be selling a computer called Mikrosha in the next suburb. But the next day, when she telephoned Radio-Technika, a voice said, 'What are you talking about? Mikrosha – they're not even in production yet.'

Finally she decided to call the Ministry for the Electronics Industry.

'You should go to the Elektronika shop.'

'But they have only application cards there.'

There was then a series of short buzzes. 'The line went dead, and I could get no further.'[50]

Similar experiences await millions of others who want to buy the latest manufactures, from Soviet-made video-recorders to new cars, of which the latest model also stands in the Economic Achievements Exhibition – long before it will go into production.

What worries the Party is that when young people buy Western-made goods on the black market, the 'traders' who make these marvellous goods available are seen to be enjoying a luxurious life inaccessible to 'true workers'. They are therefore likened to 'a cancerous tumour, which gradually saps the values of the individual and the whole of society'.[51]

Reformed speculators regularly write letters to the newspapers, describing their conversion (and, perhaps inadvertently, the pain of it). 'How do you get by on 140 roubles a month when you have been used to denying yourself nothing?' sighed a reader in Lvov, who had turned to speculation from the usual banal motives. 'I liked travelling, going to shows, seeing people, gadding about. But that sort of thing is never free – not to mention the cost of dressing decently.'[52]

Then there are the testimonies of young people themselves. Svetlana, a ninth-grade pupil, tells how 'in our *spets-schkola* there's a thriving business in records and cassettes – all obviously foreign. Our "businessmen" think that anyone who doesn't have money isn't a man.' Alexander Tchegodaev of Tblisi explains how 'you have to steel yourself morally and remember that society always rejoices when a person returns to the path'. Leonid Botchkov of Yaroslaval remembers how he was checked on the fatal slope by the last-minute thought that 'it's better to wear the same old coat and be able to look people straight in the eye'.

But there are also numerous 'realists' who see things quite differently – like Irene Oustal, twenty-one, of Tartu, who writes: 'One hears people say, "Oh, those wicked speculators," and "Oh, we must live by our moral values." But, excuse me, don't *you* ever want to go to the cinema or the theatre? Of course, everyone wants to be smartly dressed and look "with it".'[53] In fact most young people use the black market as a matter of course and envy those who are wicked enough, or smart enough, to operate there.[54]

In the debate about bourgeois influence a unique place is held by clothing fashions. Russians speak of a 'jeans psychology', in which they include appropriation by whole groups of this or that maker's label as a badge of membership.[55] Sometimes there is unpleasantness, as when clothes carry Western insignia that, on translation, turn out to have a political message, like 'Death to Nicaragua'.[56] Hoping to counter this 'bourgeois' challenge, the Soviet clothing industry has opened special shops whose creations are described at length in the newspapers. In 1987 *Sobesednik* even took on a 22-year-old fashion editor, and a great show was made of launching the Russian edition of the West German fashion magazine *Burda*.* But the industry has shown little or no sign of being able to follow needs of consumers, and particularly young consumers, who no longer take gratefully whatever comes to hand.

The couturier Zaitsev, Director of Moscow's 'House of Fashion', told us in an interview that his biggest problem was the poor materials in lifeless or violent colours that come from Soviet textile factories. *Pravda* has written of the need to improve the quality of production,[57] and *Izvestia* of bureaucratic obstacles that impede the designers' efforts.[58] At the same time some young people accuse the 'jeans psychology' of creating its own kind of formalism, almost a uniform.[59] 'Our only way is to stock up with what sailors bring back from overseas, but in the end, in our jeans, we all look alike,' complains Oksana Donskaya of Murmansk. Says one seventeen-year-old boy: 'The same cut of clothes, the same make of shoes, the same hair-styles ... there goes the colourless majority, with nothing to look forward to. They say seventeen to eighteen is when you learn to develop your personality; but *these* are just aping Western "supermen".'[60]

But perhaps in the end what worries the Party is not so much the 'copying of the petit-bourgeois world' that it talks about but the underlying urge this fashion expresses: the desire of young people to pose as a 'social sub-group', to develop ways of mutual recognition that are theirs alone, a means, almost, of separating themselves distinctly from other social layers.


In the mid-1980s the Soviet press came out with a spate of letters and articles deploring the revival of 'religious superstition'. Their writers ranged from small-town atheistic 'agitprop' groups to prominent academicians.

*Arrangements had to be revised when it turned out that the Soviet Union had no suitable machines with which to print the fashion plates, and the Russian edition had to be produced in the Federal Republic.

This militant atheism was somewhat eclipsed by gestures made towards the Orthodox Church during the 1988 celebration of 1,000 years of Russian Christianity. Not only did the atheist State return to the Church three famous monastries, but Party figures supporting reform also went out of their way to say that there was no reason why believers could not also be good Soviet citizens. A new law on religion promised to regularize this changed attitude towards the Christian Church (or Churches*) and other religious groups.[61]

Nevertheless, in 1988 many Soviet citizens, especially young ones, were still cautious of declaring themselves believers, even in anonymous surveys. Moreover, an official requirement to give advance notice of baptisms and marriages could hardly fail to deter young people from formal participation, even though among Christians of all kinds a million baptisms were celebrated annually. Another deterrent to declaring one's adherence to a Church was the association of religion with nationalism in some regions: Roman Catholicism with a nationalist revival in the Baltic republics, and Islam with nationalism in Central Asia and the Caucasus.

In the event, the main thrust of atheist propaganda was turned against Islam, which (though tolerated, and even courted, by the State while under control of a Religious Affairs Committee) was potentially a much more serious threat to socialism, through its perpetuation of restrictive family customs.

In December 1986 the head of the Uzbek Academy of Sciences delivered a broadside at the continuation of 'old, reactionary rituals' in Central Asia. He particularly singled out the saying of prayers five times a day under the pretence of physical exercises, fasting under the pretence that it was dieting, and the widespread payment of bride money (*kalim*), while 'here in Uzbekistan, under the pretext of restoring architectural monuments, mausoleums and sepulchres are being restored with the direct help of Party and government organs'.[62]

*The main churches are: Russian Orthodox, Georgian Orthodox, Armenian, Old Believers, Baptist-Evangelical Christian, Roman Catholic and Lutheran. A 1987 Western estimate put Russian Orthodox membership at 37 million, Georgian Orthodox at 2.5 million, Armenian at 3 million, Roman Catholic at 9 million and Protestant (Baptist, Pentecostal Christian, Lutheran and Mennonite) at 2.3 million. This is double the number of practising believers (8–10 per cent of the whole population) suggested in a 1985 *Pravda* article by the Director of the Historical Party Institute of Belorussia, Dr Platonov. Any figure must include a high proportion of old people, and Western estimates are liable to be optimistic.

In 1987 accusations of ambiguity towards religion caused fourteen members to be expelled from the Party in Turkmenistan, among them the manager of the Ashkabad office of Gosbank, who was found to have paid *kalim* for the bride of his son.*[63] In July the same year the Marxist philosopher N. Krivelev wrote a long article in *Komsomolskaya Pravda* attacking 'increasingly frequent' expressions of support for the idea that religion (in this case Christianity) had a monopoly of morality. He also attacked three well-known Soviet writers: the Russian author V. Astafiev, who wrote in the magazine *Nash Sovremmenik* that he deplored the 'theft' of a 'heavenly era' for which the Russian people had received nothing in return; the Kirghiz writer Chengis Aitmatov, whose latest novel *Plakha* (*The Executioner's Block*) was about a young seminarist entering a drug-ring in order to persuade its members to reform; and the Belorussian writer Vasil Bykov, who suggested in *Knijnoe Obroznenie* that the Ten Commandments were a moral code 'by which we can still live'.

In fact, what the Bible offered (thundered Krivelev) was an 'ideological basis' for murder, the slaughter of Arabs by today's Israeli soldiers. Did it not say, 'Leave not one person alive in those cities which the Lord your God hath given unto you'?[64]

A more temperate view was put to the authors by the sociologist Bestushev-Lada, who did not think there had been any real increase in the practice of religion. On the contrary, there had been a *decline* among the young. 'But today's young believers show greater conviction, and, in their efforts to proselytize, even fanaticism.'

The spread, or persistence, of religious belief has led to accusations of bureaucracy and formalism against Party officials responsible for atheistic propaganda. 'In the 1920s and 1930s the Revolution inspired atheists with a determination to extirpate religion,' complained a reader to *Sovietskaya Kultura*. 'But now we read about a survey showing that 20 per cent of intellectuals in Leningrad see no point in anti-religious agitprop.'[65]

---

*Explaining why *kalim* had not yet died out, a Secretary of the Central Committee of the Turkmenistan Party, M. Mollaeva, told *Trud* (14 March 1987) that due to the shortage of kindergarten places, and the large number of children in Turkmenian families, many women had no opportunity to go out to work. Their children received no education from the collective, and often fell captive to patriarchal values at an early age. 'In such families young men often grow up convinced that wives must be bought, and as dearly as possible, while girls who have finished their studies and even have a degree, sit at home waiting for suitors to pay a high price for them.'

'Atheist propaganda has become remote from life and needs a thorough *perestroika*,' wrote a *Komsomolskaya Pravda* reader. 'Our lecturers and agitators continue to deliver pat speeches and are quite unprepared to adjust to their audiences.' Another complained that young people seeking ideals could be drawn to religion, 'so long as lack of atheist conviction permits a revival of interest in ritual'.[66]

But it is not just lost and confused youngsters who turn to religion. Good students, Komsomol members, are known to get married in church, and then have their children baptized. Even students in higher education are liable to fall into the pit. 'After the exams, it's off to church,' as the saying has it. According to surveys, 2.8 per cent of the students at the Polytechnic Institute in Lvov are believers, as are 2.5 per cent of those at the Institute in Tallin, and 2–3 per cent in the Law Faculty of Moscow University.[67]

Often enough the basis of religious attraction is the beauty of the liturgy, which lay rituals cannot replace; but there is nostalgia too for a little-known past, idealized by young people in search of their roots.[68] And the 1988 millennium celebrations can hardly have failed to reinforce this.

The Orthodox patriarchy is generally careful to respect the authority of the State, and can nearly always be called on to speak in support of government policy at peace rallies and similar occasions. The same is true of the 'established' Islamic leaders. A more lively threat to government and Party authority comes from smaller groups and 'sects', with which Russian history has swarmed ever since Peter the Great placed the Orthodox Church under control of the State. Mistrust of 'official' priests and a popular fondness for mysticism and miracles continue to explain many such movements today.

In 1986 the Academy of Social Sciences, investigating one of the more innocent examples, found that 40 per cent of the young people of Irkutsk were practising yoga. According to a Dr P. Gurevich, writing in *Sovietskaya Kultura*, statistics from other towns were 'also impressive'. Gurevich explained the phenomenon by the fact that 'yoga promises an unprecedented development of the physical and spiritual capacities of the human being'.[69]

From Gorki, a mother told *Moskovski Komsomolyets* how her son Leonid, 'a talented boy', had discovered yoga and lost interest in everything else. 'He stopped eating meat, and lived on vegetables and fruit juice, till his friends finally shook him out of it.' The story enabled the newspaper to warn readers of the dangerous attraction of Oriental religious cults: yoga, Hare Krishna, Hinduism, Brahminism, etc. In 1987 practice of these was still identified with subversion, and yoga groups were banned in Moscow.

While most of these movements attract young intellectuals simply by their exoticism, others preach drugs, sex and bodily violence, often involving cruel or degrading initiation rites. A victim of the latter was the actor who played the Tartar prince in the Tarkovsky film *Andrei Rublev* – murdered for refusing, as a member of a sect, to execute another member on the orders of the leader.

In the *Sovietskaya Kultura* article just mentioned, Gurevich referred scornfully to the 'recently increased circulation of handwritten texts containing . . . cosmic secrets, prescriptions for improving one's health, communication beyond the grave, and magic formulas'. Why, there was even a 'certain physicist' who was famous for his talks about UFOs.[70]

Yet serious Soviet newspapers devote long articles to such matters, like the case of a young boy who was supposed to set fire to objects around him with infra-red radiation;[71] and scientific institutes across the whole country have devoted enormous energy and resources to studies of extrasensory phenomena.*

In daily life these tendencies are exhibited in a fondness for remedies based on plants and wonderful potions, and in popular recourse to magic healers. But the 'scientific society' can also provide examples of more sinister beliefs.

In the autumn of 1986 a girl called Mariana appealed for help to the magazine *Rabotnitsa*. Although living among educated and 'modern' people in her village near Moscow, she had been obliged to move to Siberia after being accused of witchcraft.

At first sceptical, the newspaper made its own investigation, and confirmed what the girl had said. A woman chemistry teacher had been the source of the allegations, which had caused Mariana's friends

---

*In 1980 claims for an extrasensory healer called Evgenia Davitashvili ('Dzhuna') led the State Committee on Science and Technology and the USSR Academy of Sciences to set up a 'laboratory for the radio-electronic research of biological objects' under an academician Gulyaev and an infra-red radiation specialist called Godik. 'Dzhuna' was permanently employed by the laboratory to take part in the experiments, and discreetly called in to treat the ailing Leonid Brezhnev (she was still 'practising' privately in 1988). Earlier the Rector of the Leningrad Institute of Precision Mechanics and a group of scientists set up a laboratory to study the healing powers of an old woman called Ninel Kulagina. According to a July 1986 article in *Izvestia*, the scientists confirmed that Kulagina could affect objects at a distance, even through a glass screen.

and acquaintances to believe that she was responsible for the death of a former friend and the malformation at birth of the chemistry teacher's baby. When her friends had taken to crossing the street in order to avoid contact with her, Mariana had been able to stand it no longer. It also appeared that pupils at the school had taught how to cast horoscopes, interpret dreams and exorcize spells cast on food.[72]

Although there are fewer eccentric and rootless persons in the Soviet Union than in the West, it still has its fair share, some of whom are treated more kindly than one might expect, even by authority. Among them are tramps (*bichi*), immediately recognizable by their ragged, dirty clothes and string-bags or rucksacks, containing scraps of food and a glass, for tea or something stronger. They can sometimes be seen on railway stations, particularly in Siberia, where their appearance attracts less attention than in European Russia and they can find casual work.

In 1986 *Sovietskaya Rossiya* carried a report from Kirov, where the authorities had started a novel rehabilitation programme. '*Bichi* are a common sight and the militia make daily swoops here,' explained the writer. 'But instead of giving them the usual thirty days for having no papers and sending them on their way, Kirov is offering them regular jobs. Of 250 taken on by factories or farms in the past year, over half are still working, and none has committed any crime.'[73]

In February 1986 a writer called Alexei Lebedev decided to live among the *bichi* for half a year. He left his passport and papers at home, put on an old coat and, with only three roubles in his pocket, set out by train from Cherepovets, 250 miles north of Moscow. He ended up by dividing the tramps into five categories: drinkers, romantic wanderers, philosophers, outlaws and mentally deranged people. Lebedev wrote:

> The romantic wanderer keeps himself as tidy as possible, always carries a razor, and does not drink to excess. He never spends more than one night on the streets, since in any new town he invariably finds a single woman and moves in with her. They live happily together for a time, the man giving a hand in the house and taking a temporary job during the day (he can turn his hand to anything). After a month or two he quietly drifts on, for he knows there are plenty of single women in other towns, while the one who has given him shelter will remember the calm, industrious, masterful man with the far-away look in his eyes for many years to come.

The 'philosopher' does not work, but neither does he harm anyone. In Lebedev's words, he is just a 'roamer'. Philosophers include religious believers, usually belonging to illegal sects, who try to convert their fellow-tramps. (A Seventh Day Adventist tried to convert him outside Gelendzhik; an Orthodox did the same outside Tashkent; and a Zen Buddhist attempted it in the Crimea. All were 'outwardly quiet and retiring, but active and erudite missionaries'.)

The third of Lebedev's categories, criminals, may be outlaws. But they may also be simply divorced husbands avoiding payment of maintenance to their wives and families.

A much more difficult situation confronts another minority: homosexuals. Early in 1987 the editors of *Moskovski Komsomolyets* received a letter from a seventeen-year-old schoolboy signing himself simply A.E. He told them:

> I am writing to you because I have nowhere else to turn. We are not used to seeing the word 'homosexual' in our newspapers – but this is what I am. This is the bitter truth. My situation is horrible. I live in a small town where everybody knows everything. My friends have turned against me and even started beating me up. Please help.[74]

The letter's publication broke one of the last taboos. Homosexuality exists in the Soviet Union as it does everywhere else. But never up to then had it been mentioned in the press, apart from a number of sinister references to 'foreign' carriers of AIDS. The newspaper gave a whole page to the topic, including observations by an 'expert' of the All-Union Scientific Methodological Centre on Sexopathology, Vyacheslav Maslov.

The reactions of A.E.'s friends were 'primitive', said Maslov. This was due to a lack of information, which had 'mostly been left to the care of medical specialists'. Because of 'distorted rumours' some people thought homosexuality was a form of insanity, an abominable villainy, or a sexual perversion, 'which is how they regard any deviation from the norm'. Some demanded tougher legislation to eradicate it. Others, confusing democracy with anarchy, took their cue from the West and argued for its legalization.

Maslov admitted that the experts themselves remained very vague when it came to explaining what homosexuality was, and why it existed in the Soviet Union. Was it a question of education? Or of chance encounters? Or a hormonal abnormality? In particular, should the homosexual be treated like a sick person, or helped to live in a society less intolerant of the abnormal?

But if up to this point the views of official sexopathology seemed amazingly relaxed, the record was quickly put straight. On one thing all were agreed, declared Maslov. It was necessary to protect children and to stop the spread of the evil. This left the problem of explaining why some homosexuals were proud to be what they were, and even had their own ideology. It was 'a question of wanting to justify abnormality. The fact is that homosexuals think they are a superior race with blue blood in their veins and other superhuman qualities.'* In an attempt to support this, they cited facts from the biographies of exceptional figures in art and culture.

Finally Maslov attacked the would-be 'legalizers' (mostly doctors wanting homosexuals to be bolder with information about AIDS contacts). Not only was homosexuality a breeding ground for AIDS and other diseases, but to push a young person towards it was tantamount to deliberately infecting him with syphilis. Legalization would create the conditions for a homosexual 'epidemic'. To the question 'What is to be done?', the answer was: 'Treat, punish, educate.' The last meant 'a father as head of the family, a tender and loving mother' and better sex-education in schools.

*For this fanciful reason homosexuals in the Soviet Union are commonly called 'blues' (*goluboi*).

# 11

# The Young Couple

*Precipitate marriage – disappointed expectations – opposition to inter-ethnic unions – reasons for young divorces – housing problems – budget problems – shortage of crèches and kindergartens – dependence on parents – lack of sex education*

Soviet citizens may marry from the age of eighteen – earlier in some republics where local custom applies or in special circumstances such as pregnancy. In the 1980s every second young person married before twenty-five and every third one before twenty.[1] For the reasons explained earlier, marriage is usually the only means by which a couple can live together.

Not only do couples tend to marry young; they also exhibit great similarity of age and background. Two-thirds of all marriage partners are from the same socio-professional category, and marriages between blue- and white-collar workers account for less than one union in five.[2]

In some parts of the country, particularly in large cities and new towns, half of all brides are pregnant. For this, the main reasons, as everyone knows, are lack of sex education, sexual precocity and the almost total absence of any acceptable form of contraception. Such contraceptive pills as are occasionally available (generally from eastern Europe) are still of an early type, producing side-effects such as obesity. It is also necessary to build up a personal supply against shortages. Contraceptives of other kinds are distinctly unreliable, and Soviet-made condoms, popularly known as 'galoshes', hardly discreet. One of the best presents the visiting foreigner can bring a young Soviet woman is a coil. Later she will have to find a doctor who can fit it.

Couples frequently plunge into marriage in a moment of passion, without waiting to get to know each other. To limit the damage, since so many divorces result from immaturity, the law imposes a one-month interval between notification and the ceremony. This is enough to discourage some hot-heads, since 10–15 per cent of fiancés never turn up for the ceremony. But many young people marry within weeks of their first meeting.

Such was the case with flirtatious and fun-loving Nina, who, as anyone but her mother could see, was no longer a child. Married by special dispensation, she became a mother herself at sixteen. In less than a year she was up before a court deciding custody of her baby. Asked what had caused the row with her husband the day she ran home to her parents, she told the judge: 'He'd promised to take me to a disco; but when the time came, he didn't want to go, and he wouldn't let me go by myself. Well, I have the right to go out, haven't I?' [3]

Not only do young people have enormous expectations of marriage and their partners, but they come to marriage with varying degrees of maturity. The boy has generally had a carefree life, without responsibilities, because of the hyper-protection provided by the family (see below). The girl is generally a little more experienced; she has seen her mother keep house and is quickly obliged to take over all the responsibilities of her new home and mother her husband. Neither finds what he or she expected in the other (she is not gentle, he is not solid), and each resents the role they are called on to play in order to make it work. 'So you begin with twenty drops of valerian, or 200 grammes of a more popular remedy, and presently your wife is asking for a divorce . . .'

In the old days husbands and wives expected to share the task of rearing a family and providing for their children's daily needs, such as food and education, and that was all. Today couples expect harmony and happiness as well. Moreover, material needs have increased, and consumption has changed the concept of the family budget, creating the need to choose and assign priorities. Not only are there endless arguments about who should manage the budget, the husband or the wife, but neither has actually learned how to do this. Palaces of Culture have waiting lists for courses in cookery and housekeeping, and newspaper columns give advice about involving small children in tasks about the home.

The 'unmarried couple' is still a rarity in the Soviet Union. Apart from a few exotic cases, 'living in sin' is as much frowned on as it still is in some Western countries. (So much for the notion of 'free love' much publicized in the early years of the Revolution.)

The near-impossibility of living together without being husband and wife explains many second marriages, which would otherwise have remained simply liaisons. It also explains many unsuccessful attempts at first ones. Cohabitation is made even more difficult by the system of housing allocation. It is almost impossible to obtain an apartment large enough for two people without being married – unless one partner has retained a flat from a previous marriage. So the unmarried couple must go in for the lottery of flat-swapping, offering to exchange two bachelor flats for a larger apartment with the same floor-space. Often, ironically, the exchange takes place with the parents of a young married couple who want separate flats, however small, in which to have some privacy.

Even writers regarded as 'modern' and open-minded reject what they call 'so-called free love', this 'Western-style non-marriage, which ends in emptiness and non-love'.[4] One of the fullest treatments of the subject is in a book by a Yugoslav writer. But the Russian translation is preceded by a convoluted note explaining that it needs to be read as an ethnographic work, 'since the customs that it describes exist, though they do not concern the reader directly'. Often too young women express concern about 'unofficial marriages that put a woman in a position of inferiority and enable the man to shirk his responsibilities, especially when she becomes pregnant'. So the unmarried couple, whose *de facto* existence must sometimes be acknowledged (without, of course, signifying that socialist society is reconciled to sexual permissiveness), is not a social entity unless and until a child arrives.[5]

Such are the considerations applying to couples in the European half of Soviet society. How different matters can be between regions was shown by the publication in 1986 of a comparative study of births and abortions in Central Asia and Moscow. Researchers questioned 300 women in a Moscow furnishing factory and 750 women in Fergana in Uzbekistan. Results showed that for every hundred girls under twenty there were seventy abortions in the Moscow group and none in the Uzbekistan group. After their first child, over 8 per cent of the Moscow women, but no Fergana women, practised some form of birth control. Later, half of the Muscovites and nearly a third of the Fergana women used unspecified contraceptive methods. But whereas in Moscow 20 per cent of first pregnancies were aborted, only 1.6 per cent were terminated in Fergana.

The majority of women in both cities bore their first child between the ages of twenty and twenty-four. But after twenty-two in Moscow, and thirty-three in Fergana, most women terminated their pregnancies. And while abortions under twenty were generally among unmarried girls, most Russian women having abortions between twenty and twenty-nine said that this was because there was not enough space for more than one child in the home.*[6]

The most divorce-prone marriages in Central Asia are said (by the secular authorities) to be those carried out in accordance with the Islamic legal code (*shariat*). 'Many weddings are just as they were in the old days', says a report by two Soviet sociologists, Kuzmina and Polyachek. 'After the registration formalities and a minute's silence at the eternal flame,† the wedding party goes to the parents' home, where the *mullah* reads verses from the Koran and pronounces the couple man and wife.' But this does not necessarily mean that they start to live together. Under a tradition known as the *kaitara*, the bride must stay with her parents until the *kalim* has been fully paid.

Once the bride price consisted of livestock. Now it usually takes the form of money. But it can also consist of household goods: a refrigerator, a television-set, perhaps a car, to ensure that the young pair begin married life in good style. Although *kalim* is illegal, its payment is still widespread. 'We only hear about it when divorces come through,' says a Deputy Justice Minister in Turkmenia. 'At the wedding, we're told nothing.'

While demands for *kalim* can cruelly complicate a possible love-match, the most harrowing stories, from both sides of Soviet society, are about young people falling in love with partners from other nationalities. A letter in *Komsomolskaya Pravda* from sixteen-year-old Jeanne, telling how her mother had forbidden her to continue her friendship with a non-Russian, brought 300 others. Most of those writing had had similar experiences, particularly young people in small ethnic groups. Nearly all the stories ended sadly, with the young person forced to choose between a family rupture or giving up the lover. 'Because my parents rejected my Russian fiancée,' wrote an Azerbaijani, 'I am today a sad father, torn between a legal wife, whom I don't love, and the Russian mother of my son.'

Such surrenders testify to the overriding strength of family bonds. In nearly all the accounts published, breaking with the family had

*On 25 September 1987 the review *Nedelia* gave the figure for abortions in 1978-9 as 102.4 per 1,000 women of child-bearing age (compared with 5.9 per 1,000 in the Federal German Republic and 11.4 in Britain). The situation in large industrial cities and new towns is more serious still. Thus, at Perm, an industrial town of one million inhabitants in the Urals, for every 1,000 women pregnant for the first time, there were 272 abortions, 140 births out of wedlock, 271 births in the first month after marriage, and only 317 children conceived within marriage.[7]

†Since the 1950s it has been the custom for Soviet couples marrying for the first time to drive from the wedding centre to the local war memorial and for the bride to lay her bouquet there.

turned out to be harder than giving up the loved one. 'You may have to fight for the one you love,' observed *Komsomolskaya Pravda*. 'But in this case it is not just anybody you're fighting, but your own father and mother.'[8]

Nevertheless, there *are* exceptions, especially in the new towns, where parents exert less influence and the determining factor is the opportunity to meet people from different nationalities. 'We've friends of all kinds in this settlement – Kazakhs, Russians, Ukrainians, Germans – and we live without worrying where a person comes from,' an enthusiast told *Komsomolskaya Pravda*. 'Most husbands and wives are from different nationalities too. The normal family is a happy family, with a brood of sturdy kids.'[9]

But what were the priorities of the 'normal Soviet family' in the late 1980s? What made for marital bliss? Answering a questionnaire, young people in Leningrad listed: material conditions, a comfortable place to live in, and mutual understanding between husband and wife.[10] But the importance attached to 'mutual understanding' drew a snort of indignation from A. Rojkova of Tashkent: 'The expression "psychological incompatibility" has become fashionable lately. One's always hearing, "We're getting a divorce – it's because of our different temperaments." What's that supposed to mean? You can't marry your double.'[11]

In the mid-1980s the Soviet divorce rate was fifteen times higher than just after the war, when divorce was made more difficult by one of Stalin's new laws. Most divorces were sought by women. Of these, according to figures in *Chelovek i Zakon* magazine, 50 per cent gave drinking as the cause, and a third cruelty, including physical violence towards themselves and their children. Other causes included infidelity, sexual incompatibility and interference in the marriage by parents. (Divorce figures also inevitably reflect the number of marriages of convenience for the sake of obtaining a residence or similar permit.)

A 1986 survey in an unnamed Soviet city of over a million inhabitants showed that half the women aged twenty to forty had been pregnant before marriage. Other findings, published in the newspaper *Sovietskaya Kultura*, were that:

– 80 per cent of divorced men remarry, compared with 50 per cent of women;
– men's much shorter life expectancy (see page 207) means a high proportion of widows;
– women's marriage prospects are commonly harmed by their in-

tellectual superiority, particularly in the Russian Federation, where the ratio of women to men with higher education is 10:4;

– one in two Soviet women are married by twenty-one, while from twenty-three the chances of finding a husband fall rapidly;

– half the fathers of the 500,000 children born annually out of wedlock acknowledge paternity but do not marry the mothers – 'mature women who want a child but not the burden of a husband'.

In the case of young couples the most common reason given for divorce is accommodation. Since childless couples have no housing priority, 70 per cent must live for at least the first year of their marriage with parents. As a result nearly 40 per cent of divorces within the first year are attributed to 'housing difficulties' or 'family rows'.[12] Later, if the marriage survives and the couple get a flat, parents and children tend to stay close to one another. (A third of subsequent home-moves are for this reason.[13])

At the same time there are plenty of examples of successful 'mucking in', where each member of the family makes his or her contribution. A typical case is that of a couple with a two-room flat who took in a pregnant elder daughter during her husband's military service. On his demobilization communal life continued, since the young couple had still to wait at least a year for a flat. 'No problem,' explained the grandfather cheerfully.

> We're a bit short of space, but the place has never been so lively. My daughter, still on maternity leave, does the cooking, which makes it easier for my wife after her work. My second daughter adores her niece, the young couple can go out in the evening without needing a baby-sitter, and, finally, I have a son. If ever there's a little tension, I always take a walk in the nearby wood, and it passes.

In the parents' flat, typically of two rooms, the parents usually move into the living-room and use a fold-away bed for sleeping, giving the couple the bedroom. 'Living' is done in the small kitchen. The only other room is a minute bathroom.

However, getting a flat at last doesn't mean an end to the housing problem. There are still likely to be complaints – not about the *type* of accommodation (a flat in a high-rise is all that most couples aspire to)[14] but about its size, the near-impossibility of any privacy, and the general absence of facilities for bringing up children.[15]

In the new flat the couple will have only one room plus a kitchen in which to do everything. (They cannot expect a two-room flat till the child grows up, or they have a second.) The lack of intimacy and general stress will be compounded by the invariably poor sound-proofing, the noises from neighbours, windows on higher floors that cannot be opened without admitting a gale, and municipally con-trolled heating that cannot be regulated. These minimal standards must be borne in mind when the government announces, with every sign of satisfaction, that although some 20 per cent of Soviet families are still without homes of their own, the problem of housing will be solved by the end of the century.

Among the devices tried out to help speed a solution of the prob-lem has been the new Youth Housing Complex scheme (MJK) that started at the end of 1986. Under this trade unions and similar bodies are required to give a hand to young people who want to build their own homes or renovate old buildings. The administration deals with the technical and financial problems and helps voluntary associations of amateur builders to draw up plans, both for housing and for amenities such as shops, schools and green spaces. It is then up to the volunteers to negotiate with their employers for whole- or part-time leave during the building work.

Priority for the creation of MJK groups has been given to regions such as Siberia and the Far East, where, as we have seen (chapter 5), painfully assembled work-forces continually melt away because young married couples cannot find anywhere to live. Not missing a chance to educate the masses, the MJK makes the husband respon-sible for each couple's participation, so as to strengthen his image as the head of the family.[16]

An older device, dating from 1981, is the authority given enterprises to make interest-free loans of up to 1,500 roubles to couples with young children to help them buy furniture, an expense that would otherwise mean calling on parents. But not everyone is eligible, as Galina Blinova of Moscow found out when she and her husband were offered a three-room flat for themselves and their newly born twins. 'The key is still on the hook,' she says. 'Perhaps in the end we'll scrape together a hundred roubles to buy some stuff for the kitchen, but goodness knows where.' When they applied, they found that her husband's factory did not make loans, but distributed its social funds quite differently. 'We use our money to build housing,' an official told a journalist alerted by Galina. 'If her husband earns so little, it's because he changed his job.' The journalist compared the situation with that at the Uralmash factory at Sverdlovsk, where young people need only to fill in a form giving a few personal details.[17]

A teacher of the 'Ethics and Psychology of Family Life' course, V. Tcherdnichenko, asked a meeting of parents of final-year pupils at her school in Dnepropetrovsk: 'Who should be in charge of the family budget?' She herself thought it was high time that the duty should cease to fall entirely on the wife. But 80 per cent of the parents disagreed.

When she asked her pupils how they would manage, the difference between boys and girls became clear. She posited a monthly budget of 220 roubles,* typical for a couple of unskilled workers just starting or a student couple. The husband would have a forty-rouble study grant. The girl, on maternity leave, would get thirty-five roubles. Each would receive fifty roubles from their parents, and the husband would earn an additional forty-five roubles by doing odd-jobs.

The way the boys divided the expenditure was: 115 roubles for food and daily expenses; 27 roubles for heating and services; 33 roubles for leisure; and 45 roubles for clothing, furniture and holiday vouchers. The girls' division was: 91 roubles for food; 35 for services; 14 for leisure; and 80 for clothing, etc. – a difference that 'went far to explain the frictions that arise among couples, and the current insistence of educators on the need to share responsibility'.[18]

Bringing up young children on a tight budget can be hard indeed, when the mother cannot go out to work because there are no crèche or kindergarten places, and the family loses half its income. Supply has still to catch up with demand, particularly in new districts, where social facilities lag far behind housing. Young parents now demand crèches and kindergartens at their work-places, and factories are finding that this is the only way to attract and keep young specialists. *Pravda* gives the happy example of a working couple newly arrived in Ivanov, near Moscow, who went to their trade union committee and were given places for their two children almost the same day. But the same article points out that there can still be enormous difficulties, depending on the region. In some parts of the country 99.8 per cent of the able-bodied population is working, for example

*In 1987 about £200 but (see page 18) within a system where many basic expenses are borne by the State.

in new towns. Moreover, many existing crèches are located in old, decaying buildings – often so decrepit they need to be closed for health reasons.[19]

If pushed too far, parents can rebel – like those at the Solnychko crèche and kindergarten near Saratov. When it was closed without any clear explanation, and the factory declined to help, they took their infants and went from crèche to crèche throughout the town. Some found places, others left their children with grandparents. The rest, after much discussion, decided to take their children to work with them. 'Which is why little Nadia goes off with her father to his job every morning and runs round the surgical department of his hospital all day – an ultimatum to the head doctor,' noted *Izvestia*.[20]

Hence the slips of paper stuck to bus-stop shelters and the small ads in local newspapers, like the following in Vladimir: 'Exchange place Crèche Number 85 for place in Crèche Number 87, alternatively kindergarten place Voroshilov or Balakirev districts. Child aged one year two months,' followed by the writer's address and telephone number.[21]

Nearly two-thirds of young couples continue to receive money from their parents, often for a very long time after marriage. About half of it goes towards furnishing and equipping the flat, the rest for clothing and bringing up the children.[22] Wise parents limit their assistance to what is immediately necessary, and try to avoid creating a relationship of permanent dependence. 'My son received presents that would be useful,' wrote L. Kasianova to *Sovietskaya Kultura*, giving linen and crockery as examples. 'It's the best kind of help. The young people get what they need, and have the happiness of knowing that it's a gift. If you keep giving them money, they take it for granted.'[23] But theories vary enormously; witness the wealth of advice to fellow-readers:

– 'You need more than just love before starting a family.' – K. Tokarena, Azov
– 'Shame on children who fleece their parents.' – Rovina, Moscow
– 'Every young person must shoulder his responsibilities towards our future society.' – S. (engineer), Leningrad
– 'How can you *not* help them? If they're still students, they absolutely depend on you. And young specialists do scarcely any better.' – T. Voikova, Moscow

But there are also cases of real abuse, like that of the mother in Alma-Ata, whose son and daughter-in-law worked in a research institute.

Wanting to buy a car, they took it in turns to lay siege to the mother, who emptied her bank account and then, to make up the balance, sold all she could lay hands on. Once they had the car, she never saw them again.[24] These 'crows', as they are called, may not be the general rule, but their numbers are swollen by the misguided generosity of parents who have had a hard life and want their children to 'have things better'. When the children are single, they buy them everything they want – from smart foreign clothes to tape-recorders. When they marry, the parents' generosity continues. Then grand-children come along, equally avid for good things. Social authorities can be very bitter when describing these doting elders, especially single mothers 'who don't know how to say no'.*

As mentioned earlier, a major cause of family problems is the absence of any practical and psychological preparation for a shared life. Dr Boris Malakhov, chief sexologist of Leningrad City Health Director-ate, admits to the difficulty of giving precise figures because of the embarrassment of subjects being interviewed. But he quotes a survey in which 15 per cent of divorced Soviet wives confessed to having lacked sexual harmony with their husbands, and 35 per cent avoided giving a straight answer. 'Since people give an evasive reply when not wanting to reveal their most intimate experiences, there are grounds for supposing that these too lacked harmony in intimate rela-tions.'

Malakhov notes that most divorces are sought by women, who

more commonly than men, are the victims of this lack of harmony. A man often think's he's in 'fine form', whereas it's he who should see the

---

*A 1986 round table was given the following results of a survey among young couples about to get married in Moscow:

– 58.6 per cent of brides were under twenty-one, and 28 per cent of men under twenty-two;

– 44 per cent expected to live with their parents after the wedding;

– 24 per cent expected to live in separate flats paid for by their parents (such flats being generally rented from people away on contract, usually in Siberia, at a cost, in 1988, of about fifty roubles per room per month);

– 9.7 per cent expected to rent a separate flat for themselves;

– 10 per cent expected to live in a room in a communal flat;

– 10 per cent expected to live in a dormitory;

– 66 per cent of the men and 68.9 per cent of the women expected their parents to help look after the grandchildren.

sexopathologist. Often all that's needed is to open his eyes to some aspect, and harmony will be achieved. If husbands thought more about their wives in these matters there would often be no problem.

Many young people think that once they get married, 'everything will be fine', but often there's nothing fine about it. Thanks to poor teaching, the majority of our married couples don't know what it is to reach harmony. The woman first feels dissatisfaction, then irritation, then sometimes plain hatred, towards the person who has promised her so much. So the marriage goes through a crisis and ends by breaking up.[25]

Malakhov is just one of the growing number of Soviet specialists who recognize that the relationship between sex and society is a matter for urgent action. The city of Leningrad now has a 'sexological service', and the medical faculty of Kirov State University runs a special course of sexopathology for psychologists, gynaecologists and urologists. Several other large cities have marriage guidance clinics, like that of Dr N. Vilikova in Gorky, where, according to *Meditsinskaya Gazeta*, 'everything is done to put couples at their ease', including the playing of suitable music during psychotherapy sessions.[26]

But, as the name 'marriage guidance' all too obviously implies, these services are mainly for the married. 'Perhaps a newspaper really shouldn't mention the subject, but, if not, who will?' wrote Irina Andreevna to the editors of *Komsomolskaya Pravda*. 'Whether we like it or not, pre-marital sex – generally a bitter experience – happens among our children too! When a young girl, unprepared for motherhood, has a baby, she finds herself alone with a host of problems – not the least of which, sometimes, is she simply didn't know where babies came from.'[27]

One of the problems about sex education in Soviet schools is the near-total feminization of the teaching profession, whereas sex education for boys is, naturally, reckoned to be a man's job. To make things worse, due to the high divorce rate (thirty-five divorces for every hundred marriages in 1984) millions of boys are having to grow up without a father, while many will never even know who their father was, because of pre-marital desertions. 'Men must be brought back into the schools,' cried Andreeva, adding, 'We need a complete sex-education programme, and marriage-guidance services in every town and village. We need to publish handbooks about it.'

Another letter in the same issue (one of 700 the newspaper received after publishing an article entitled 'Love without Love') was from a social economist, V. Perevedentsev. He too deplored the fact that pre-marital sex was becoming commonplace, 'particularly in big cities', yet on no other subject was there so much silence and sancti-moniousness. 'It is absolutely essential that bodies like the Ministries of Health and Education face up to it.'

In the end this lack of information about physical relations and their possible consequences goes counter to the desired result. Not only do young people have early, and often very early, sexual contact, but it is unsatisfying and unexciting. A *Moskovski Komsomolyets* re-porter, making inquiries at a clinic specializing in the treatment of venereal diseases, was struck by the young age of many patients and the variety of their family backgrounds. When he asked some young girls 'how it had happened', he received answers like, 'He wanted it. I had nothing against it. It was all the same to me.' Or, 'Why should I refuse? After all, it's natural, isn't it?' [28]

It was to remedy this state of affairs that in 1985 Soviet schools were instructed to give the 'Ethics and Psychology of Family Life' course (see chapter 2), which nevertheless has received nothing but abuse – either because teachers are too prudish to give the set lessons properly, or because the course itself is so feeble and evasive. 'Weigh-ed down with abstract edifications, while questions about how to deal with intimate life [i.e., sex] are not raised at all,' was how Vera Alekseeva, a senior Party official, described it. And when the State publishing house Progress brought out the Russian edition of a much praised Czech book, *The Young Woman's Encyclopedia*, the vital chapter on sex was omitted altogether.

In 1987 'Ethics and Psychology of Family Life' came in for its most withering attack yet: by the prominent sociologist Professor Igor Kon. 'The situation regarding the enlightenment of teenagers is particularly bad,' he wrote in the quarterly *Sotsiologitcheskie Issle-dovania*.

Although the new course includes sections on sex education, this subject is treated extremely coyly and superficially. Subjects outlined in the syllabus are often missing from the text-books, and the teachers them-selves have insufficient knowledge. The Academy of Pedagogical Sciences concentrates, as always, on the 'ethical and aesthetic' aspects of sex educa-tion. But how can we talk about moral education when teenagers are denied truthful answers to the most elementary questions about their psycho-sexual development?

It was said at the Twenty-seventh Congress of the CPSU that the family must be strengthened. But we shall not achieve this by just moraliz-ing. What we need here is the same realism and radical restructuring that we are seeing in other areas of life.

Deploring low standards of professional advice on sex and marital relations, Kon proceeded:

> Lectures and consultations are often given by people without any special training. Indeed, in many places such training is almost unobtainable. Soviet psychology practically puts up a 'no entry' sign when it comes to the question of male–female relationships of any kind, let alone sexual ones. Sexology is generally identified, quite incorrectly, with sexopathology.

As an example of gratuitous secrecy, he referred to a standard medical work, the *Handbook on Sexopathology*, edited by G. S. Vasilchenko, which had still not been put on sale openly. 'You even require special permission to see it in scientific libraries.'

In another interview,[29] Kon attacked the 'coyness' of the authorities over contraceptives. Teachers and parents might protest that telling teenagers about these was likely to encourage early sexual relations, he told *Argumenti i Fakti*. 'But many teenage schoolchildren start sex without their parents' permission. And their inexperience often leads to an unwanted pregnancy, usually terminated by an abortion.'

The Soviet Union had one of the world's highest abortion rates. 'Surely it would be better to teach young people a less harmful method of contraception.'* The 'unhealthy silence' on sexual matters was a legacy of teaching by the Orthodox Church.

> Russian Orthodoxy is very ascetic – the icons portray faces, but the body itself does not exist as such; it is completely covered. Try to find an Orthodox icon of the Virgin breast-feeding her child like a Renaissance madonna. Today the source of this taboo is forgotten, but clearly it persists in our subconscious.

Sexology had three branches, he said: medical, social and psychological.

> But in the Soviet Union hardly anybody studies sexual sociology and psychology. Nor is there any systematic sociological research into the sexual behaviour of youth. This subject remains as taboo as ever among

---

*But in a later statement (to the same magazine) about publicizing the use of contraceptives, Kon foresaw problems with 'outraged' teachers and parents, especially as 'many adults in our society do not know how to use them'. In it he quoted a survey of 1,000 married couples in Moscow, Ufa (in the Urals) and Saratov (in Moscow *oblast*) in 1983–5, in which up to 59 per cent of the men and 68 per cent of the women turned out to not know what he called 'the best methods'. Popular ignorance was shared by many doctors, who tended to warn people against the use of the Pill.[30]

the human sciences. In other words, instead of three branches, we study only one – and that intermittently. Even educated people confuse sexology with sexopathology, or even with pornography.

An all-Union scientific methodological centre on sexopathology exists in the USSR. There is a growing network of consultation centres. But neither future doctors nor future teachers receive even the most elementary sex education. And it is they who are to treat and educate the young people of the twenty-first century!

Born of ignorance and the absence of preventative measures, 'contraception by abortion' (legalized since 1955) has become one of the country's gravest scandals. 'There are more abortions than births in our country,' wrote V. Vasyenka, a teacher in Tallin, Estonia. 'In the Russian Federation the figure is double. Three-quarters of all Soviet women have had at least one.' In fact, if only legal abortions were counted – seven million a year, according to the Soviet Health Minister, Yevgeny Chazov, in November 1987 – the figure would be slightly under. But legal abortions are only part of the picture. The intimidating treatment afforded by State clinics drives hundreds of thousands of women to have pregnancies terminated elsewhere.

'A woman who comes into the clinic for an abortion is deeply unhappy,' says Vasyenka. 'But the next few hours are going to depress her even more. Nobody is going to talk to her; she is part of a faceless stream. Most women ask for an anaesthetic – a mask or a jab in the arm. But there is not enough. Often she gets nothing. Is it possible that the cruelty of the system is intended to teach women a lesson?' Vasyenka agrees that performing abortions is not popular with doctors. 'It's the same operation again and again. Your hands lose their sensitivity after the fifth or sixth. You have to do dozens a day; eight minutes for each – who's fastest? But it should be made more human.'

Another deterrent is the lack of confidentiality. It is impossible to have an abortion without one's employer knowing – unless (Vasyenka was assured) you are a doctor yourself. 'A pregnant doctor can arrange for a colleague to perform it, without having forms to fill in or tell-tale sick leave. But anonymity can be purchased for cash. For thirty or so roubles you can get it done discreetly – and with the coveted anaesthetic.'[31]

An equally grim picture of legal abortion clinics was given by a young student, signing herself A. Perevalova, in *Moskovski Komsom-*

*olyets*. Perevalova said she went to a clinic to talk with women and girls in the queues. What she found was 'a fear of hospitals and the horror of being humiliated'. 'The first thing a girl sees when she enters a clinic is a poster saying, "Mother, Don't Kill Your Baby!" Healthy women come looking for help, and are greeted with the words, "It's not for you. You're already twelve weeks gone." But it's obvious the woman will go ahead anyway, if that's what she's set her mind on.'

Perevalova went to the clinic when it opened at nine. But there was a one-hour wait before a nurse first appeared and bawled through the door, 'Who's for pregnancy termination?'

'Why all this humiliation?' she asked the newspaper, adding how a girl in the queue was told that in order to have an abortion she would have to produce her passport.

Yuri Tinismyagi, the Tallin Deputy Prosecutor, is another who blames lack of anonymity and 'degrading procedures' for the number of young women who resort to illegal operations. A recently published book *Demographic Factors of Health*, by M. Bednyi, gives the ratio of illegal to legal abortions as 1:2.7. But the ratio is much higher among teenagers. According to the author's figures, 70 per cent of town girls and 90 per cent of country girls terminate their first pregnancies with a criminal abortion – often with fatal consequences. This is despite the fact that today such illegal operations are generally performed at night or at weekends in State hospitals by qualified State doctors, undeterred by the risk of a two-year sentence to 'corrective labour' if discovered – or eight years if the woman dies or suffers 'other grave consequences'.*

With *glasnost* inspiring so many questions about sex, pregnancies, abortion, divorce and other problems in the Soviet press, one is

*In February 1988 a deputy Soviet Health Minister told *Sovietskaya Rossiya* that more than half the country's gynaecological clinics had no heat or plumbing. Gynaecological assistance for young women was virtually non-existent. Consequently one in every eight young women needed treatment. Statistics were even more alarming among older women: selective studies showed that 300–350 per thousand had gynaecological problems. The Minister further disclosed that one out of every fifteen couples was infertile, but that doctors could not perform fallopian tube surgery for lack of special instruments. Moscow women also found that gynaecological clinics knew nothing about painless vacuum abortions, and hospitals lacked the equipment for these too. While girls under seventeen were now a higher percentage of those seeking abortions, it was not unusual for an older woman to come for her tenth or eleventh.

driven to inquire, what is the attitude of Soviet society towards extra-marital relations generally?

Private conversation leaves little room for doubt that despite problems of privacy, and the ever-watchful eye of the Party and Komsomol, most of today's Soviet citizens, at least in European Russia, have had sexual relations at an early age, and that the discretion that normally surrounds sexual affairs is no bar to uninhibited activity in this respect. Indeed, a survey by three women sociologists, Zena Yankova, Yevgenia Achildi and Olga Loseva, found that only 12.6 per cent of Soviet men and 40 per cent of Soviet women fail to have sex before marriage, and that 28 per cent of men and 75.5 per cent of women marry their first sexual partner.[32]

In official literature socialist morality demands fulmination against anything suggesting licentiousness. But in the real life of ordinary people, sexual relations tend to be seen as a demand of nature, in a country where nature is always right.

'When the time for love arrives, there's nothing parents can do to prevent it,' wrote a fifty-year-old newspaper reader, recalling his first experience, before his sixteenth birthday. To which he added: 'I'd been ready much earlier than that.'[33]

'Alternative love', i.e., extra-marital relations, is even regarded with a certain amount of fatalism nowadays, since 'psychologists have demonstrated that the individual falls in love a dozen times in his life'.[34] But this passing passion is not perceived as any ultimate threat to the affection supposed to exist between husband and wife, who are 'married once and for all'.[35] In any case, marital infidelity is far from being a principal reason for seeking divorce, at least among women (see chapter 3).

Such are the facts of human nature behind the statistics turned up by sociological surveys, as when, among Leningrad teenagers, more than half the boys and 14.5 per cent of the girls tell social researchers that they have had sexual relations; and 50 per cent of 'happily-married' women say they accept the idea of 'infidelity'. In fact, 'modesty' seems a fairer word than 'prudishness' when speaking of the mores of Soviet society.

Certainly it is not prudery that keeps individuals from broadcasting the details of their private lives – or inspires the hostility of the young towards official organizations, usually the Komsomol, which seek to poke a finger into their intimate affairs. Rather it is a jealous concern for the all too often invaded privacy of the person.

Concern for other people's affairs 'may be the mark of a society in which each feels responsible for his neighbour,' observed *Komsomol-skaya Pravda* apropos of a case in 1987. This can induce a marvellous solidarity, but it can also induce a shocking right of inquisition. And in cases like this one must show tact and understanding.'[36] The newspaper was talking about a girl who had been accused by the Komsomol of abandoning her newly born baby. In fact, the child was the result of a rape a few weeks before her marriage; but in a town where everyone knew everyone else, she had shrunk from making a charge, or even telling her fiancé. When the Komsomol broadcast the 'abandonment' across the whole town, she finally decided to confide in her husband. But he, unable to face the shame, had already left her.

# 12

# The Generation Gap

*Changed status of parents – problems of retirement – neglect of the elderly – nostalgia for the past – neo-Stalinism – debate on 'moral values' – the 'lost' and the 'super-lost' – problem of reintegrating the young in politics*

After the tensions described in earlier chapters, it might seem super-fluous to add that in many ways Soviet society suffers from a wide generation gap. But this gap is more complex than one might first suppose. To understand what 'generation' means in the Soviet Union, it is necessary to speak not of two generations but of three.

The generation brought up immediately after the war and under Khrushchev was highly politicized. It believed in Progress, technological, political and cultural, and knew what the war had meant, often from first-hand experience. Times were hard, with very few material goods in which to take an interest. But every small additional comfort was seen as proof of Progress. In every way things were going to be better than they had been yesterday.

It had, however, to pass through the period of Khrushchev's 'deStalinization', which for some was further encouraging evidence that everything was getting better, but for others a severe shock, as if the exposure of Stalin meant the end of the Party. The generation brought up under Brezhnev was depoliticized, cynical and bent on material consumption. At the same time, there was an unprecedented stress on the study of 'social science' in schools. It was obligatory to study the speeches of Brezhnev and his cronies, every one of which caused the student to withdraw further and further from politics. This was the high season of cynicism and pretence in the Komsomol, when young people joined wholesale in their last year at school for the naked purpose of improving their chances of a place in an institute.

The longer Brezhnev stayed in power, the worse it became, since the gerontocracy blocked every means of young people's progress, and every relationship became based on deceit and corruption. (To give an example, under Khrushchev any group of pupils or students could invite a writer, poet or similar representative of the intelligentsia to come and give a talk. In this way young people came to know Yevtushenko, Trifonov, Vosnessensky and others. But under Brezhnev, the procedure was deliberately complicated, making it necessary for the Director or Dean, no longer the students, to submit the invitation for the approval of the local *raikom*, saying what would be discussed. As a result, these meetings simply stopped.)

Regrettably it was this 'lost generation' that brought up the present generation. And because it had no ideals to transmit, no compelling example to set, and lived in hypocrisy, it fathered what some people call the 'super-lost generation'. That is to say, while those who came to maturity under Brezhnev may have lost their faith, their children, today's generation, have in most cases never had a faith to lose in the first place.

Those who perceive the truth of this tragic situation place their hopes on 'unblocking' history, so that today's young people may see what happened – and react. (A major development was the sudden decision in 1988 to scrap existing history textbooks, even though this meant a wait of up to two years for new ones to be introduced.)

Of course, after fifteen years of stagnation, the younger generation sees nothing to get excited about. Nevertheless, Gorbachev is obliged to lean on these teenagers, counting on their being attracted by technological change, and on their interest in the rejuvenation of leadership and management, and reforms in general.

One of his problems is the absence of young leaders. In Khrushchev's time, the young had young models (particularly in literature). Khrushchev himself encouraged the creation of 'young leaders' groups': and it is from these circles (demoted to third-rank positions under Brezhnev) that Gorbachev has drawn so many of his 'vanguard', like Yakovlev, Bovin and Smirnov.

Whether the young can be expected to return to politics, in the spirit of earlier days, is a hotly debated point between optimists and pessimists. Both can claim some support from the facts. True, some young people have bitten on the reforms, seeing the new leaders and the anti-corruption campaign as giving politics a kind of new virginity. But most of the 'super-lost' generation are more likely to respond (if they respond at all) out of material self-interest. The mobilization of youth for the good of society is therefore likely to depend, for some time yet, on appeals to the profit motive and not on 'ideals', and Gorbachev knows this very well.

In the meantime there are other, quite different 'moral' problems.

An old Russian proverb tells how a peasant is tearing up a loaf and throwing the parts away. A passer-by asks what he is doing. 'One part I throw to the wind,' he says, 'a second into the water. A third I eat myself. With the fourth I pay off a debt. The fifth is a loan.' The explanation is as follows: bread thrown to the wind means paying taxes. Throwing it to the water means feeding his daughter, who will one day grow up and swim away. Payment of a debt means feeding the parents who have nurtured and raised him. Making a loan means feeding his son, who will one day look after him in his old age.

Modern ways of life have shattered this idyll. The average young Soviet citizen depends wholly on his parents until he is twenty, compared with the peasant of the past who was fully independent at fifteen. At the same time, an insufficient birth rate, an ageing population and the prevalence of one-child families in many parts of the Soviet Union has made the elderly dependent, not on their children but on the often uncertain care of the State.*

The change in material status has been accompanied by a change in attitudes. Of course, respect for the elderly still exists. You still find it in villages (if the young have not deserted them). And in the cities, though people mutter angrily at pensioners who use their privilege to jump queues, they still give up seats to them in buses and help them carry parcels in the streets. Even sales girls, perennial weather-cocks of Moscow's ill humours, have been heard to say, 'This way, grandma,' as they steer an old woman through the crowd. In the Caucasus and Central Asia respect for age survives so strongly as to be almost suffocating for young people. But in recent years the Soviet Union has witnessed something quite new: cases of parents completely forgotten or neglected by their children.

Retired people form an increasingly large part of the population. In 1940 there were 200,000. In 1961, 5.4 million. In 1981, 34 million. At the time of writing (1988) there are some 50 million, with everything set for a gerontological 'boom' (70 million) during the thirteenth Five-year Plan in 1991–5.[1]

*Figures published for the first time in 1986 showed that between the mid-1960s and the late 1970s the life expectancy of men had dropped from sixty-six to sixty-two years, and that of women from seventy-three to seventy-two. But in December that year it was claimed that the anti-alcohol campaign had helped to raise the figure for a man to sixty-four.

ЛАОКООН, или ОТЦЫ и ДЕТИ.                                Рисунок Л. ФИЛИППОВОЙ.

The modern Soviet Laocoön, father and sons caught in the
coils of consumerism.

As in the West, retirement is often regarded as a misfortune rather
than a reward. 'Many of the 50 million people thus "given" free time
feel oppressed by it,' says Professor Boris Grushin, a specialist in the
subject. 'Twenty-five out of every hundred in Moscow have no
family to take care for them. In Tallin the figure is even higher –
thirty-one, and in Leningrad, thirty-seven. In other words more than
15 million people, a third of all Soviet pensioners, are alone.'

Saving up for a possibly bleak future is now an everyday topic
says Grushin, who would like to see a percentage of everyone's pay
deducted as savings. There should also be an all-Union council for
pensioners' welfare, an improvement in old people's homes and the
organization of old people's clubs. 'These 50 million must not be left
to feel thrown on the scrap-heap; they should stay active in our
society to the end of their days.'

In some cases, thanks to the country's labour needs, there are small
moves towards this. As we noted in chapter 5, pensioners are encouraged to continue at least part-time work after their retirement
date, and a quarter do so. And many apartment blocks have set up
'pensioners' collectives', by means of which the retired can keep in

touch and be on hand for small jobs, like looking after small children. Pensioners were also in the mind during the framing of the 1986 law on individual enterprise; and many have taken advantage of it to resume work like dress-making, hairdressing, take-away cooking and light household repairs.

There are several reasons why the authorities want to keep old people usefully engaged. The first is social: no group must be allowed to exist outside the main body of society. The 'old' are required to hand on their 'work-experience', either as individuals or as members of the new 'veterans' association' formed from the previously separate war- and labour-veterans' organizations. The second is economic: it will be the end of the century before the number of young people entering employment is equal to the number of workers retiring on pension, and by continuing to work the retired can help bridge the gap. The third is financial: the need to compensate pensioners for the thirty years, up to 1986, when wages increased by 250 per cent but pensions remained static. 'The elderly are paying the same prices as the rest of us, from a third of the income,' wrote Vyatcheslav Basjic in *Literaturnaya Gazeta*.[2]

And after the 1987 Central Committee plenum, promising 'more realistic' prices, economists like Abel Aganbegian were obliged to call for pensioners (and parents of large families) to be compensated if the socialist character of society was to be preserved.

But, above and beyond these practical considerations, the condition of the elderly confronts Soviet society with a moral and social problem. Old people used to be 'heeded, feared and respected, but times have changed and this classical hierarchy has been broken', observed *Sobesednik* in December 1986. 'Today we are attempting to put the old into homes, and the young into apartment blocks with other young people. Those responsible are no doubt fired with the best of intentions, but by segregating age groups they are breaking one of nature's most important laws.'

The magazine told how a 75-year-old woman had been installed in a flat in a Moscow old people's home, for which she was totally unsuited, both physically and psychologically. According to her middle-aged daughter, 'an ambulance would appear at the door of the building with frightening regularity, seven inmates having died within one year'. The woman's one bright spot was the company of an elderly gentleman who quietly courted her and for whom she would sometimes cook – till one day there was a small disagreement, and she did not call on him for two weeks. When finally she became worried at not seeing him out walking and raised the alarm, it was discovered that he had collapsed on the floor and died a fortnight before. 'My mother was right about one thing,' the daughter told a reporter, 'during the arrangements for his funeral, the belongings of this man without a family disappeared without trace.'

*Sobesednik* called attention to the increasing loneliness of old people; even grandmothers living with the family could nowadays be excluded from family affairs. Invited to supper with a family one evening, the magazine's reporter had found the *babushka* in the kitchen sipping tea. 'My son's afraid I'll pick up the wrong end of my spoon,' she told him. 'When there are guests, I usually make myself scarce and watch television; it's the best way if you're old.'

It went on to describe what happened to mothers who sold up their houses in the village and went to live with their children in town.

> Usually they give them the money to buy furniture and a car – and then spend the rest of their days doing cooking and housework and queuing at the shops. The children no longer think of them as a real part of the family circle: they don't take them to the park or the cinema when they go. So the old people feel alone, even among their own.[3]

It also told about another old woman, living 'very poorly' on her miniscule pension on the outskirts of Moscow. She wore 'just any old clothes' and 'seemed to live on air'. But when she died, it turned out that she had saved 3,000 roubles, to be distributed between a shop-assistant who had regularly saved her a carton of *kefir*,[g] neighbours to pay her funeral expenses and her son – who had not been to see her for five years.

In 1986 the trade-union newspaper *Trud* published a withering description of the way old people were treated in hospital. The author, a woman doctor, explained how, because of staff shortages and a general unwillingness, the relatives of geriatric patients had to turn to work as cleaners and orderlies. She proposed that some hospital wards should be made 'pay wards', where the old could pay to be treated properly, and that 'We shouldn't be afraid of using the word "pay".' She explained how it was difficult to get old people into hospital for 'statistical reasons' – because their need of additional attention and medication made their treatment less 'profitable'. The staff manning 'pay wards' should get extra pay, as in already existing 'self-financing polyclinics', where patients (or their families) paid according to their means.[4]

But the youngest are equally victims. For reasons including the low standard of medical treatment, out of every 1,000 babies born in the Soviet Union, eighteen die immediately and thirteen fail to survive their first year. These figures put the country in fiftieth place in the international infant mortality table, below Barbados and, in the case of certain regions, on a level with Paraguay and Thailand.[5]

But when *Literaturnaya Gazeta* asked for the statistics in April 1987, its reporter was told that they could be given only to certain 'competent specialists' – and in any case not by the Ministry of Health but only by the Central Statistics Board. When he appealed to the Deputy Head of the Central Statistics Board 'health section', he was fobbed off with obsolescent data – for 1985, when the rate was 'only' twenty-six deaths per 1,000.

*Literaturnaya Gazeta* blamed the appalling figure partly on poor doctoring. 'The standards of medical science have gone up, while those of treament have fallen far behind.' It went on to slam the long-standing custom of maternity clinics taking babies from their mothers and putting them in huge wards, 'like pickled cucumbers out of the same jar'. From here they were trundled out at feeding time, their names written 'from shoulder to wrist' with a ball-point pen, for the sake of convenience. All of this occurs despite a growing recognition that it would be safer to leave them in the wards with their mothers.

Medical equipment was also years behind, said *Literaturnaya Gazeta*. For instance, while the rest of the world had long been using ultrasound techniques to screen pregnant mothers, 'such equipment in the USSR can be counted on the fingers of one hand'. As for the antiquated bureaucracy that forbade parents' visits to sick children, in some hospitals mothers were getting permission to visit the wards by offering to do menial work such as scrubbing floors and cleaning toilets.[6]

The backward condition of Soviet medicine affects every age group. In 1986 a fourteen-year-old boy, Kalibek Ainazharov, who had lost both legs as a result of an incorrect diagnosis, took the ultimate revenge on Soviet medicine by driving his new invalid carriage to the hospital in Alma-Ata where the mistake had been made, and shooting the surgeon responsible. Shortly afterwards it was revealed that one-third of the 30,000 appendixes removed annually in Moscow turned out to be normal, and that a medical survey-team questioning 242 doctors from seven different medical institutes had found that 'not one knew the basic facts that should be within the ken of every physician'.

Referring to the way in which students are accepted for medical training, *Literaturnaya Gazeta* observed:

> Some, who have a real calling, tend to be excluded on the pretext of 'campaigning against negative phenomena' [such as nepotism], while youngsters from the country are accepted almost without having to take entrance exams in the hope that they will return to the village when qualified. But why should a village have a semi-trained doctor who has, so to speak, been dragged there by the ear?

Behind this dark picture is the question of pay: while a handful of 'stars' make large sums of money treating patients from the elite and from abroad (for example, the Soviet Union leads the world in laser eye-surgery), the general run of doctors receive a pittance. 'Why do surgeons' wages not approach those of a bus driver?' asked one writer. The same goes for the wages of nurses and auxiliary staff, a factor contributing to the universal system of bribery,

In August 1986 a reader wrote to *Moskovski Komsomolyets*, describing his experience after an operation. In a ward where post-operative patients were unable to move, and totally dependent on assistance from the staff, 'each menial service comes with a price: one rouble for changing the bed linen, one for changing the towel, another for fetching food – brought by relatives – from the refrigerator. It costs three roubles to be taken to another room for treatment, and so on. Usually it is the visiting relatives who pay – right at the entrance by the lift.'

Soviet society is susceptible to bouts of nostalgia, both social and political. The older generation is predictably most prone, making it a factor in the generation gap. But the young have their own forms too.

There has always been a nostalgia for the families of yesterday, when children had nearby grandparents, and brothers and sisters, and uncles and aunts, and it was easier to give them a decent upbringing.[7] Today this nostalgia looms large in a widespread fear among older people (and some younger ones as well) of the changes taking place in the society around them. Some even speak with nostalgia about the old days of communal apartments, when, they now remember, there was a feeling of human warmth and solidarity that has since vanished. Newspapers regularly print letters explaining how people in modern apartment blocks simply don't know one another; and the consequent lack of 'social control' is regularly given as a reason for the increase in drinking, drugs and delinquency.[8]

But while the nostalgia of the old is a simple case of regret – of remembering how girls used not to smoke, and people were polite and cultured, and social rituals served as a protective fence – the nostalgia of the 'sophisticated' young takes a different form. Theirs has been responsible for a whole succession of backward-looking fashions, beginning in the mid-1970s with the wearing of crosses at the neck of open shirts, and later Tolstoy beards and other devices. As in the West, there have also been periodic 'returns to the land' (preferably in a *dacha* with heating and a bathroom), and vogues like that described earlier for collecting objects to pass off as heirlooms, since it is no longer shameful to have had a noble ancestor before the Revolution.

However pretentious it may be, all this is harmless. More disquieting have been two quite different manifestations of nostalgia, derived from perverted romanticism and ignorance of history.

The first began with an historical association, Pamyat, founded in the early 1980s with the entirely respectable aim of preserving the Russian cultural and architectural heritage. But within a short time a group of individuals within the association had begun to peddle a sinister brand of Russian ultra-nationalism.

By 1986, using the cover of Gorbachev's *glasnost*, they had all but taken it over; but, since the authorities were loath to suppress them directly, the job of exposure was given to the press. In June two *Izvestia* reporters obtained a recording of a Pamyat meeting at which speakers allegedly quoted from the notorious anti-Semitic document known as the *Protocols of the Elders of Zion*. The *Protocols* purport to be a verbatim report of a congress at the beginning of this century at which Jewish leaders planned to seize world power. Published in 1905 by the right-wing extremist Union of the Russian People, they were later taken over and used by the Nazis to justify the Holocaust.

'The *Protocols* have a dirty and sinuous history, yet Pamyat considers them the key to a "real" understanding of the past, present and future of the country in which we live,' said *Izvestia*, whose reporters also visited the home of a prominent Pamyat supporter, D. D. Vasiliev.

> The flat where our conversation took place looked like a museum. On the walls were icons, pictures and old photographs, including a photo of the Tsar and [his minister] Stolypin. But on the table was a volume of Lenin.

How can one reconcile these things – Stolypin on the wall and Lenin on the table? Later we found that Stolypin is considered by Pamyat to have been a progressive reformer, whose experience should be used in today's *perestroika*.

Though *Izvestia* could hardly admit it, this assessment of Stolypin is shared by a number of liberal Western historians. But Vasiliev appears to have volunteered a wealth of crackpot ideas – for example, that a mention in the *Protocols* of 'underground passages' meant that Jewish leaders were planning to use the Moscow Metro to blow up the seat of Soviet power in the Kremlin. Pamyat leaders were also said to be convinced that 'dark powers' had a hand in editing Gorbachev's speeches, so that every good reference to the Russian people was cut out.

By 1988 the source of poison appeared to have been capped. Measures included the expulsion of members of Pamyat from the Moscow Party; public ridicule also played a part. The irony was that Pamyat should have been one of the first tests of *glasnost*. But the authorities resisted the temptation to suppress it.

The second disconcerting manifestation of nostalgia is for the 'order' and 'stability' of thirty years ago; a naïve nostalgia that causes its middle-aged adherents to say of the pot-holed Moscow streets that 'it wasn't like that in Stalin's time', and younger ones, truck drivers, to paste pictures of the dictator in the windows of their cabs.

People must be told the truth about Stalin if we are not to become a passive society, declared the head of the State Archive, Professor Yuri Afanasyev, in March 1987. 'It is time to put the study of his personality cult on a proper basis. We do not have a single research paper on this question. Our television often portrays him as a leader crowned with wisdom and authority. Let us give the younger generation a chance to form their own ideas.' Afanasyev also criticized the caricatures drawn of past enemies of socialism, such as the White Guard General Kolchak and Tsar Nicholas 11 – portraits so one-sided that 'ordinary citizens begin to feel sympathy for them'.*[9]

---

*Accusing television of 'containing some of the most "unreconstructed" members of the Soviet intelligentsia', Afanasyev instanced the TV film *My Contemporaries* (*My Sovremenniki*), in which the young Gagarin returns to earth, walking down a long red carpet. It was clear from history that he should end up being greeted by meeting Nikita Khrushchev; but for political reasons Khrushchev was not portrayed. 'Khrushchev was a complicated man. But how much longer can we pretend that he never existed. Gagarin had to walk off the screen without meeting him, from "space" into another kind of space.'

People who actually witnessed the cruelties of the Stalinist period are less inclined to nostalgia, but others, who were children at the time, can be desperately muddled – like a 38-year-old truck driver writing in 1987 to *Sotsialistitcheskaya Industria*. Although he 'fully supported the *perestroika*', Ivan Karasev thought it wrong to try and blacken Stalin's name, which 'should be carved in granite, or even gold'. 'It's not Stalin's fault that people made a cult of him. Stalin did many things for his people, and the people did much for him and for their country. They lived and worked as one great Soviet family for the good of the Motherland.'[10]

In answer to another piece of nonsense, a repetition of the myth that in the Great Patriotic War soldiers had died glorifying Stalin in their battle cries, the newspaper published a letter from the historian Alexandr Samsonov. The truth, explained Samsonov, was that the relatives of the fallen would receive a letter with the standard phrase: 'He died like a true patriot with the words "For the Motherland, for Stalin!" on his lips.' This hackneyed picture was a travesty of people's true feelings. The widow of one of Samsonov's own friends, Nikolai Kulikov, had received such a letter, even though her husband had always experienced the deepest antipathy for Stalin.[11]


In the later 1980s a spate of plays, novels and press articles appeared that dealt either obliquely or directly with the period of Stalin's repression. These are some of the most important results of *glasnost* and the *perestroika*. But to observe the extent of popular hunger for a look into the closed book of history, one can hardly do better than go on any weekend to Moscow's Novodyevichy cemetery, reopened to the public after ten years in 1986.

All Russian cemeteries are places of pilgrimage, even in winter. But four-centuries-old Novodyevichy is special. In it lie buried some of Russia's greatest figures from both before and after the Revolution: writers and poets, composers and musicians, inventors and aviators, scientists and generals. A guide printed in 1970 sold out within days. But when a second edition was proposed, the Moscow Executive Committee forbade it on the grounds that Novodyevichy was not open to visitors 'and therefore this sort of informative historical literature is not needed by anyone'.

Today's visitors are most interested in the resting places of political figures. Hence the crowd forever before the tomb of Nikita Khrushchev, and that of Stalin's unhappy wife, Nadezhda Alliluyeva.

This quest by broad sections of Soviet society for an insight into the past, and through this an understanding of the present and future, is enough to show that what divides Soviet society is not a simple 'generation gap'. Rather there is a division between those who look forward and those who look back.

The letters that fill the Soviet press on the subject of human values fall into two halves. There are those that bewail a loss of manners and 'morals', but in reality show a fear of change and the loss of reassuring landmarks. And there are those that recall the past, not in order to turn back the clock but to discover where society took the wrong turning, and to regain the path. As the reformists in the Party see it, this was in the early 1920s.

The debate is typically Soviet in the balance (or more frequently imbalance) between emotion and logic. Official Soviet society knows perfectly well what kind of citizens it wants today and tomorrow – an image that was created in the first years of the Revolution. It wants:

– collectivists (with values entirely in terms of the interest of society);
– self-disciplinarians (forever ready to subordinate personal needs to the common good);
– workers (ready and able to tame nature);
– patriots (capable of loving without distinction the millions of people who constitute their country);
– internationalists (putting Soviet citizenship above individual nationality);
– atheists (rejecting religion because of the certainty of their scientific life-view).

The trouble, as endless letters to the press testify, is the gap between these requirements and today's reality. One of the first perceived evidences of the decline in Soviet values has been the appearance of the profit motive where before there were simply acts of humanity.

In 1986 Vladimir P., a teacher from Moscow, described a summer holiday visit to the north Caucasus town of Kirillovka. In the past, local people had done an honest business letting rooms. But now, in the scramble to make money, they were ready to sell any kind of space – from sheds to balconies – for the same price. They charged for gas, water and electricity, which had formerly been free, and crammed twenty to fifty guests into houses that had come to resemble camping sites. The only visitors the locals bothered to talk to were those whose jobs gave them access to 'deficit' goods. They had given up cultivating their vegetable plots, because letting floor-space was more profitable. The young wore black-market clothes and looked for jobs with easy money; they could reel off the names of current pop stars, but once, when he had asked a group, not one knew the words of the Soviet national anthem.

Another correspondent recalled how, in contrast to others' generosity, at the time of the exodus from Chernobyl some Caucasian locals had promptly put up rents.

'It's a scandal how self-interest has eroded the traditional good-neighbourliness of the village,' wrote V. Fedorov of Pskov *oblast*. 'Nowadays if an old person asks for a hand, even with little things, like mending a fence, he's expected to fork out a bottle. Perhaps that's why so many *samogonchiki* are pensioners. The good old ways have quietly disappeared – like getting together to build a house or dig a well.'

Anna Vasilievna, sixty-five, thought that men had 'lost all conscience'. Whenever she asked a fellow-villager for a small favour nowadays, he'd say, 'Give us a bottle, granny!' A bottle was the only currency recognized. 'And how many bottles one parts with in one summer!' [12]

'What worries me is that people are no longer interested in cultural values,' wrote Veniamin Kaverin, a contributor to *Literaturnaya Gazeta*. 'What are the roots of this frightening phenomenon?' he went on, instancing the growth of dishonesty, calculated flattery, 'careerism' and abuse of trust. 'The trouble starts with childhood. Parents are at work all day, and there's no proper family atmosphere. Schools should be doing something, but they're not.'

Pre-revolutionary schools had a higher standard of teaching.

> For all their faults, the old gymnasia gave a much better education. There was no 'Academy of Pedagogical Sciences' then, no endless succession of 'reforms' to prevent the development of firm traditions.
>
> The most destructive thing I see in our culture is superficiality and estrangement. We are gradually losing those spiritual values that existed throughout history and were tangibly evident in the Great Patriotic War. Neither before nor since have we felt the same bond between people, the same feeling of comradeship. [13]

'What can be more shameful than a lack of respect for the glory of one's fathers?' asked a writer in *Sovietskaya Rossiya*, calling for less 'formalism' in patriotic education and more respect for elders within families. Why, parents even sometimes talked unflatteringly about war veterans, and made fun of their medals in front of the children.[14] The same writer described how two Volgograd (Stalingrad) youths had burgled a veteran's flat and stolen and sold his medals. Even worse was the case of a 75-year-old woman, 'a veteran wearing two medals on her sweater', bowled over and left unconscious by a party of youths stampeding through a Volgograd underpass. The party turned out to have been part of a P T U group on their way to the war museum.

Nevertheless, the system continues to put trust in the educative value of heroes. Soviet hagiography provides one suited to the needs of every age, yet always endowed with the same basic qualities: respect for elders, readiness to help the young, to rescue those who 'stray from the path'; a good son, later a model husband, a diligent worker forever good for a laugh and a song, always 'ready' when danger calls or the motherland needs to be defended.

Such is the example of the military instructor who, during a secondary-school training exercise, discovered that the demonstration grenade was a live one, and died throwing himself on top of it to save the lives of the class.[15] Or the kindergarten hero, little Volodya (he is not yet called Lenin, or even Vladimir Ilich), already ever-gentle and polite, helping others, obeying his parents, working hard at school.

Then there are the heroes of literature, either characters or authors, like Alexander Pushkin, honoured in 1987 on the 150th anniversary of his death as a model of honour, love and liberty. And the heroes of the Revolution and the Great Patriotic War, including (a sign of the times) increasingly frequent references to those whose path was not always straight (like revolutionary émigrés who subsequently fought Fascism); the heroes of Afghanistan, made the object of stories that are as often human as heroic–internationalist; and the heroes of everyday life – heirs of the working-class romanticism that was a mark of the Revolution, people who have 'done their bit' in the workshop or *kolkhoz* and now say 'Don't call me a hero, it's nothing special.'[16]

And, of course, there are those who have *really* achieved something with which to inspire young people's dreams and give them a model. Of these the example *par excellence* remains Gagarin, the son of a peasant family, with a picture-book wife and children, who, succeeding by force of work and courage, has given two generations of Soviet youngsters the longing to be cosmonauts.

In 1987 the twenty-fifth anniversary of his epic first space flight ('a victory for Soviet science and technology, for our social system, and for the whole Soviet people')[17] enabled the press to spell out the lesson that is still transmitted by Gagarin's successors: that the hero is he who assumes his responsibility in society, no matter what his station, 'when a man is not afraid to face risks, whether an aviator or a fitter', explained the cosmonaut Pavel Popovich.[18]

And sometimes events take it on themselves to complete, tragically, the pantheon of heroes. Chernobyl provided a host of examples: the fatally injured but still fighting fire-brigade captain, the helicopter pilot smothering the burning reactor with sand, the miner volunteering to tunnel underneath it, the doctors, accident-investigators, truck-drivers, young soldiers – all the volunteers 'who couldn't stand by with arms folded'. Then, almost immediately afterwards, the sailors rescuing passengers from the *Admiral Nakhimov* as it went to the bottom of the Black Sea.

But today's young people are tired of these classic heroes. Not only do they create their own quite different ones, who may be far from attractive to the older generation, but they regard the traditional heroes in a quite different light. 'When today's young people read *War and Peace*, it's not the love of Bolkonski and his search for a sense in life that they remember; it's the story of Natasha and Anatoly Kuragin,' wrote a young Moscow student.[19]

# 13

# The Millennial Vision

*Prospects for the year 2000 – Russia's 'American dream' – productivity and redeployment – a new NEP? – publication of statistics – scope for East–West collaboration – consequences of failure*

Where is the Soviet Union going? In July 1988 a special Party conference approved major changes in the political system, including a move to separate the powers of Party and State. One of the purposes was to give ordinary non-Party citizens a visible role in the process of reconstruction. Time would show effectively the changes would be applied, but the openness of the proceedings was the surest indication that now there could be no going back and that, whatever the difficulties, Gorbachev's projections for the twenty-first century had become lodged in the national consciousness.

One of the most plausible expressions of the Soviet vision came not from any Party speech but from one of the country's most articulate publicists. Lean, relaxed, and highly sociable, 54-year-old Vladimir Posner is in frequent demand by US television networks to deliver a coherent Soviet view on current affairs. His father, a Jewish accountant, left revolutionary Russia in 1920 and settled in France. In 1940 the family escaped Hitler by fleeing to America, and Posner senior found work in Hollywood. After the war, father and son moved back across the Atlantic – first to Berlin, where Vladimir took a job with an East German film company, and later to Moscow, where he joined the State broadcasting organization.

In 1986 Posner told Soviet readers of *Argumenti i Fakti* about differences between the Soviet and American ways of life. He started by explaining that there were 'separate kinds of shops' for rich and poor in the United States – which prompted his interviewer to say that 'some of our readers think that in America there is real abundance, while in our own country we still have many shortages'. Well, said Posner, the Soviet Union did have shortages, 'And they come from a combination of two things: first, our own bungling, and secondly because we have tried to ensure that everyone has everything of about the same quality.'

He recalled how he had once told American television viewers:

You Americans have absolutely everything. Your shop windows have marvellous displays of beautiful things that people want to buy. But they have no money with which to buy them. That is one sort of stress.

In our country unfortunately many things are lacking. Either the quality is bad, or there are not enough. We have money – but nothing to spend it on. That is another kind of stress. But when I think which stress is more terrible, I come to the conclusion that it is the first.

A reader had asked: 'How do Americans live? What sort of houses do they have? Who does their plumbing repairs? Why, on television, do they seem relaxed, and never to be carrying heavy shopping-bags like us?' Posner explained how many Americans bought their own homes with a mortgage. 'And there's a network of shops where nearly everything can be bought for doing your own repairs. Then there is the co-operative condominium, where families buy their own flats. Other flats are rented, and the landlord does all the repairs. Finally, there are the slums, where the poor live, which are not repaired or serviced at all.'

The Soviet Union could learn from the Americans in a whole range of things, he admitted. For example, the organization of public services. One rarely saw an American struggling home with heavy bags, because most of them had cars and did their weekly shopping at one go.

But when it came to the point, Posner, for all his 'Americanness', was unyielding. He quoted the time-honoured dictum that to give a few people a high living standard is simple, and to give more people a tolerable one is possible, but that to give everyone a high standard has so far been beyond any society: 'I believe our society is approaching this last, while the Americans do not even set themselves such a goal. I like America – it is part of my past. But today's America does not have what I consider most important – a future. I believe in communism, although I don't know when we shall build it.' [1]

One of the ironies of popular expectations in Gorbachev's Russia is what might be called the Soviet 'American Dream'. Among its symbols are ubiquitous machines selling Soviet-made drinks under the Pepsi-Cola franchise (supplemented in 1988 by a similar agreement with the rival Coca-Cola company and the McDonald's Hamburger chain). Soviet 'Pepsi' may not taste quite authentic (perhaps it is too watered down), but young Russians drinking from the familiar red, white and blue paper-cups buy the momentary illusion of being part of the American scene. American models are also evident in the all-pervading pop music, despite efforts to develop a Soviet pop with supposedly native roots.

Among the young a further American Dream symbol is the cult of the motorcycle (bought with parents' help), whose wilder manifestations were described in chapter 10. Other 'cult' imports have included foreign names in the fashion world – a Pierre Cardin shop that, nevertheless, up to July 1988 had not actually opened for business – and, yet more bizarre, a 1987 Yves Saint Laurent retrospective exhibition at the Moscow exhibition centre.

In Moscow, more exposed than other cities to Western life-styles, the urge to be 'with it' and Western is evident in numerous other ways, from the ownership of dogs (with regular shows and pedigree clubs) in flats already too small for their human occupants, to the early-morning jogs of track-suited citizens newly awakened to the cult of the waist-line. Indeed, one could almost think that inside every new Russian there is an American waiting to get out. But for the moment the country is occupied with serious matters.

The launching of the *perestroika* in 1985–6 promised a transformation of nearly every branch of life, beginning with the economy. The goal remains intact. But already changes have met resistance in factories and on farms, where, under the 1987 law on State enterprise, many workers are having to work harder for less pay because the enterprise is required to become 'self-financing'. Perhaps this will change as work standards improve. But behind the drive for greater efficiency, automation and higher productivity lies the threat of what Soviet workers have always been led to believe is uniquely a vice of the capitalist system: job competition and redundancies.

The economist Abel Aganbegian estimates that there will be no problem of redundancies before 1992. But some other Soviet economists think Aganbegian's approach to the country's huge problems is too gradual, and that unless Gorbachev takes additional powers to speed up the process at the cost of some 'socialist values', the whole *perestroika* will run out of steam.

Clearly, if the Soviet Union is to compete economically with the West, it will have to reduce its huge army of unproductive workers. (In 1986 Professor Vladimir Kostakov, writing in the magazine *Rabotnitsa*, estimated that increased labour productivity would require 13–15 per cent fewer workers in production industry, i.e., a cut of 15 million. The change would begin to be felt in the twelfth five-year period of 1991–6 and would particularly affect women.[2])

It will also be necessary to redeploy many of the 18.6 million civil servants, whose numbers were growing till 1988 at an average 300,000–500,000 per year.[3] In his 1987 'Jubilee' speech Gorbachev said plans to create new jobs in the service industries were already in hand. But nine months later there were still no clear indications as to how this would be done, or sign of a general solution to the problem of motivation.

Since 1985 Gorbachev has spoken about a technical and managerial revolution. But he has before him a new generation for whom the old manufacturing jobs have lost their allure. Since the mid-1960s engineering has lost out to science and medicine. Today, in the late 1980s, it has still not regained its standing, and students continue to despise and reject it despite the many newspaper articles eulogizing turners, mechanics and welders.

Moreover, though Gorbachev speaks of technological progress in the factories, he knows quite well that the tooling of industry is hopelessly out of date. In the 1970s (significantly this type of statistic has ceased to be published) more than 40 per cent of workers in the mechanical engineering industry had only their bare hands to work with. The majority were thus a far cry from conditions ripe for 'technological progress'. And as long as this is so, it will be impossible for industry to attract today's young workers, who are both better educated and more selective.

He also knows that the failure of a succession of earlier attempts at reform has imbued older workers with deep scepticism and an overriding mood of 'wait and see'. Hence the importance attached to new measures accompanying the reforms:

– *Glasnost*, so that people do not hear one thing and discover another;
– the reorganization of pay to promote quality of output and relate wages to work actually done;
– the campaign against bureaucrats who put their own interests before the general good;
– the drive against corruption, which perverts social relations and the system of values, and causes shortages.

To achieve the transformation he needs, Gorbachev depends absolutely on youth, including the very youngest. If he can win their support, numbers are in his favour. Although only 8.7 per cent of the working class fall into the category of the 'workers' intelligentsia' (those who have completed higher education or middle and specialized), 32 per cent of these are under thirty. So the slogans make a point, for once: youth is the most educated part of the Soviet population.

But education by itself is not everything. The young workers 'up to the year 2025', on whom the economists pin such high expectations, are supposed to have kept the 'tradition of work' better than their predecessors.[4] Yet studies in 1986 for the Central Committee of the Komsomol produced some disconcerting figures: one young worker in ten was not fulfilling his plan; one in five was turning out defective products or failing to keep up with the production line; one in three was guilty of poor work discipline or without any feeling of identity with his enterprise. The same inquiry showed that the majority took no part in any of their factory's voluntary activities, had a 'pragmatic and disinterested attitude' towards work, and sought only to get the most for the least effort. And this in a country in which work is valued in terms of 'socially useful activity' and 'taking one's place in society', and in which to regard it as a means of earning money, as in a capitalist system, is wrong.

At the same time, any progress towards achieving the economic revolution is bound to have two-edged social consequences. Among these must be a further erosion of family and personal relationships. Such values as have survived the effects of professional and geographic migration will be exposed to the strains that rack competitive Western society. Almost overnight, one kind of strain will be exchanged for another, for which society is quite unprepared.

Social economists insist that the rationalization of industry must be accompanied by safeguards to 'preserve socialist values', and prevent hardship. But, again, how this is to be done, beyond professional retraining and tinkering with some family allowances to offset rising prices, is not clear.

Against all this it is necessary to set the momentous positive changes that have marked Gorbachev's first years. Second only to the opening up of the press (which we speak of below), the most dramatic have been in the arts. At the beginning of our book we mentioned the cinema, which inaugurated a new era with the first encoded attack on Stalin and Beria in Chengiz Abuladze's *Repentance*. Since then the exposure of Stalin has come full circle with a whole series of films explicitly depicting the Great Terror. In publishing, *Novy Mir* has serialized Anatoly Rybakov's *The Children of the Arbat*, which describes the horrors of Stalin's purges and mass deportations – a book written more than twenty years ago, but forced by censorship to remain in the author's drawer. In 1988 the same magazine published Boris Pasternak's *Doctor Zhivago*. And *Oktyabr* has published Vassily Grossman's *Life and Fate*, a searing account of Stalinism in the war years.

Setting his personal seal on all this, Gorbachev donated 50,000 roubles, the royalties on his own books abroad,* to erect a statue to the late editor of *Novy Mir*, Tvardovsky, who fought to give his readers true literature (including Solzhenitsyn's *One Day in the Life of Ivan Denisovich*) in Khrushchev's day.

There have also been real changes in material matters.

– *In planning*. After years of national obsession with the gigantic, economists have denounced the building of huge complexes, created without regard to local conditions (such as the world's most powerful hydro-electric scheme, Bratsk, without local users, and the world's largest truck factory, Kamaz, without the work-force to run it at full production level).

– *In environmental protection*. Against the romantic, but destructive, tradition that man's function is to 'tame nature', scientists have recognized nature as an asset for the twenty-first century. 'Its protection concerns us all, especially the young,' the sociologist Tatiana Zaslavskaya told *Komsomolskaya Pravda* in 1987.[5] And 1985–7 saw a series of historic victories: the rescue of Lake Ladoga from destruction by development projects; of Lake Baikal from poisoning by a paper factory; and (biggest of all) the defeat of the scheme to reverse the flow of the northern rivers so as to irrigate parts of Central Asia.

– *In decentralization*. In addition to freeing enterprises from rigid central planning, the Party has recognized the need to adapt to local conditions, for example, by setting up of 'village factories' in Central Asia where widespread unemployment is masked by a patriarchal social system.

– *In housing*. Every leader since Khrushchev has promised a home for everyone within a decade. Gorbachev has made his target the year 2000. What is new is a drive by young architects who in 1987 deposed their union president for failing to give active support to plans for better housing and called for a radical change in design.[6]

In our book we have described the problems of the family, and their underlying social causes; the failures of the education system, the problems of young men returning from Afghanistan, and the discouragement met by young workers in industry. We have explained

---

*The donation coincided with the sale of foreign rights in his book *Restructuring and New Thinking for Our Country and the Whole World* to the American publishers Harper & Row.

how socialist society, no less than the 'decadent' West, faces problems of crime and corruption; and how bureaucracy, for example in the Komsomol, frustrates the involvement of the people in the process of social renewal. Finally we have tried to describe the problems of living with the system, and to put into perspective the differences of outlook between generations.

Unless these problems are solved, there can be no going forward. But any estimate of Russia's potential must take account of the Soviet talent for improvisation and 'muddling through', without which the whole economy would long ago have ground to a stop.

Huge enterprises, making everything from lorries to pharmaceuticals, make do with machinery and production systems that would be the despair of almost any Western work-force. Others could set standards for the West. The Moscow Metro is an obvious, if now somewhat dated, example, with its network of trains running every two to three minutes.

When one comes to the human potential, it is necessary to recall once again the contradictions of the complex Russian character: the coexistence, often within the same person, of quite opposite tendencies: to authoritarianism, yet also to spontaneity; to indolence, yet also to surprising bursts of initiative; to self-denigration, yet also to fierce national pride. Moreover, Soviet society is an optimistic society, in which tomorrow's people will always be better than today's; a society sustained by an inner conviction that conflicts stem only from the denial of dialogue, and that one has only to *understand* the other person in order to find a solution.

It is also an irrational society, in which emotion is of great importance. Hence political speeches with emotional passages – 'heart-to-heart' appeals to individual listeners or the whole population – that would expose any West European speaker to ridicule. And in this society, where words may lack the precise significance of a Cartesian discourse, and the press is liable to combine a high moral tone with a touch of exaggeration, it is sometimes necessary to stand back a little.

The debate about loss of values, increasing violence and bad upbringing must be seen in this context if it is not to be misunderstood. With obvious exceptions – chiefly petty figures in authority – Russians as a whole remain deeply attached to a scale of moral values (like culture and respect for the person). These may be in decline at the moment, but they are often more in evidence in the Soviet Union than in the West. Today one sees forms of criminal violence not previously encountered, but they are still at levels that almost any Western authority would envy. Burglaries may be increasing, encouraged by easy opportunities, but one has only to look at the luggage left unattended at railway stations, or hear the hue and cry over the theft of a purse, to understand that in Russia standards of personal security are higher than in some other countries.

As for the 'badly brought up children' so frequently complained about in the press, young Westerners meeting young Russians outside organized tours tend to find them, on the contrary, 'too polite, too well behaved and too much "mother's darlings"'.

Another contradiction. The lack of daily work ethic to which we have so often had cause to allude is liable to be offset by extravagant bursts of professional romanticism, as when collective farmers — scarcely the most zealous beings normally — suddenly become harvest-time 'shock workers', doing double shifts with their tractors and lorries under the proud slogan 'The Nation's Bread Depends On Us', uttered without a trace of black humour.

Finally, it is a society of great solidarity. One might argue that this is necessary for survival among the system's failings and shortages. But the latter could as easily have led to cut-throat struggle for existence. In fact, the opposite has happened. Friends are instantly ready to cancel holidays to help one another, to spend a weekend searching for a scarce medicine (often at the other end of the country, which means a stranger has to bring it by train) or to give up their day off to find an urgently needed book.

And in case of big problems (divorces, children running off, crises at work) there is always somebody ready to spend a night listening to it all. (An art student recalls how one day she received permission to go to Yugoslavia to see the work of a painter, but hadn't a penny for the fare. Without her asking, classmates clubbed together and lent her the necessary sum, 'not even asking when I could repay it'.)

Many in the West believe that the only way the Soviet Union can attain its goals is by abandoning the principles of Leninism. Had Russia followed the social–democratic path of the February Revolution, they argue, it would now be much further advanced. In one field, agriculture, this is possible. Before the First World War, Russia was one of the world's principal grain exporters, whereas today the Soviet Union is obliged to rely on huge imports from the Americas.

But like all great 'ifs' of history, the social–democratic scenario begs too many questions. The future can be discussed profitably only on the basis of existing facts.

There is a lively debate as to whether the New Economic Policy

(NEP) introduced to revive the economy in the early 1920s was intended by Lenin as a temporary or a permanent measure. Most of the evidence suggests the former. But there is just enough to support the contrary view. It is thus possible to invoke Lenin (who was constantly changing his mind, but to whose pronouncements Soviet leaders must still pay almost biblical deference) as authority for the development, under the *perestroika*, of a Soviet mixed economy.

An optimist might see the seeds of such a development in measures introduced after the June 1987 plenum of the Central Committee: the law on individual enterprise, new rules for co-operative enterprises, permission for collective farms to sell their 'surplus' on the market, invitations to foreign firms to participate in joint enterprises, and so on.

He might also hope that further injections of democracy and openness will enable Gorbachev to conduct his 'revolution' not only from above, by strengthening his control of the Politburo and Central Committee, but also from below, by ensuring the election of reformists in local sections of the Party and on the factory floor.

A pessimist, however, would find much to contradict this. He would note the huge weight of the bureaucracy opposing the *perestroika* (not least among many who pay the reforms lip-service). He would see the resistance of interlocking systems, the inertia of working traditions, and the difficulty of rousing interest in monetary rewards, when the goods on which to spend them (better food, fuller shops, worthwhile leisure facilities) do not yet exist. Above all he would have noted the scepticism of the majority of young people, still smothered (in 1988) by an authoritarian education system, and inheriting nothing from their parents but a taste for the trappings of a quasi-Western consumer life without responsibilities.

Perhaps the only way forward is for Gorbachev to adopt a much tougher stand than he has so far been willing or able to do. The model sometimes suggested is Peter the Great, who autocratically opened Russia to Western technology and culture and brought it into the mainstream of European life. But such a course would almost certainly mean curtailing *glasnost*, something that Gorbachev has not yet brought himself to do.

In launching the *perestroika*, Gorbachev faced a novel problem: how to know what the people looked for. Without this, there could be no 'democratization', no development of a sense of personal responsibility.

Thanks to the 'Party = People' equation, there had until then been no need to ask. No need of opinion polls. No need of market research. In so-called samples of public opinion, the organizers knew that individuals would answer almost anything, or whatever they thought would sound pleasing to the pollster or the authorities. The questions were idiotic, and honest replies potentially dangerous.

Getting people to talk, in expectation of being listened to, is not something to be improvised overnight. There has to be a renewal of confidence between leaders and people. This is what has most occupied the Soviet leadership ever since the Twenty-seventh Congress. The task of opinion-sounding has been largely taken on by the press. This is particularly evident in Moscow, where the city authorities have used Party newspapers to sound out opinion on just about everything, from the restoration of pre-revolutionary street names to the scrapping of the monstrous memorial planned to commemorate the city's stand against Hitler.

Under the slogan 'No democracy without *glasnost*. No *glasnost* without information' the press has reached out to cover a whole range of subjects that were formerly taboo, from drugs to official corruption. Journalists hope to become, in the words of one aspirant, 'the ambulances of Soviet society'. More and more, people look to newspapers as a means of exposing injustices.

Thus, when in June 1987 some Moscow students organized a 'sit-in' (a novel enough happening) to protest against the removal of their wall newspaper, they persuaded *Komsomolskaya Pravda* to come along and publicize their protest. This use of the press as a kind of embryonic ombudsman is quite without precedent. And in shops and queues one may now hear managers and assistants being threatened with 'a letter to the papers'.

Some newspapers, like *Moscow News* (published in five languages, including Russian), are snapped up the moment they hit the streets. Readers complain that kiosks are sold out by 7 am, and there are even queues in front of the wall posters. Among senior secondary-school students, 'journalist' has moved to the top of the career popularity list, alongside 'actor'.

Certainly some Soviet journalists have shown courage that any Western reporter must admire, pressing on with their investigations in spite of anonymous telephone calls, promises to make trouble for them with their employers, even threats of violence against their families. And what is true in the big cities is doubly true for journalists on local newspapers more vulnerable to blackmail from local authorities.

Needless to say, the press is not overtly critical of the Party and the system. (All newspapers are under government or Party control.) But it can be critical of methods, and is constantly critical of abuses within society. In 1987 this led to accusations that it was systematically destroying a whole series of organizations, undermining the social and moral foundations of the country, and creating the impression that the country was 'one huge brothel', where all was corruption and nothing worked. But *glasnost* survived.

The idea of newspapers approaching former bosses, the police and the judiciary to unearth past scandals is not to everybody's liking. And it is not only those with something to hide who are frightened. Ordinary citizens too can be scared about 'where it will all end'. It is these who most often accuse the press of 'giving young people bad ideas' by writing about drugs, prostitution, homosexuality, the black market, etc.

There has also been a heated debate about publishing or not publishing certain statistics. After much argument, 1987 saw the first publication of figures for price increases and for life expectancy, and 1988 those for crime and delinquency. The year 1988 also saw the opening of 700,000 of the million files hitherto closed to researchers in the State archive, plus half the documents of the State Bank and a third of those of the Central State Planning Committee (Gosplan).*

The opponents of such openness naturally include partisans of the former system. But even 'liberals' think it difficult, after so many years of silence, to publish such statistics without putting weapons into the hands of one's enemies.

In Soviet Asia and parts of the Caucasus *glasnost* is mistrusted for different reasons. Articles in the all-Union press about nepotism and corruption in Armenia or Georgia, or the economic blunders of Baku or Alma-Ata, or the bribery scandals of Uzbekistan, are often seen locally as attacks on national honour. Even articles about drugs and the clandestine poppy fields of Central Asia are taken in this sense – and the fact that most of the journalists in the all-Union press are Europeans does not help.

*

*There were fears among historians that a number of these files had been not merely closed but destroyed. And in November 1987 a senior historian, academician Yuri Poliakov, referred to the disordered state of national and regional archives in connection with the rehabilitation of victims of Stalinism.

Of course there is no guarantee that the *perestroika* will succeed. But of one thing there can be no doubt: Gorbachev is right to make *glasnost* its cornerstone. And now that so many know so much, it would be hard for even the most determined opponent to put it all back in the box and out of the public mind.

The trouble with nearly all dreams of political leaders is their time-scale; and by making the year 2000 the target for completion of renewal, Gorbachev is in danger of attempting on a global scale yet another of those heroic, romantic 'campaigns' that, as we noted earlier, have been a characteristic of post-revolutionary history – drives often leading to repeated disappointments and a cruel waste of enthusiasm and resources.

The problems we have explored (with the help of the country's own media) should be warning enough that Gorbachev's transformation will take much longer than the rest of the century. The changes needed are not merely of management and technology but of people – for it will take more than a generation before the Soviet character is liberated from the habits of thought instilled not just by Brezhnevism or Stalinism but also the condition of Russia before 1917.

What would already be a very considerable success by the year 2000 would be to bring the Soviet Union up to the economic and social level of Western Europe in the early 1950s, albeit in the context of Soviet socialism and culture, and without the cruder features of capitalism in the West. To many who wish the *perestroika* well, this might seem like the language of defeatism. But it is not. For the 1950s were a period to which the West could now profitably look back as a period of opportunity, subsequently betrayed. At that time it might still have been possible to avoid the folly of the arms race, mindless consumerism, the ruin of the environment and a general loss of social conscience.

At the outset we drew attention to the parallel nature of many of the problems of the East and the West. The comparison bears repeating as we finish. The fact is that both our societies are seriously afflicted by sickness. Both face huge difficulties, generally of different natures but of equal urgency. And without drifting into a simplistic belief in 'convergence', it is possible to see opportunities for each of us learning something from the other.

Of one thing, at least, there can be no doubt, if only by looking at the logic of economics. That is the sincerity of the Soviet leaders' wish to throw off the shackles of the past, not only on the domestic scene but also in international relations. For, if *glasnost* is one cornerstone of the *perestroika*, the removal of the enervating arms burden is another.

The West now faces a simple question: does it want the *perestroika* to succeed or not?

'No' would mean voting for a Soviet return to secrecy and suspicion, a state of repression that could be ended only by violence and bloodshed – something that can hardly seem attractive, except to the fanatics of the Western 'far-right'.

If the answer is 'yes', then the question is what can the West do to help. There is, of course, a practical answer, of mutual benefit: and that is to pursue energetically the process of *détente* and arms reduction to which Soviet initiatives have made a substantial contribution. But more than that, it is necessary to realize that the faults of Soviet society we have described here are the product of a particular environment, now hopefully changing; that they are not endemic but open to cure – and that the will to cure them exists.

Anyone who agonizes over what will come out of it all, should meanwhile take encouragement from a passage in Chekov [7] where, in the mouth of a doctor, he delivers a verdict on his own generation and the next. The house-surgeon, Korolyov, has been sent to treat the insomnia of a stricken young girl, heiress to a group of factories whose senseless exploitation of the workers brings no joy even to her mother, who owns it.

'Your insomnia is something *honourable*,' he tells her.

> Whatever you may think, it's a good sign. In actual fact this conversation we're having would be unthinkable for our parents. They never discussed things at night but slept soundly. But *our* generation sleeps badly, we become weary and feel we can find the answers to everything, whether we're right or wrong. The problem whether they are right or wrong will already have been solved for our children and grandchildren. They will see things more clearly than us. Life will be good in fifty years' time and it's a pity we shan't live till then. It would have been interesting to see.

# · Glossary ·

*apparat:* Body of officials (about 1,500 in the case of the Central Committee) responsible for all but the largest administrative decisions on behalf of Party organs or their departments.

*BAM (Baikalo–Amurski Magistral):* Baikal–Amur mainline railway, constructed as a strategic alternative to the Trans-Siberian further from the Chinese frontier, and to open up eastern Siberia.

*blat:* Sometimes translated as 'exchanging favours' but without the implication of active corruption. Based on the principle, 'I do you a good turn, you do me one', it operates through a network of parents, friends and friends of friends.

*brigade:* Factory or farm work-team.

*Central Committee:* Highest authority, below Congresses, of the Soviet Communist Party. Meets twice yearly to discuss and approve proposals and decisions of the Politburo (q.v.).

*Collective:* Defined by the *Great Soviet Encyclopedia* as 'a group of people linked by a community of work, interests and overall purpose'.

*Communal flat:* Older type of flat, now disappearing, consisting of rooms whose occupants share cooking and sanitary facilities with neighbours.

*Congress:* Meeting every five years for delegates of the whole Party (or republic party, Komsomol, etc.) in order to adopt major lines of the Plan for the coming five years.

*CPSU:* Communist Party of the Soviet Union.

*Dom kulturi:* See House of Culture.

*DOSAAF:* The armed services' auxiliary association. The Russian initials stand for 'Association for Assistance to the Army, Air Force and Navy'. Principal activity is giving of military training courses.

*druzhiniki:* Literally 'comrades in arms'. Volunteer auxiliary police organized in the 1950s to 'enlist working people in the cause of protecting public order'. Recognizable by their red arm-bands, *druzhiniki* have police powers entitling them to demand to see passports and other papers, enter buildings and make arrests.

*dushman:* Literally, 'enemy'; applied to Afghan guerrillas.

*Gosagropom:* 'Food and Agriculture Complex', created in 1985 to regroup, in the interests of efficiency, the several ministries concerned with agriculture.

*Great Patriotic War:* Second World War on Soviet fronts.

*G TO:* Preparation for work and defence programme. Russian initials stand for 'Ready for Work and Country'. Offers a programme of sports activities for the general public.

*house, housing:* The standard urban residential building is the *dom*, literally 'house', in fact an apartment block. Modern blocks are mostly of sixteen to twenty-two storeys and, like older buildings, are usually sited so as to enclose a large 'courtyard' or play area. A *dom* may contain anything up to 220 flats.

*House of Culture:* Community building in each urban neighbourhood and village, serving as centre for recreation and 'improvement'.

*institute:* Higher educational establishment, with status equal to university, but tending towards professional, as opposed to scientific, training.

*internat:* Boarding school for children in State care.

*internationalism:* Harmonious co-existence of different Soviet nationalities.

*isba:* Traditional single-storey peasant house that still dominates the country-side of European Russia.

*karakteristika:* Student's record of social involvement, important for promotion, admission to elite schools, posts in research organizations, etc.

*kefir:* Drink made of soured milk and cream.

*kolkhoz:* Collective farm with average agricultural area of about 6,700 hectares, generally taking labour from a number of villages and under control of a committee and manager.

*Komsomol (Young Communist League):* Youth organization for ages fourteen to twenty-eight.

*lay magistrates:* Citizens elected to sit with the judge in court cases.

*military commission:* Board responsible for administering conscription.

*militia:* Civil police. The full title is 'People's Militia'. So named after the Revolution to distinguish them from the Tsarist and bourgeois police. Departments include uniformed branch, criminal investigation department and traffic police (G A I).

*minors' commission:* Tribunal for young offenders. Also decides cases involving interests of children, e.g. in the event of parents' divorce.

*nationality:* Indicated in the citizen's passport (identity book). In addition to their Soviet citizenship, all citizens have a nationality inherited from their parents. In the case of 'mixed' marriages, the nationality of one parent or the other is chosen at the age of sixteen, when the passport is first issued.

*OBKhSS:* Department of the Campaign Against Offences involving State Property. Responsible to the Ministry of the Interior.

*Obkom:* Regional (*oblast*) committee of the Communist Party.

*oblast:* Soviet administrative division, the equivalent of W European region or province, or state in the USA.

*Oblomov(s):* So called after central character of Goncharov's novel of the same name, a young man always at home and doing nothing.

*Palace of Culture:* Grander version of House of Culture (q.v.).

*Party Conference:* Special Party gathering, second only to Congresses.

*Party Congress:* Supreme policy-making gathering of the Soviet Communist Party, held every five years.

*Pioneers:* Children's organization for ages ten to fourteen.

*plenum:* Plenary meeting of Party, trade union or similar organ, most importantly of the CPSU Central Committee.

*Politburo:* Political bureau of the Party Central Committee, responsible for the work of the latter between plenary sessions.

*PTU:* Vocational–technical, or trade, school for training skilled workers.

*RAF:* Russian initials stand for Riga Automotive Factory.

*raikom:* Rayon Party committee (see *rayon* below).

*rayon:* Soviet administrative division, rural district.

*remont:* Renovation or repair applied at frequent intervals of all Soviet buildings, machines, etc., generally putting them out of use for extended periods.

*republic:* One of fifteen federal states of the Union, having government and Party structures parallel to the latter, except in the case of the Russian Federation (q.v.), which has no separate Party.

*Russian Federation (RFSR):* Largest of the Soviet republics, containing three-quarters of the area, and approximately half the population, of the Soviet Union, including many non-Russian territories.

*samogon:* Home-made spirit, 'moonshine'.

*sanitary days:* Days, generally once a month, when public buildings are closed for cleaning and/or disinfection.

*service centre:* Shop providing services such as household equipment and shoe repairs.

*sobriety society:* Voluntary group formed to discourage drinking by advice and example.

*social funds:* Funds put aside by enterprises for assisting workers' housing, holidays, welfare, etc.

*sovkhoz:* State farm in which all property is owned by the State, as opposed to a *kolkhoz*, where it is collectively owned by the members.

*special school (spets-schkoly):* School specializing in languages, mathematics, etc. for purportedly gifted pupils.

*specialist:* Skilled worker holding diploma or lesser qualification.

*S S O:* Russian initials stand for 'Student Work Brigade'.

*subbotnik:* Free day (usually Saturday) when citizens work voluntarily for nothing or donate what they earn to a public cause. Tasks commonly include cleaning up the factory, farm or city in advance of events such as Lenin's birthday.

*tekhnikum:* Secondary specialized school teaching intermediate technical subjects, e.g. electronics.

*vuz(y):* Higher educational establishment(s), i.e., universities and institutes.

# · Notes ·

## 1 · Children of the *Perestroika*

All figures concerning the composition of the Party are from *1917–87: Gody Truda i Pobed* (Moscow, 1987), pp. 312–54 and those concerning the population from the same work, pp. 272–84.

1. *Moskovskaya Pravda*, 12 December 1986.
2. Rutkevich, M. N., *Soverchenstvovanie Sotsialno-klassovoy Struktury Sovietskovo Obchestva na Etape Razvitovo Sotsializma* (Moscow, 1981), p. 7.
3. Rutkevich, M. N., *Towards Social Homogeneity* (Moscow, 1984), p. 162.
4. *Literaturnaya Gazeta*, 24 June 1987.
5. *Izvestia*, 10 June 1987.

## 2 · The Cradle of Society

1. Kharchtev, A. G., *Brak i Semia v SSSR* (Moscow, 1979), pp. 6–7.
2. Zubenko, L. A. and Jazikova, V. S., *Rol Semi v Sisteme Kommunistitcheskovo Vospitania* (Moscow, 1984), p. 12.
3. *1917–87: Gody Truda i Pobed* (Moscow, 1987), p. 242.
4. *Literaturnaya Gazeta*, 1 October 1986.
5. *Sotsialistitcheskaya Industria*, 24 May 1987.
6. *Nedelia*, no. 50, December 1984.
7. *Komsomolskaya Pravda*, 3 December 1986.
8. *Smena*, no. 22, November 1987.
9. *Pravda*, 8 June 1986.
10. *Sobesednik*, no. 41, October 1986.
11. ibid.
12. *Smena*, no. 22, November 1987.
13. *Ogonyek*, no. 52, December 1986.
14. *Izvestia*, 13 January 1985.
15. *Sobesednik*, no. 45, December 1984.
16. ibid., no. 41, November 1984.
17. *Komsomolskaya Pravda*, 3 December 1986.
18. *Sobesednik*, no. 35, August 1985.
19. *Knijnoe Obozrenie*, no. 35, August 1985.
20. *Interview na Nravstvenuiu Temou* (Moscow, 1985).
21. *Pravda*, 2 February 1987.
22. *Nedelia*, no. 38, September 1984.
23. *Izvestia*, 6 February 1985.
24. *Nedelia*, no. 38, September 1984.
25. *Izvestia*, 27 January 1985.
26. *Sobesednik*, no. 52, December 1986.
27. *Literaturnaya Gazeta*, 10 October 1984.
28. *Komsomolskaya Pravda*, 17 November 1985.
29. *Pravda*, 18 February 1987.
30. *Izvestia*, 18 June 1986 and 2 June 1986.
31. *Pravda*, 26 January 1987.
32. *Kommunist*, no. 8, May 1987.
33. *Komsomolskaya Pravda*, 21 January 1987.
34. ibid., 5 February 1987.
35. ibid., 22 January 1987.
36. *Moskovski Komsomolyets*, 22 October 1986.
37. *Smena*, no. 12, June 1986.
38. *Literaturnaya Gazeta*, 7 October 1987.
39. *Sobesednik*, no. 49, December 1986.
40. *Sovietskaya Rossiya*, 9 December 1986.
41. *Sovietskaya Rossiya*, 9 December 1986.

## 3 · A 'Communist Education'

1. Redulova, A., 'Le Développement des enfants sous tous les aspects', *Sciences Sociales*, no. 4, 1979, pp. 243–50.

2. *Pravda*, 17 November 1984.

3. *Izvestia*, 5 January 1986.

4. *Komsomolskaya Pravda*, 3 December 1986.

5. ibid., 22 May 1987.

6. *Izvestia*, 22 April 1986.

7. *Komsomolskaya Pravda*, 16 May 1986.

8. *Uchitelskaya Gazeta*, 18 February 1985.

9. *Vechernaya Moskva*, 10 January 1985.

10. Prokhorova, Z. P., *Sotrujestvo Semi i Chkoly v Vospitani y Chkolnikov Navykov i Umenii Utchebnovo Truda, in Vospitanie u Chkolnikov Kultury Truda* (Moscow, 1977), p. 5.

11. Juravlev, V. I., *Rol Chkoly, Semi i Obchestvennosti v Ideynopolititcheskom Vospitanie Utchachikhsia* (Moscow, 1977), p. 13.

12. *Pravda*, 20 November 1984.

13. *Smena*, no. 15, August 1986.

14. *Moskovskaya Pravda*, 21 September 1986.

15. *Pravda*, 6 February 1985.

16. *Komsomolskaya Pravda*, 26 December 1984.

17. *Sobesednik*, no. 14, April 1986.

18. *Trud*, 13 February 1987.

19. *Pravda*, 24 June 1986.

20. *Moskovski Komsomolyets*, 5 November 1987.

21. *Pravda*, 10 January 1987.

22. *Izvestia*, 12 May 1987.

23. Avanesov, V. S., 'The Problem of Psychological Tests', *Soviet Review*, vol. XXII, no. 1, spring 1981, pp. 97–106.

24. Lomov, B. R., 'O Sostoyanii i Perspektivakh Razvitiya Psikhologitcheskikh Nauk v CCCP', *Voprossy Filosofii*, no. 5, 1977, cited by Avanesov, op. cit., pp. 97–106.

25. *Pravda*, 24 June 1986.

26. *Komsomolskaya Pravda*, 24 June 1986.

27. *Smena*, no. 15, August 1986.

28. *Komsomolskaya Pravda*, 22 November 1984.

29. Juravlev, V. I., *Trudovoe Vospitanie Chkolnikov* (Krasnodar, 1981), p. 34.

30. Kumanev, V., 'L'Instruction publique en URSS dans les conditions de la révolu-

tion scientifique et technique', *Sciences Sociales*, no. 4, 1979, pp. 121–8.

31. *Smena*, no. 15, August 1986.

32. *Pravda*, 5 February 1985.

33. *Ogonek*, no. 15, April 1986.

34. *Komsomolskaya Pravda*, 14 May 1986.

35. *Moskovskaya Pravda*, 18 February 1987.

36. *Sovietskaya Rossiya*, 22 February 1987.

37. ibid., 1 March 1987.

38. *Uchitelskaya Gazeta*, 14 March 1987.

39. *Moskovskaya Pravda*, 18 February 1987.

40. *Ogonek*, no. 15, April 1986.

41. *Uchitelskaya Gazeta*, 22 July 1986.

42. *Moscow News*, no. 27, 12–19 July 1987.

## 4 · Defenders of the Faith

1. *Nedelia*, no. 44, 1985.

2. Gabriel, R. A., *The New Red Legions* (Newport, Conn., 1980), vol. I, p. 88.

3. *Literaturnaya Gazeta*, 25 February 1987.

4. Chubkin, V. N., *Sotsiologitcheskie Opity* (Moscow, 1970), p. 190.

5. Vodzinskaya, V. V., cited in Osipov, G. V. and Schepanski, I. A. (editors), *Sotsialnye Problemy Truda i Proizvodstva* (Moscow, Warsaw, 1969), pp. 47–53.

6. Treiman, D. J., *Occupational Prestige in Comparative Perspective* (New York, 1977), pp. 342–415.

7. Rittersporn, G. T., *Détente* (February 1985).

8. ibid.

9. Suvorov, V., *The Liberators* (London, 1978).

10. *Izvestia*, 10 January 1985.

11. Utkin, V. F., 'Vospitatelnaya Rol Sovietskikh Voorujennikh Sil v Usloviakh Rasvitovo Sotsializma', *Voprossy Filosofii*, no. 1, 1984.

12. Kerblay, B., *La Société sovietique contemporaine* (Paris, 1977), p. 50.

13. Tikhodumoff, I., *Annuaire de l'URSS* (Moscow, 1969), p. 288.

14. *Sobesednik*, no. 48, November 1985.

15. *Pravda*, 9 September 1986.
16. *Krasnaya Zviezda*, 30 January 1985.
17. *Komsomolskaya Pravda*, 27 January 1985.
18. ibid., 27 April 1986.
19. ibid., 16 January 1985.
20. ibid., 21 May 1986.
21. ibid., 27 April 1986.
22. ibid., 17 October 1986.
23. *Pravda*, 27 May 1986.
24. *Komsomolskaya Pravda*, 12 December 1986.
25. *Sobesednik*, no. 2, January 1986.
26. *Izvestia*, 15 April 1987.
27. *Pravda*, 27 May 1986.
28. *Sobesednik*, no. 45, November 1986.
29. ibid., 6 February 1987.
30. *Komsomolskaya Pravda*, January 1986.
31. *Molodoya Gvardia*, August 1987.
32. *Komsomolskaya Pravda*, 17 October 1986.
33. ibid.
34. ibid.
35. *Sobesednik*, no. 47, November 1987.
36. *Pravda*, 4 April 1987.
37. *Kommunist Tadjikistana*, 29 August 1987.
38. *Moskovskaya Pravda*, 15 November 1984.
39. *Pravda*, 20 April 1987.
40. Pavlov, S., 'La Culture physique et le sport dans la société socialiste', *Sciences Sociales*, no. 2, 1982, p. 15.
41. ibid.
42. *Sotsiologitcheskie Issledovania*, no. 1, 1987.
43. *Komsomolskaya Pravda*, 6 January 1987.
44. *Izvestia*, quoted by Reuters, 21 September 1987.

## 5 · The Worker-bees

1. Rutkevich, M. N., *Towards Social Homogeneity* (Moscow, 1984), p. 172.
2. *Pravda*, 7 February 1987.
3. Rutkevich, M. N., *Tendentsii Razvitiya Sotsialnoi Struktury Sovetskovo Obchestva* (Moscow, 1975), p. 4.
4. ibid., p. 8.
5. *Sobesednik*, no. 48, November 1987.
6. Polis, A. F., 'Emotsionalnoe i Norma Povedeniya Litchnosti', *Voprossy Filosofii*, no. 5, 1984, pp. 111–12.
7. Osipov, G. V. and Rutkevich, M. N., 'Sociology in the USSR 1965–75', *Current Sociology*, vol. 26, no. 2, summer 1978, p. 10.
8. Trufanov, I. P. and Sivak, A. F., *Molodoi Rabotchi v Trudovoy Kollektive* (Leningrad, 1981), p. 24.
9. Balaondin, I., 'Formation chez les jeunes d'une position de vie active', *Partinaya Zhizn*, no. 22, November 1984, p. 55.
10. *Komsomolskaya Pravda*, 17 January 1985.
11. *Sobesednik*, no. 45, December 1984.
12. ibid., no. 44, December 1984.
13. Diamanova, P. B., *Molodoi Rabotchi i Kollektiv: Problemy Vzaimootnochenii* (Frunze, 1981), p. 17.
14. Antipev, A., *Sotsialnoy Portret Komsomolskovo-molodiejnovo Kollektiv* (Perm, 1983).
15. Nasirov, K. A., 'Rol Sotsialatisticheskovo Truda v Stanovlenii i Razvitii Razumakh Potrebnostey Litchnosti', *Nautchni Kommunist*, no. 1, 1985, pp. 35ff.
16. Zintchenko, G. I. and Popov, A. N., *Sotsialistitcheski Trud i Katchestvo Raboty* (Moscow, 1980), p. 15.
17. Bliakhman, L. and Chkaratan, O., *Man at Work* (Moscow, 1977), pp. 62–3.
18. Iadov, V. A. and Dobrynina, V. I., *Molodej i Trud* (Moscow, 1970), p. 11.
19. Rutkevich, M. N., *XXVI Siezd KPSS i Voprossy Sotsialnovo Razvitiya Sovetskovo Obchestva* (Moscow, 1981), pp. 28–32.
20. *Literaturnaya Gazeta*, 17 October 1984.
21. *Komsomolskaya Pravda*, 2 December 1984.
22. ibid., 22 January 1985.
23. *Sovietskaya Rossiya*, 22 September 1985.
24. ibid.
25. *Sobesednik*, no. 42, October 1985.

26. *Sovietskaya Rossiya*, 13 April 1984.

27. ibid., 5 February 1986.

28. *Sobesednik*, no. 48, November 1986.

29. ibid., no. 30, July 1986.

30. *Komsomolskaya Pravda*, 5 June 1985.

31. Bondarenko, V. I., *Formirovanie i Razvitiya Trudovykh Kollektivov na Udarnykh Komsomolskykh Stroikakh* (Moscow, 1983), pp. 4ff.

32. *Sovietskaya Rossiya*, 20 October 1984.

33. *Sobesednik*, no. 40, September 1986.

34. ibid., no. 50, December 1986.

35. *Komsomolskaya Pravda*, 14 December 1986.

36. ibid., 13 February 1987.

37. ibid., 10 November 1987.

38. *Literaturnaya Gazeta*, 4 June 1986.

## 6 · The Drones

1. *Komsomolskaya Pravda*, 2 November 1986.

2. *Sotsialistitcheskaya Industria*, 2 August 1986.

3. *Moskovski Komsomolyets*, 19 November 1986.

4. ibid.

5. *Komsomolyets Kirgizii*, 27 January 1988.

6. *Moskovski Komsomolyets*, 19 November 1986.

7. ibid.

8. ibid.

9. *Sovietskaya Estonia*, 16 October 1987.

10. *Sovietskaya Belorussiya*, quoted in *Argumenti i Fakti*, no. 34, 1986.

11. *Komsomolskaya Pravda*, 9 October 1986.

12. *Krokodil*, no. 17, June 1986.

13. ibid.

14. ibid.

15. *Sovietskaya Rossiya*, 31 July 1986.

16. ibid., 2 August 1986.

17. *Trud*, 21 October 1986.

18. ibid.

19. ibid.

20. *Sovietskaya Rossiya*, 10 September 1986.

21. *Izvestia*, 3 November 1986.

22. ibid.

23. Case known personally to the authors.

24. *Izvestia*, 29 May 1986.

25. *Sovietskaya Kultura*, 24 December 1986.

26. *Literaturnaya Gazeta*, 29 March 1987.

27. *Sovietskaya Rossiya*, 24 December 1986.

28. *Sovietskaya Kultura*, 10 March 1987.

29. *Trud*, 19 September 1986.

30. *Nedelia*, no. 47, November 1986.

31. *Pravda Vostoka*, 30 August 1986.

32. *Krokodil*, no. 32, October 1986.

## 7 · Bureaucracy or Democracy?

1. Vojstrochenko, A., 'Otbor v Partiyou i Vospitanie Molodykh Kommunistov', *Partinaya Jizn*, no. 4, February 1985.

2. Riabuchkin, T. V., *Sovietskaya Sotsiologia*, vol. II (Moscow, 1982), pp. 42–9.

3. All figures concerning the Party from *1917–87: Gody Truda i Pobed* (Moscow, 1987), pp. 312–54.

4. All Soviet newspapers of 27 June 1987.

5. *Sotsiologitcheskie Issledovania*, no. 2, 1987.

6. 'Obchestvienno–polititcheskaya i Utchebnopoznavatelnaya Aktivnost Rabotchey Molodeji', *Informasionni Buleten* (Chelyabinsk, 1978), p. 12.

7. Antipeva, A., *Sotsialnoy Portret Komsomolskovo-Molodejnovo Kollektiva* (Perm, 1983), p. 30.

8. *Pravda*, 23 January 1985.

9. ibid., 27 April 1987.

10. *Sobesednik*, no. 38, September 1986.

11. ibid., no. 45, November 1986.

12. ibid., no. 38, September 1986.

13. ibid.

14. ibid.

15. ibid., no. 50, December 1986.

16. *Komsomolskaya Pravda*, 13 February 1987.

17. ibid., 28 February 1985.

18. ibid., 29 January 1985.

19. *Pravda*, 3 May 1987.

20. *Komsomolskaya Pravda*, 10 January 1987.

21. *Sobesednik*, no. 50, December 1985.

22. *Komsomolskaya Pravda*, 1 February 1987.

23. ibid., 28 December 1984.

24. ibid., 29 January 1985.

25. *Moskovski Komsomolyets*, 27 December 1984.

26. *Komsomolskaya Pravda*, 11 January 1987.

27. *Moskovskaya Pravda*, 24 June 1987.


**8 · Leisure**

1. *Bulletin du BIT*, October 1979, pp. 73–80.

2. Vasilevski, A. A., *Znanie Roditeley Utchachikhsia Vojnoe Uslovie Effektivnosti Vospitateloy Raboty Vo Vneutchebnoe Vremia* (Moscow, 1977), pp. 16–19.

3. *Sovietskaya Kultura*, 1 July 1986.

4. ibid., 13 June 1987.

5. *Sotsiologitcheskie Issledovania*, no. 4, 1986.

6. *Knijnoe Obozrenie*, no. 37, 11 September 1987.

7. *Komsomolskaya Pravda*, 19 July 1986.

8. *Sovietskaya Rossiya*, 19 February 1986.

9. *Komsomolskaya Pravda*, 4 June 1986.

10. ibid., 19 July 1986.

11. ibid., 9 December 1986.

12. *Rabotnitsa*, no. 6, 1986.

13. *Komsomolskaya Pravda*, 30 May 1986.

14. *Izvestia*, 6 December 1986.

15. *Moskovskaya Pravda*, 28 December 1986.

16. *Moskovski Komsomolyets*, 28 December 1986.

17. *Sovietskaya Rossiya*, 30 October 1986.

18. *Komsomolskaya Pravda*, 5 December 1986.

19. *Sovietskaya Kultura*, 6 December 1986.

20. ibid., 5 February 1985.

21. *Nedelia*, no. 33, August 1987.

22. *Moskovski Komsomolyets*, 28 December 1986.

23. *Vetchernaya Kazan*, 11 August 1987.

24. *Komsomolskaya Pravda*, 12 January 1985.

25. *Sovietskaya Kultura*, 10 January 1985.

26. *Sobesednik*, no. 49, December 1985.

27. *Moskovski Komsomolyets*, 11 November 1984.

28. *Komsomolskaya Pravda*, 12 January 1985.

29. *Sobesednik*, no. 35, August 1985.

30. Quoted by Reuters, 10 March 1988.

31. *Sovietskaya Kultura*, 24 January 1987.

32. *Knijnoe Obozrenie*, no. 14, 4 April 1986.

33. *Sovietskaya Kultura*, 18 December 1984.

34. ibid.

35. *Sovietskaya Rossiya*, 26 October 1986.

36. ibid.

37. *Sovietskaya Kultura*, 10 June 1986.

38. *Komsomolskaya Pravda*, 26 October 1986.

39. *Komsomolyets Uzbekistana*, 16 October 1987.


**9 · 'Negative Leisure'**

1. *Moskovski Komsomolyets*, 31 May 1986.

2. *Smena*, no. 6, March 1986.

3. *Pravda*, 31 October 1987.

4. *Sobesednik*, no. 48, November 1987.

5. *Izvestia*, 5 December 1986.

6. *Sovietskaya Rossiya*, 19 July 1986.

7. *Trud*, 15 August 1986.

8. *Literaturnaya Gazeta*, 17 September 1986.

9. *Izvestia*, 5 December 1986.

10. *Sovietskaya Kultura*, 10 August 1986.

11. *Sobesednik*, no. 11, 1986.

12. *Trud*, 25 March 1986.

13. *Tchelovek i Zakon*, no. 4, April 1986.

14. *Selskaya Jizn*, 3 September 1986.

15. *Literaturnaya Gazeta*, 3 December 1986.

16. *Izvestia*, 12 May 1987.

17. *Sobesednik*, no. 49, December 1986.

18. *Pravda*, 6 January 1987.

19. *Vechernaya Moskva*, 23 November 1987.

20. *Literaturnaya Gazeta*, 20 August 1986.
21. *Argumenti i Fakti*, no. 38, 1986.
22. *Vechernaya Moskva*, 5 September 1986.
23. *Uchitelskaya Gazeta*, 15 January 1987.
24. *Sovietskaya Rossiya*, 3 December 1986.
25. *Uchitelskaya Gazeta*, 27 November 1986.
26. ibid.
27. *Ogonek*, no. 50, December 1986.
28. Connor, W., *Deviance in Soviet Society* (New York, 1972), pp. 86–8.
29. *Izvestia*, 11 February 1985.
30. *Komsomolskaya Pravda*, 9 January 1985.
31. *Sovietskaya Rossiya*, 31 October 1984.
32. Kassof, A., *The Soviet Youth Program: Regimentation and Rebellion* (Cambridge, Mass., 1965), p. 35.
33. Gledov, L. D. and Ustinov, V. S., *Otvetstvennost za Khuligantstvo* (Moscow, 1973), pp. 3–4.
34. *Pravda*, 26 November 1973.
35. *Komsomolskaya Pravda*, 15 January 1985.
36. *Izvestia*, 11, February 1985.
37. *Sobesednik*, no. 42, December 1984.
38. *Moskovski Komsomolyets*, 21 August 1987.
39. *Soviet Union*, July 1987.
40. *Komsomolskaya Pravda*, 14 December 1986.
41. *Ogonek*, no. 5, February 1987.
42. *Sobesednik*, no. 7, February 1987.
43. *Sovietskaya Rossiya*, 4 March 1987.

## 10 · Living with the System

1. Osipov, G. V. and Rutkevich, M. N., 'Sociology in the USSR 1965–75', *Current Sociology*, vol. 26, no. 2, summer 1978, p. 10.
2. Rutkevich, M. N., *Sotsialistitcheski Obraz Jizni* (Moscow, 1983), pp. 4–5.
3. Efimov, N. I., *Dva Mira – Dva Obraza Jizni* (Moscow, 1981).
4. Juravlev, V. I., *Rol Chkoly, Semi i Obchestvennosti v Ideynopolititcheskom Vospitanii Uchachikhsia* (Moscow, 1977).
5. Rutkevich, M. N., *XXVI Siezd KPSS i Voprossy Sotsialnovo Razvitiya Sovietskovo Obchestva* (Moscow, 1981), pp. 3–4.
6. Bestushev-Lada, I. V., *Molodost i Zrelost* (Moscow, 1984), p. 108.
7. Dontsov, I. A., *Samovospitanie Litchnosti* (Moscow, 1984), p. 283.
8. Rutkevich, M. N., 'Enseignement comme facteur de la mobilité sociale en URSS', *Association sociologique de l'URSS: rapport du sixième congrès de sociologie internationale* (Moscow, 1966), pp. 3–8.
9. Aza, L. A., *Tsennostnye Orientatsii Rabotchey Molodeji* (Kiev, 1978), p. 17.
10. Kossov, V. V. and Tatevossov, R. V., 'La mobilité géographique de la main d'œuvre en URSS', *Revue internationale du travail*, vol. 123, no. 1, January to February 1984, pp. 95–105.
11. Kerblay, B., *La Société sovietique contemporaine* (Paris, 1977), p. 75.
12. ibid., pp. 68–70.
13. see note 10 to this chapter.
14. *Komsomolskaya Pravda*, 18 December 1984.
15. ibid., 5 January 1985.
16. *Sobesednik*, no. 42, December 1984.
17. *Komsomolskaya Pravda*, 24 January 1985.
18. ibid., 27 December 1984.
19. *Sobesednik*, no. 41, November 1984.
20. *Komsomolskaya Pravda*, 17 January 1985.
21. *Izvestia*, 10 February 1987.
22. *Komsomolskaya Pravda*, 11 June 1986.
23. ibid., 7 May 1986.
24. ibid.
25. ibid., 11 June 1986.
26. *Sobesednik*, no. 41, November 1984.
27. *Argumenti i Fakti*, no. 13, 1987.
28. ibid.
29. *Leninskoe Znamia*, November 1987.
30. *Komsomolskaya Pravda*, 27 October 1986.
31. ibid., 8 August 1987.
32. *Trud*, 14 November 1987.
33. *Izvestia*, 13 December 1986.
34. *Pravda*, 23 February 1987.

35. *Komsomolskaya Pravda*, 3 February 1985.
36. *Sobesednik*, no. 45, December 1984.
37. *Komsomolskaya Pravda*, 17 January 1985.
38. *Sobesednik*, no. 38, September 1986.
39. ibid., no. 2, January 1987.
40. *Komsomolskaya Pravda*, 5 April 1986.
41. ibid., 6 September 1986.
42. ibid., 18 January 1985.
43. ibid.
44. ibid., 6 July 1986.
45. ibid., 15 January 1985.
46. ibid., 12 February 1985.
47. *Sovietskaya Kultura*, 23 October 1984.
48. *Moskovski Komsomolyets*, 28 December 1984.
49. ibid.
50. *Komsomolskaya Pravda*, 11 January 1987.
51. *Sobesednik*, no. 42, October 1985.
52. ibid.
53. *Sobesednik*, no. 2, January 1986.
54. *Literaturnaya Gazeta*, 2 September 1987.
55. *Sobesednik*, no. 5, January 1984.
56. *Moskovski Komsomolyets*, 28 December 1984.
57. *Pravda*, 25 April 1986.
58. *Izvestia*, 11 May 1986.
59. *Komsomolskaya Pravda*, 6 December 1986.
60. *Moskovski Komsomolyets*, 24 October 1986.
61. For a 'reformed' Soviet view, see Lobachev, V. and Pravotorov, V., *A Millennium of Russian Orthodoxy* (Moscow, 1988).
62. *Sovietskaya Kultura*, 18 December 1986.
63. *Trud*, 14 October 1987.
64. *Komsomolskaya Pravda*, 30 July 1986.
65. ibid., 31 January 1986.
66. *Pravda*, 23 January 1987.
67. *Nauka i Religia*, no. 11, November 1986.
68. *Moskovski Komsomolyets*, 31 January 1986.
69. *Sovietskaya Kultura*, 11 October 1986.
70. ibid.
71. *Moskovskaya Pravda*, 12 June 1986.
72. *Rabotnitsa*, no. 11, 1986.
73. *Ogonek*, no. 8, February 1987.
74. *Moskovski Komsomolyets*, 27 March 1987.

## 11 · The Young Couple

1. Kerblay, B., *La Société sovietique contemporaine* (Paris, 1977), p. 120.
2. ibid., p. 119.
3. *Sovietskaya Rossiya*, 19 February 1986.
4. *Sovietskaya Kultura*, 10 February 1987.
5. ibid.
6. *Sotsiologitcheskie Issledovania*, no. 4, 1986.
7. *Smena*, no. 22, November 1987.
8. *Komsomolskaya Pravda*, 30 June 1987.
9. ibid.
10. *Young People, Be Happy* (Leningrad, 1986), quoted by Boika, V. in *Komsomolskaya Pravda*, 'Four Questions about Love'.
11. ibid.
12. Rujje, V. L., Elisseeva, I. I., Kadibur, T. S., 'Struktury i Fonktsii Semeynykh Groupp', *Finansy i Statistika* (Moscow, 1983).
13. Baranov, A. V., 'Potrebnosti v Jilicha Kakie Oni Sevodnia?', *Stroytelstvo i arkhitektura* (Leningrad, 1969), p. 18.
14. Baranov, A. V., *Sotsiologitcheskie Problemy Jitelstva* (Leningrad, 1969), p. 17.
15. ibid.
16. *Pravda*, 9 June 1986.
17. *Komsomolskaya Pravda*, 23 May 1986.
18. *Izvestia*, 18 May 1986.
19. *Pravda*, 3 May 1986.
20. *Izvestia*, 10 May 1986.
21. *Vladimirskoe Nedelia*, 18–24 August 1986.
22. Khartchev, A. G., *Brak i Semia v SSSR* (Moscow, 1979), p. 243.
23. *Sovietskaya Kultura*, 5 December 1985.
24. ibid.
25. *Zhurnalist*, no. 9, 1986.
26. *Meditsinskaya Gazeta*, July 1986.

27. *Komsomolskaya Pravda*, July 1986.
28. *Moskovski Komsomolyets*, 24 February 1987.
29. *Argumenti i Fakti*, no. 5, 1987.
30. ibid., no. 7, 1987.
31. *Nedelia*, 25 September 1987.
32. See their book *Muzhchina i Zhenshchina v Semve* quoted by Cherednichenko, V. I. in *Zdorovye*, no. 5, 1987.
33. *Komsomolskaya Pravda*, 23 January 1985.
34. ibid.
35. *Sobesednik*, no. 38, November 1984.
36. *Komsomolskaya Pravda*, 23 January 1987.

## 12 · The Generation Gap

1. *Sobesednik*, no. 48, November 1986.
2. *Literaturnaya Gazeta*, 24 June 1986.
3. *Sobesednik*, no. 49, December 1986.
4. *Trud*, 6 December 1986.
5. Tabolin, V., corresponding member of the Academy of Sciences, in *Sovietskaya Rossiya*, 23 October 1987.
6. *Literaturnaya Gazeta*, 24 June 1986.

7. *Sovietskaya Rossiya*, 23 December 1984.
8. *Komsomolskaya Pravda*, 3 June 1986.
9. *Sovietskaya Kultura*, 21 March 1987.
10. *Sotsialistitcheskaya Industria*, 24 May 1987.
11. ibid.
12. *Selskaya Zhizn*, 7 December 1986.
13. *Literaturnaya Gazeta*, 18 June 1986.
14. *Sovietskaya Rossiya*, 3 August 1986.
15. *Komsomolskaya Pravda*, 26 February 1985.
16. ibid., 2 May 1986.
17. *Izvestia*, 12 April 1986.
18. *Komsomolskaya Pravda*, 13 April 1986.
19. *Sobesednik*, no. 50, December 1986.

## 13 · The Millennial Vision

1. *Argumenti i Fakti*, no. 38, 1986.
2. *Rabotnitsa*, no. 3, 1986.
3. *Sovietskaya Rossiya*, 21 May 1987.
4. Illinski, I., 'Razvitie Sotsializma i Molodej', *Kommunist*, no. 6, April 1986.
5. *Komsomolskaya Pravda*, 15 May 1987.
6. ibid., 28 May 1986.
7. 'A Case History', *The Kiss and Other Stories* (Penguin, 1982).

# · Index ·